DRED SCOTT'S CASE

ORIGINALLY PUBLISHED BY FORDHAM UNIVERSITY PRESS

Dred Scott's Case

BY

VINCENT C. HOPKINS, S.J.

ATHENEUM 1971 NEW YORK

Published by Atheneum
Reprinted by arrangement with Fordham University Press
Copyright 1951 by Fordham University Press
All rights reserved
Manufactured in the United States of America by
The Murray Printing Company
Forge Village, Massachusetts
Published in Canada by McClelland & Stewart Ltd.
First Atheneum Printing November 1966
Second Printing November 1971

INTRODUCTION

THE DECISION GIVEN BY THE UNITED STATES SUPREME COURT ON
March 6, 1857, in the case of Dred Scott vs. Sanford has been, from
that day to this, the subject of much acrimonious discussion. It
was a decision on which much more than the freedom of Dred
Scott, his wife, Harriet, and their two daughters, Eliza and Lizzie,
depended. To decide their fate, the judges felt compelled to discuss, among other issues, the citizenship of free Negroes, the power
that Congress could legitimately exercise over the territories of
the United States, and the relationship that existed between the
States at that particular stage of the development of the Federal
Union. These questions were the vital issues of that day and the
answers men gave to them were various and conflicting. Who were
citizens in the sense in which that word was used in the Constitution of the United States? Of what manner of country were persons entitled to call themselves citizens members? Men were not
then, and to some degree, are not now neutral on these issues.
Neither were they nor are they neutral on the persons involved
in formulating the decision.

The present study is an attempt to approach the case *sine ira
et odio*. To achieve this effect, a genetic method has been used,
particularly in the chapters which deal with citizenship, congressional power in the territories, and the relationship of one State to
another, technically, interstate comity. Granting that to understand all does not necessarily imply pardoning all, yet a fuller
comprehension of the origin and development of the axioms, syl-
logisms and other arguments of the judges, a scrutiny of the
sources on which they relied, or might have relied, an understanding of the necessities of the times to which they felt constrained
to yield, should help "the cool and the candid," in Madison's
phrase, to a more kindly appreciation of the positions taken by
the judges in 1857. The case was not of their making. It had to be
heard. Interested parties exerted pressure to secure an opinion on
the more important political question involved, the power of Con-

gress over slavery in the territories. Public opinion appeared to demand that the judges pronounce on it. All but one of the justices thought that this question belonged to the case and could be dealt with by the Court. If they had not spoken, they would have been attacked as delinquent. If there had been no decision, men would probably ask, in the years to come, why the last peaceful means of settling the issue that precipitated the Civil War had not been tried.

The case, originating in the Circuit Court of St. Louis County, Missouri, in 1846, passing from that court to the Supreme Court of the State in 1852, being transferred to the Federal Court for the Missouri District in the following year, and finally coming to the Supreme Court of the United States where it was argued twice, was rather mysterious from the start. The present writer regrets that certain phases of it still remain so. How Dred Scott, called, at least till 1833, Sam, obtained his more celebrated and euphonious name—why Mrs. Emerson refused to allow him to buy his and his family's freedom—why the Blows, the sons of his first master, took such a deep interest in him—why the young lawyer, Edmund La Beaume, approached Roswell Field to find out how the case, decided against the Scotts by the Missouri Supreme Court, could be carried to the Federal courts—these are but some of the interesting questions which receive, in the present study, but tentative and, consequently, unsatisfactory answers.

On the other hand, the chase and the quarry have been rewarding. Events receive their form from the history of ideas and share in their intelligibility. The judgment given by the Supreme Court of the United States in the Scott case is an event, and, to understand it as fully as it is given to men to understand such things, many ideas have had to be traced. The natural yearning of an enslaved human being to be free—the anxieties, hesitancies and compromises of a group of men drawing up a constitution, the organic law of a new nation—the interpretations given to that document by their successors—the final meeting of the primitive desire of the slave and the complex forces contending for the mastery of a continent before the last court of appeal in the country—all these considerations may well serve as a memory and an experience for the use of the prudent and as justification for the present essay.

The obligation to acknowledge his debt to those who investigated the Dred Scott decision before him lies heavily on the present writer. It was they who gave the necessary clues, suggested possible sources of further research and provided much of the material incorporated in the present study. In particular, he would like to acknowledge his dependence on the work of John D. Lawson, editor of the *American State Trials,* on that of Frederick Trevor Hill and Mary Louise Dalton, whose investigations of the Scott Case, preserved at the Missouri Historical Society, were of great value, on the researches of the late Stella Drumm, of the Missouri Historical Society, on the writings of Charles Warren, Senator Beveridge, and Edward S. Corwin, and on the studies of Professor William E. Smith and John A. Bryan on the Blair and Blow families respectively. The writer would also like to record the assistance he received from many kindly individuals. He would like to thank especially Miss Helen Newman, Librarian of the Supreme Court of the United States, Mr. Charles van Ravenswaay, Director of the Missouri Historical Society, Mrs. Rufus Lackland Taylor and Mr. Louis La Beaume, of St. Louis, Mo., the staff of Kent Law Library, Columbia University, and Professors Henry Steele Commager and Allan Nevins, of the Columbia University Graduate School.

TABLE OF CONTENTS

DRED SCOTT'S CASE

"Let the case of the slaves be considered, as it is in truth, a peculiar one . . ."—JAMES MADISON, The Federalist, No. 53

1

ORIGINS

To tell the story of a slave is, of necessity, to tell the story, largely, of his masters. The latter usually left some records: they married, paid taxes, served in the armed forces, drew up last wills and testaments. Of the former, as a class, we have only chance references in the papers of their masters. The early history, then, of the slave who was called Dred Scott must be the history of the Blow family, his first masters, whose fortunes Dred Scott for many years shared.

Peter Blow was forty-two in 1819. By this time he and his wife, Elisabeth, had been married for nineteen years and the children were growing up, those who had lived. Mary Anne was seventeen —Tom would have been fifteen; Elisabeth Rebecca was thirteen— the twins had died. But there still were Charlotte, Martha Ella, called Patsy, Peter and two-year-old Henry.[1] Eight hundred and sixty acres of land in Southampton County, Virginia, poor and worn out from years of cultivation, were not much to support such a family.[2] There was good land to the west. But the county had always been his home; he had been born there, married there. He had done his brief bit of soldiering in the War of 1812 as a lieutenant in a county regiment, the Sixty-fifth Virginia Militia. His cousin, James Blow, had been the captain of his company.[3] But perhaps, despite all these ties, it was better to sell out and move on. In all probability that was what the first Blow to come to this country had thought when he left Sussex and England for Virginia well over a century before.[4]

So Peter Blow, like many another hard-pressed Virginia planter of "the era of good feelings," that period when the disruptive personal animosities of the statesmen of the next thirty years were incubating and the lines along which they would divide were already faintly drawn, sold his lands in the east for whatever he could get for them and passed over the mountains, settling down near Huntsville in northeastern Alabama.[5] His oldest daughter, Mary Anne, stayed behind—she was now Mrs. Key—but all the other children made the journey. With them was at least one of the slaves whom Peter Blow had owned in partnership with Henry Moore, a short, stocky young fellow named Sam.[6]

Soon after their arrival, Elisabeth Blow, on March 26, 1820, gave birth to another boy and he was named after her family, Taylor. The Blow family was proud of this Taylor connection. Charlotte and Henry had their mother's maiden name as their middle one and Peter and Martha Ella had it for a third name. Two years later, the last child of Peter and Elisabeth Blow was born and was called William Thomas. For some eleven years the Blows farmed in Alabama. But either the promised land had not been as bountiful as they had hoped or the lure of greater possibilities for his children in growing St. Louis caused Peter Blow to decide to move on to that key outpost of the west. It may have been merely the natural restlessness of the pioneer. Huntsville was left behind and the Blows and their Negroes, among them Sam, traveled, this time, northwest.[7]

By frontier standards St. Louis was already old, having a past as well as a future. In 1763, Pierre Laclede Liguest had picked the limestone bluff right below the junction of the Missouri and the Mississippi Rivers as the site for what he hoped would be the center of the trade and industry of the vast region drained by them. The town had been founded the next February. This outpost with the royal name had passed from France to Spain and back to France before it was purchased, in 1803, by the United States. Soon after its acquisition, the predominantly French settlement experienced a large influx of speculative Yankees and the searching of titles and the contesting of claims became and long remained one of the chief means of support of the town's lawyers. But the south also came and Virginia, Kentucky, the Carolinas contributed their share of men. With the coming of the southerners, the number of the town's slaves increased; in its early days they constituted about one-third of the inhabitants. Their masters had been among those who saw to it that Missouri had entered the Union, in 1821, as a slave State, although, to secure its admission, the nation had been distracted for two years, thoughtful men had been seriously alarmed, and a limit to the future extension of the institution, which was already beginning to be regarded as "peculiar," had been placed at the northern boundary of the State. The appearance of the steamboat on the western waters knotted more closely the town's original bonds with New Orleans and the bustle along the river front could compare with that of the parent city. It was a place of contrasts and each opposing force was to work itself out. In no small measure they would resolve themselves about the person of one of the Negro slaves of Peter Blow, young Sam.

At this point where north met south and, together with the east, turned to face the west that was to be made, Peter Blow's four boys would have plenty of opportunities. The future appeared bright, but there was the immediate problem of feeding several children. The slaves brought from Alabama were no help to a planter without land. So all, except two who were quite old, were hired out, among them Sam, who worked, for the next year or two, up and down the river as a roustabout. The Blows opened a boarding house, known as the Jefferson Hotel, in a large dwelling hired from Peter Lindell for twenty-five dollars a month.

They seemed settled. But on July 24, 1831, Elisabeth Taylor Blow died. The following November, Charlotte married.[8] Her husband, Joseph Charless, Jr., came of a family well known in St. Louis. His father, a refugee from Ireland after the failure of the rebellion of Lord Edward Fitzgerald, had learned printing in Philadelphia in the office of his fellow countryman and exile, Mathew Carey. On the advice of Henry Clay he had gone to Kentucky and had come from there to St. Louis in 1807. He established the first newspaper in the town, the *Missouri Gazette,* in which he espoused the prohibition of slavery in Missouri. In 1822 the paper was taken over by his son, Edward, and renamed the *Missouri Republican.* The senior Charless, having taken a final fling at those of his opponents who had failed to distinguish between the restriction of slavery by the people of Missouri, which he had advocated, and congressional coercion of a State, which he had denounced, went into the wholesale drug business with his son, Joseph, who, on his return from Transylvania University, had tried the law but found it uncongenial. Charlotte Blow had made a good match.[9]

On June 23, 1832, a few months after he had leased the former home of John B. C. Lucas, with whose son the baroque senator from Missouri, Thomas Hart Benton, had fought a bitter duel some years before, Peter Blow died.[10] In his will he named his son-in-law, Charless, the administrator of his estate and to his care and affection he left his six orphan children. The inventory of his property mentioned only household furnishings and five slaves.

The latter were listed as Solomon, who died soon after his master, Hannah, described as very old, Luke, William and, last, Sam. On the back of this inventory, Elisabeth Rebecca Blow noted that she had received all the listed goods and had sold them, after she had taken out what was necessary, "with the exception of the negroes which have been and are still hired out to support the family." Blow had left whatever he possessed to his two unmarried daughters, Elisabeth and Martha, and to his two younger boys, Taylor and William. Peter and Henry, eighteen and fifteen, did not share in the will.[11] However, they did receive their share of the care and affection of Joseph Charless, who took both the older boys into his drug company, Peter shortly after his father's death and Henry after he had finished at St. Louis College.[12]

One of the first acts of Charless, as administrator of the estate of Peter Blow, was to sell Sam, who will hereafter be called by his more famous name, Dred Scott, for five hundred dollars to Dr. John Emerson, a graduate of the University of Pennsylvania in the class of 1824 and now resident in St. Louis.[13] Dred's initial relations with his new master were not happy. He ran away at the time of the sale, was found in the Lucas Swamps, a favorite Negro resort near St. Louis, and returned to the doctor.[14]

Shortly before his purchase of Dred, Emerson had established his first connection with the army. On September 28, 1832, General Atkinson at Jefferson Barracks wrote to Captain Joshua B. Brant, who was stationed at the St. Louis Arsenal, that Dr. McMahon, the post physician, was ill and instructed the captain to hire a civilian physician without delay. Brant hired Emerson. Life at the Barracks, a string of stone buildings set on high ground along the Mississippi several miles south of the city, must have pleased the doctor. His wife, Irene Sanford Emerson, through her sisters who had married into the service, had many army connections. Her brother, John F. A. Sanford, an agent for the Pratte, Chouteau Company, one of the great fur firms of the country, and son-in-law of Pierre Chouteau, Jr., had many friends stationed at the various frontier posts. Whatever the reason, letters soon began to arrive at the office of the then Secretary of War, Lewis Cass, and at that of the Surgeon General, Thomas Lovell, seconding Emerson's original request of November 27, 1832, for an appointment as an assistant surgeon. General Atkinson and Captain Brant commended the doctor highly. Senator Benton, Senator Buckner, Dr. Samuel Merry all used their influence in his behalf. A petition was forwarded from members of the Missouri Legislature. Finally, in December, 1833, the desired commission was issued.[15]

With the commission came orders for the doctor to report to Fort Armstrong, situated on Rock Island, one of a chain of frontier defences erected after the War of 1812 and part of the free State of Illinois. There Emerson went, accompanied by his slave, Dred Scott.[16] But Fort Armstrong did not suit Emerson and all during his stay there he importuned the powers at Washington for leave and transfer. His health was undermined, he himself wrote to the Surgeon General and the Secretary of War. Senator Hendricks and Congressman Ashley, of Missouri, used their influence with the latter to secure the appointment of surgeon at the St. Louis Arsenal for Emerson. Lovell, the Surgeon General, found all this pressure little to his liking and he reprimanded the doctor for going over his head in the matter. Emerson apologized and pleaded ignorance. As it turned out, neither the influence of the Missouri congressmen nor the prestige of a group of citizens of Pittsburgh, who petitioned Cass in his favor, gained the coveted position at the St. Louis Arsenal for Emerson.[17] In 1836, when Fort Armstrong was decommissioned, the unwilling doctor, whose commission was due in some degree to Benton's influence, departed for Fort Snelling, a post established by Calhoun in 1819, taking Dred Scott with him.[18]

Fort Snelling stood on the west bank of the Mississippi, below the Falls of St. Anthony, at the junction of the Minnesota and the great river, a part of the Louisiana Purchase north of the line thirty-six degrees, thirty minutes, and north of the State of Missouri, territory in which, by the Act of 1820, slavery had been prohibited. Lieutenant Zebulon Pike had picked the site and Colonel Henry Leavenworth had established the post. There the doctor set up quarters and there Dred, away from whom a wife had been sold, met Harriet, a slave in the possession of Major Laurence Taliaferro, the Indian agent at Fort Snelling.[19] Dr. Emerson bought Harriet from Taliaferro and the couple, with his permission, married.[20]

Emerson did not remain long on the upper Mississippi, leaving there in October, 1837. Dred and Harriet did not accompany him on his rather hazardous descent of the river, three hundred miles of which, so he told the Surgeon-General, were made in a canoe.[21] They remained at the fort, hired out as servants, till April, 1838, when they, too, left Snelling. On their trip down the river, their daughter, Eliza, was born on the steamboat, *Gypsy*, north of the northern boundary of Missouri.[22]

Emerson, after a short stay at Jefferson Barracks, had proceded to Fort Jesup, Louisiana. But Jesup proved bad for his health, the heat aggravating his rheumatism, and from December, 1837, to July, 1838, he asked, in a series of letters, for a transfer back to Fort Snelling. Not only his health troubled him, but certain investments he had made in lands, both in Illinois and in Iowa Territory, were endangered. "Even one of my negroes in St. Louis had sued me for his freedom," he told the new Surgeon General, Lawson. His request was granted and, on October 22, 1838, he informed Lawson of his arrival at Snelling. But another winter in the north country found him ready for a change and he again requested an appointment at Jefferson Barracks or the St. Louis Arsenal. He followed this letter with another, asking for leave to attend a public land sale at Dubuque and investigate the condition of his holdings at Davenport. During 1841 and 1842, Dr. Emerson was in Florida, serving in the Second Seminole War and still trying to get back to St. Louis. On September 23, 1842, he found himself without an appointment, the medical staff of the army having recently been reduced. A reappointment seemed in the offing, but Emerson died at Davenport on December 30, 1843, before it was issued.[23]

With the death of their master, Dred and his family passed to Mrs. Emerson, "for the term of her natural life," like the rest of his estate. After her death, they, with all his other possessions, were to go to his daughter, Henrietta. His widow was empowered, if she judged it expedient, to "sell all or any part" of his lands and tenements and to appropriate the proceeds to her own or her daughters' support or to re-invest it. Her brother, John Sanford, and George Davenport, the son of the founder of the city of that name in Iowa, were named executors.[24]

The movements of Dred, Harriet and Eliza, in the years after 1838, are obscure. They may have joined Dr. Emerson at Fort Jesup.[25] They did not accompany him on his return to Fort Snelling nor were they with him in Florida. While Emerson was in Minnesota and with the troops in Florida, his wife was living with her father, Alexander Sanford, on an estate outside St. Louis, called "California." The Scotts, most probably, were somewhere in the vicinity of St. Louis, hired out as servants.[26] Captain, later Colonel, Henry Bainbridge, a brother-in-law of Mrs. Emerson, who was stationed at Jefferson Barracks during 1843 and part of 1844, left that post for Camp Wilkins in the latter year, moving on from there to take part in the military occupation of Texas.[27] Dred was with him as his servant. Before the captain went with General Taylor into Mexico, he sent Dred back to St. Louis.[28]

Notes

1. James A. Bryan, "The Blow Family of St. Louis," Ms., Jefferson National Expansion Memorial, National Park Service, Department of the Interior, St. Louis, Mo. Hereafter referred to as: Bryan, "The Blow Family."

2. In 1818, Peter Blow paid taxes on this amount of land: Southampton County Tax Lists, Virginia State Library, Richmond, Va.

3. "Peter Blow," Records, War Department, National Archives.

4. Bryan, "The Blow Family."

5. In 1819, Peter Blow deeded 860 acres to Robert Nicholson: Southampton County Tax Lists, Virginia State Library, Richmond, Va.

6. In 1818, Peter Blow and Henry Moore were listed as owning three Negroes over twelve years of age and one over sixteen. Sam, the later Dred Scott, most probably was one of these slaves. He was born while the Blows were still in Virginia. He described himself as brought up in the Blow family and his statement was corroborated by one of them. Cf. Southampton County Tax Lists, Virginia State Library, Richmond, Va., *Washington Daily Union*, April 11, 1857, Julia Webster Blow to Mary Louise Dalton, March 13, 1907 (Dred Scott Collection, Missouri Historical Society, St. Louis, Mo., hereafter referred to as Dred Scott Collection).

7. Bryan, "The Blow Family."

8. Stella M. Drumm and Charles van Ravenswaay, "The Old Courthouse" (*Glimpses of the Past, 7*, January-June 1940), pp. 26-27; Bryan, "The Blow Family."

9. Richard Edwards and Menra Hopewell, M.D., *Edward's Great West and Her Commercial Metropolis*, (St. Louis, Published at the Office of Edward's Monthly, 1860), pp. 586-587.

10. Bryan, "The Blow Family."

11. "Peter Blow," Files, Probate Court, St. Louis.

12. Bryan, "The Blow Family."

13. The evidence that Dr. Emerson bought a slave from the estate of Peter Blow is definite. That it was Sam is only a little less clear. Luke continued to belong to the Blow family (Julia Webster Blow to Mary Louise Dalton, March 13, 1907, Dred Scott Collection). Henry Blow said that Emerson bought Dred from his father (Dred Scott Collection, evidence of Henry Blow at the first trial). Sam was sold, most probably, a short time after Peter Blow's death when the family needed ready money. Peter Blow died in 1832. Among the Peter Blow papers there is a summons, calling on Charlotte (Blow) Charless and Peter E. Blow to appear in a matter of controversy, "wherein John Emerson is plaintiff and Peter Blow's Executor [Charless] is defendant," dated August 8, 1833. This may have concerned Dred's flight when he was sold. The first annual settlement and inventory of Blow's estate is dated 1834, Charless having been remiss in filing it. Miss Elisabeth Blow's endorsement of the inventory does not mention the sale of one of the Negroes. After Sam's name on this list there are added the words, "sold—$500." Sam was sold, most probably, between June, 1832, and December, 1833, the dates of Blow's death and Emerson's commission. Somewhere between 1834 and 1846, Sam took or received the name Dred Scott. The circumstances which led him to change his name are not known.

7

14. John D. Lawson, *American State Trials* (St. Louis: Thomas Law Book Co., 1921), 13, p. 220. Hereafter referred to as *13 American State Trials*.

15. "John Emerson," Records, War Department, National Archives.

16. Testimony of Miles H. Clark, Dred Scott Collection.

17. "John Emerson," Records, War Department, National Archives.

18. Testimony of Miles H. Clark, Dred Scott Collection.

19. "Laurence Taliaferro," Records, War Department, National Archives. Two contemporary accounts, that in the Washington *Union* for April 11, 1857, and that in *Frank Leslie's Illustrated Newspaper* for June 27, 1857, say that Harriet was Dred's second wife, his first wife, by whom he had no children, having been sold from him. They also say that Dred had two sons, who died, as well as Eliza and Lizzie. There seems to be no reason for doubting the accounts, both of which were based on interviews with Dred. Who his first wife was and by whom she was sold are not known. Harriet was one of several slaves in Taliaferro's possession at Fort Snelling (Elbert W. R. Ewing, *Legal and Historical Status of the Dred Scott Decision*, Washington, D.C.: Cobden Publishing Co., 1909, p. 31).

20. Benjamin C. Howard (ed.), *Reports of the Cases Argued and Adjudged in the Supreme Court of the United States, December Term, 1856* (New York: Banks Law Publishing Co., 1903), 19, p. 398. Hereafter referred to as 19 Howard.

21. "John Emerson," Records, War Department, National Archives.

22. Testimony of Catherine Anderson, Dred Scott Collection; *13 American State Trials* 250. Lawson, the editor of the *State Trials*, owned a copy of the pamphlet issued after the trial in the Federal Court in 1854 in Scott's interest. An anonymous annotator noted, in regard to Eliza's age, "This daughter is sixteen years old and was born just before the master took the family across that magic line that transmutes persons into things."

23. "John Emerson," Records, War Department, National Archives. No record of the trial mentioned in the text could be found. Mary Louise Dalton to Frederick Hill, Feb. 22, 1907, citing a letter from Judge James Bollinger, District Judge, Davenport, Iowa, Dred Scott Collection.

24. "John Emerson," Files, Probate Court, St. Louis. From these papers it appears that the qualified administrator of Emerson's estate in Missouri, which consisted of nineteen acres of land and some household furnishings, was Mrs. Emerson's father, Alexander Sanford. He was named such on August 13, 1844, Benammi Garland and John Sarpy going bond for him for four thousand dollars. Mrs. Emerson's brother, John, never qualified as executor in Iowa. There is no mention of slaves in the Missouri papers. There may have been in the Iowa papers but, if there were, it has since disappeared; cf. Mary Louise Dalton to Frederick Hill, Feb. 22, 1907, Dred Scott Collection.

25. Testimony of Catherine Anderson, Dred Scott Collection. Mrs. Anderson was under the impression that the Scotts, when they left Snelling in 1838, went to Fort Gibson. Emerson was at Fort Jesup at this time, in western Louisiana. Fort Gibson was in what is now eastern Oklahoma.

26. Notes taken in conversation with Mrs. Louisa Berthold Sanford by Mary Louise Dalton, Dred Scott Collection. Due to his military duties and his ill health, Dr. and Mrs. Emerson rarely lived together.

27. George W. Cullum, *Biographical Register of the Officers and Graduates of the United States Military Academy at West Point* (Boston: Houghton Mifflin Co., 1891) I, pp. 218-219.

28. Scott's petition to the St. Louis Circuit Court, Dred Scott Collection.

8

2

MISSOURI PHASES

IT WAS A DIFFERENT CITY TO WHICH DRED RETURNED. THE FRENCH hamlet of 1803, the frontier town of 1830, was now becoming, as Laclede, its founder, had hoped, the commercial metropolis of the west. The change was apparent in the careers pursued by the sons of Peter Blow, the Virginia planter. Peter, the eldest son, had left the firm of Charless, Blow and Company, forsaking the drug business for lead mining in Washington County, Missouri. Henry, who, at the age of nineteen, had become a partner in the Charless Company, was responsible for the expansion of the firm into oils and paints. In 1844, he founded the Collier White Lead and Oil Company.[1] With his father-in-law, the wealthy saddler, Thornton Grimsley, whose daughter, Minerva, he had married in 1840, he took an interest in railroad development.[2] The younger boys, Taylor and William, after finishing their schooling, had entered their brother-in-law's business.[3] Joseph Charless had proven an excellent guardian to the children of Peter Blow. The latter's move from Alabama to St. Louis and the benign interest of their brother-in-law had turned four future farmers into four already well-established manufacturers and merchants. With their change of occupation, the Blows may have changed their opinion of the worth of slavery. It was a phenomenon appearing all over the north and west at this time where the southern system of labor was of no value to growing industry.

The political situation in Missouri was also in a state of flux. Senator Benton was still a dominant figure, but his position was being threatened. It was now some four years since Samuel Treat had written his editorial on "The Right of Private Judgment" in the *Missouri Reporter*. This attack, occasioned by Benton's denunciation of Treat for differing with him on a currency measure, was regarded by the latter as the beginning of Benton's downfall in Missouri.[4] The national implications resulting from this encounter can be gauged from Calhoun's directive to Treat of April 14, 1845, in which he stressed that nothing was to be done to give aid or comfort to the Van Buren-Benton-Blair wing of the Democracy which had been defeated in Baltimore at the convention of 1844 in which Polk had been nominated.[5]

Into this struggle for power the slavery issue was to be injected with ever-increasing violence. On this question Missouri was not of one mind. She seems never to have been. But the issue had always become involved with other problems. In 1820, it had been the imposing of conditions on a sovereign State. Once that question had been settled, it seemed possible that the institution would be judged on its own merits. A bipartisan meeting for this purpose, attended by politicians from the entire State, took place in Missouri in the late twenties. Benton and Judge Barton, the Democratic and Whig leaders of the State, were there. It was unanimously agreed that a memorial, drawn up at the meeting, was to be presented to the voters of the State and that both parties were to urge the acceptance of the resolutions, urging emancipation, contained in it. Unfortunately, one of the Tappans of New York picked this moment to indulge in a rather ostentatious bit of philanthropy, driving, it was said, in his carriage with his daughters and some Negroes whom he had entertained at dinner. This incident, equally unfortunately, outraged public sentiment in Missouri and it was judged inopportune to present the memorial.[6]

The arrival of the sons of Francis Preston Blair, Montgomery and Frank, in St. Louis to practice law and politics there under Benton's sponsorship was to be full of consequence for the city, the State and the nation. Montgomery Blair had come in 1837. When Frank arrived in 1842, his brother was mayor of the city. Both were strongly opposed to the further extension of slavery in the territories, though both were slave-holders. Of equal, if not greater, consequence was the interest being aroused in projects for a transcontinental railroad, with St. Louis, Memphis and Chicago as the leading contenders for the position of eastern terminus.[7]

Shortly after his return from Texas to this scene of rapid change, Dred had endeavored to buy his own and his family's freedom from Mrs. Emerson, offering to pay part of the price down and giving security for the rest. She refused.[8] Dred's next move, on April 6, 1846, was to petition Judge Krum, of the St. Louis Circuit Court, for permission to bring suit for his freedom on the grounds of his residence in Illinois and in the Minnesota

Territory. He asked for ten dollars damages. Krum, who had had the unpleasant experience of being the mayor of Alton, Illinois, when the abolitionist Lovejoy was killed, granted the petition and issued a court order that Scott be allowed to sue with the usual conditions, that he give security for all costs, that he have the right of free access to counsel, and that he be not removed out of the jurisdiction of the court. At the same time, similar papers were filed and similar proceedings took place in the interest of Harriet Scott. Dred's attorney, Francis B. Murdoch, executed a bond for the costs, a summons was issued by John Ruland, the court clerk, which was served on Mrs. Emerson the next day, April 7, by Deputy-Sheriff Henry Belt. Several days later, George W. Goode appeared in the circuit court in St. Louis and moved that the suit be dismissed, arguing that the conditional order of the court, the posting of the bond, had not been complied with, a motion that Judge Krum refused to entertain for the simple reason that the bond had been posted by Murdoch.[9] Goode was a fellow resident of St. Louis County of Mrs. Emerson and her father, Colonel Sanford, and, like them, a Virginia emigrant. He was a bit of a fox-hunting country squire of decided pro-slavery beliefs, who had no general legal practice in Missouri, confining himself to a few cases in which he was particularly interested.[10]

Events, nationally, were moving as they were manifestly destined to. Before activity in the Scott case was renewed, the country had gone to war with Mexico. Polk had sent his War Message to Congress on May 11, 1846. On August 8 of the same year, David Wilmot had introduced his "Proviso," stipulating that slavery be prohibited in any territory acquired as a result of the war. No man to let a challenge pass, Calhoun retorted in February, 1847, with his famous resolutions. Wittingly or not, the south was taking to its last line of political defense when its largely self-appointed apologist asserted the powerlessness of Congress to prohibit slavery in the territories of the United States. Any attempt along the lines of Wilmot's proposal was unconstitutional, Calhoun declared. To Benton, who had recently been instructed by the Missouri Legislature to support the Missouri Compromise of 1820, such statements were "firebrand." He saw in them, "as Sylla saw in the young Caesar many Mariuses," many "nullifications."[11] In the midst of all this excitement, Goode, on November 19, 1846, filed a plea of "not guilty" for Mrs. Emerson in answer to Scott's charge of assault.[12] More than ten years were to pass before the issues

11

raised in Congress by Wilmot and Calhoun and the train of events set in motion by Mrs. Emerson's plea were to meet.

It was on May 7, 1847, however, that action was resumed in the Scotts' case. Charles D. Drake, the son of the well-known frontier physician and the husband of Martha Blow,[13] gave notice on that day that he was taking depositions on behalf of the Scotts at William Anderson's house on Myrtle Street, in St. Louis. Goode acknowledged the notice the same day. On May 13, he served a similar notice that depositions would be taken at his office.[14] James R. Lackland, a Marylander who had migrated to Missouri in 1828 and who had been recently admitted to the bar, for which he had prepared in Drake's office,[15] wrote to Samuel Russell, the current employer of Dred and his wife (who had, about this time, been blessed by the birth of a second daughter, Lizzie), requesting information as to when he had hired the Scotts, to whom their wages had been paid, and similar data. Russell replied on June 2. On June 24, the witnesses were summoned. Russell was called. Catharine Anderson, who, as Mrs. Thompson, had hired Harriet from Dr. Emerson at Fort Snelling, Miles Clark, a soldier in the army who had known Dred both at Fort Armstrong and Fort Snelling, Henry T. Blow, the son of Dred's first master, Thomas O'Flaherty, Captain Thomas Gray and Major A. D. Stuart were also cited. On June 26, John and Stewart Carter were summoned.[16]

On June 30 the trial commenced in the long, rectangular room at the west end of the still uncompleted courthouse in St. Louis. Judge Krum had retired and Pennsylvania-born Alexander Hamilton was now the Judge of the St. Louis Circuit Court.[17] The Scotts were represented by the well-known firm of Field and Hall, of which the senior partner, Alexander P. Field, was a prominent trial lawyer. Before coming to Missouri he had been the Secretary of State of Illinois. Threatened with removal from that office, Field contested the governor's right to remove him, thereby precipitating a nice constitutional battle and an early example of court packing. He yielded only when the legislature passed a bill adding five new justices to the State Supreme Court.[18] Lyman D. Norris and Hugh A. Garland appeared for Mrs. Emerson. Garland had had as colorful a career as Field. A Virginian, he had been Professor of Greek at Hampden-Sydney College, a member of the Virginia Legislature from 1833 to 1838, and, in 1839, clerk of the national House of Representatives. It was in this role that

12

Garland, who had always been a strong Jacksonian, struck a blow for the Democracy. He declined to call the names of five Whig members from New Jersey, whose seats were contested, and thereby gave the Democrats a majority. The uproar which resulted continued for several days and only ceased when John Quincy Adams was elected chairman *pro tempore*. In 1840, finding himself financially straitened because of a too liberal endorsing of his friends' notes, he emigrated to St. Louis.[19] Van Buren spoke of him, apropos the speeches Garland attributed to John Randolph of Roanoke in his life of that statesman, "as a man of rare abilities—one fully equal to the task of preparing a speech adapted to the occasion."[20] His speech at the trial must have been one of considerable power because, to the surprise of the opposition, the jury, through its foreman, John Sappington, returned a verdict for Mrs. Emerson.[21]

But more than the eloquence of Mr. Garland had entered into the verdict. The defense had seriously impaired Samuel Russell's testimony on cross examination. It was on his statements that the Scotts' lawyers had depended for proof of the fact that Mrs. Emerson really held and treated Dred and Harriet as slaves. Russell had written to James Lackland that he had hired Dred and Harriet from Mrs. Emerson. At the trial he said that his wife had made all the arrangements. The all-important fact that Mrs. Emerson had acted toward the Scotts as though they were her slaves was left hanging, legally, in the air. S. Mansfield Bay, at one time a pupil of Salmon Chase and, from 1837 to 1843, Attorney-General of the State and editor of its Supreme Court decisions,[22] and who, along with Drake, Lackland, Murdoch and Goode, took an interest in the case at this stage, immediately moved for a new trial. He renewed his motion on the following day, July 1, alleging, apart from the ritual charges that the law and the evidence did not support the verdict, the concrete point of surprise at Russell's testimony. Judge Hamilton granted the retrial. Mrs. Emerson, through counsel, excepted to this grant and her bill of exceptions was signed by the same judge.[23]

On July 2, the day that Mrs. Emerson received her bill of exceptions to the State Supreme Court, Scott, through his lawyers, filed another petition, thereby starting the case of Scott vs. Alexander Sanford, Samuel Russell and Irene Emerson, alleging that his detention at Fort Snelling was a violation of the Missouri Compromise and asking three hundred dollars damages. His request was granted, the husband of Charlotte Blow, Joseph Charless, Jr., signing the bond for the costs. Similar proceedings were instituted in Harriet's interest. In naming the father of Mrs. Emerson, who ordinarily took care of her affairs and who had been the man with whom the Russells dealt, the Russells who had hired the Scotts, and Mrs. Emerson as defendants, no loophole would be left through which Garland, that "man of rare abilities," could wriggle. The Scotts now had two cases on the docket of the circuit court and on July 31, 1847, the court ordered them to choose between them. They elected to take the retrial and the case of Scott vs. Sanford, Russell and Emerson was quashed, while that of Scott vs. Emerson was continued. On March 14, 1848, Mrs. Emerson filed a motion to hire Dred and Harriet out, which the court granted. The Scotts were hired, for one year, or till the termination of the suit, for five dollars a month by Edmund C. La Beaume, a young St. Louis lawyer, whose sister, Eugenie, had married Peter E. Blow. La Beaume signed the necessary bond as principal, Henry Blow, the second son of old Peter, going security for the sum of six hundred dollars. The Blow family had not abandoned Dred Scott.[24] During the same month of March, the Missouri Supreme Court dismissed Mrs. Emerson's bill of exceptions because, a retrial having been granted, there was no true judgment.[25]

While the case of Dred Scott and his family continued to hang over in the Missouri courts, the slavery issue continued to vex the nation. The stakes now were the recent acquisitions of territory from Mexico by the treaty of Guadalupe-Hidalgo—California and New Mexico. Finally, after wrangling that seemed interminable, Senator John M. Clayton, of Delaware, asked, on July 12, 1848, that the question of slavery in the territories be referred to a committee of eight, four representatives from the north, four from the south, to be selected by ballot. The motion passed; Clayton was named chairman and Calhoun was a member. Polk, who hoped that the question would be solved by the extension of the Missouri Compromise line to the Pacific, had confided this desire to a friend of the Senator from South Carolina, Frederick H. Elmore, who arranged a meeting between the two. Calhoun told Polk that a suggestion had been made at one of the committee meetings with which he was in agreement or, at least, was willing to accept. This plan would have left the existing laws prohibiting slavery to continue to operate in Oregon, which Congress was also trying to organize at this time, until they were changed by the territorial legislature. On the other hand, the local governments of California and New Mexico were to be prevented by Congress from touching the subject at all. If the question arose, it would be handled by the local judiciary. On the next day, Calhoun told the President that the committee was, in general, agreed but that the northern members insisted that appeals lie from the local courts to the Supreme Court of the United States whenever slavery was involved. Calhoun was not in favor of this addition but, on Polk's urging, he yielded. On July 18, Clayton reported his bill, incorporating the right of appeal. This attempt at compromise, which had the support of senators of both sections, was, in reality, a surrender of the whole question to the judiciary. The bill passed the Senate but failed in the House. Nevertheless, this solution of the territorial question remained the favorite of the conservative elements of the country who regarded talk about the dissolution of the country over slavery "as nonsense or something worse." [26]

Back in Missouri, the anti-Benton war had grown in fierceness. The State Legislature, now controlled by his enemies, presented Benton with a set of resolutions which thoroughly aroused that veteran. Known as the Jackson-Napton Resolutions, they were the work of Claiborne Jackson and Chief Justice William Barclay Napton, of the State Supreme Court, and were, in substance, those of Calhoun of the preceding year. Benton refused to be instructed by the Legislature, saying that the resolutions did not embody the will of the people of the State, being but "the speckled progeny of a vile conjunction." Pausing in Washington to propose his Transcontinental Railroad Bill, Benton then hurried back to mend his badly neglected political fences in Missouri and to carry the war into Africa against, what he termed, "the few black jack prairie lawyers" who dared oppose him.[27]

In St. Louis, preparations were being made for the new trial of the Scotts' case. All through 1849, various witnesses were being summoned. At one time it was Major Stuart, who could not be found. Later, Mrs. Russell and Miles Clark could not be reached. In December, 1849, Henry Blow was not available. At last, on January 12, 1850, the second trial began.[28] Before it started, however, Alexander Sanford had died and Mrs. Emerson had left St. Louis to make her home with her sister, the wife of General Barnes, in Springfield, Massachusetts, leaving her affairs in St.

15

Louis to be cared for by her brother, John, through his agent, Benammi S. Garland.[29]

The evidence at the second trial was the same as at the first, with the exception of that of Mrs. Russell which had been taken by deposition and was read by counsel. Mrs. Russell confirmed Mrs. Emerson's ownership of the Scotts. After all the evidence had been taken, Scott's counsel prevailed upon the court to instruct the jury that hiring as a slave was the same as holding as one, that "it is no answer to such hiring that the defendant acted as the agent of others, and that residence in the Louisiana Purchase north of thirty-six degrees, except the state of Missouri, and the Northwest Ordinance entitled a slave to his freedom." The defendant's counsel argued that the Scotts were really under military jurisdiction when they were in free territory, since Dr. Emerson had gone to such territory under orders. Of greater interest was Norris's argument on the effect on his status of Scott's return to Missouri. He admitted that the authorities were in conflict, but held that "The voluntary return of the slave places him under the operation of our local laws and the rights of his master, if ever divested, reattach the moment they are again in a State that recognizes the institution of domestic slavery." The jury returned a verdict in favor of the Scotts. Harriet's case had been joined to her husband's. So the whole family was now declared free. Hugh Garland then moved a new trial, a motion Judge Hamilton refused. A bill of exceptions for an appeal to the State Supreme Court was then requested by the defendant and this the judge signed on February 14, 1850.[30]

The following October 24th, Edward Bates, a prominent Missouri Whig and an able lawyer, noted in his diary that the Supreme Court was to have met the preceding Monday at St. Louis, but that low water in the Missouri prevented the arrival of two of the judges. Judge Birch was the only one in town. Bates feared that the term would lapse. But the other judges arrived and the court sat for the first time on the 26th. One of the judges, John Ryland, a man "of kind heart and pacific disposition, prone to discourage suits involving feeling," [31] gave Bates some news that upset him considerably. This was that his colleagues, Judges Napton and Birch, two of the "black jack prairie lawyers" who opposed Benton, were about to make use of the Scott case, now on the Supreme Court's docket, to give an opinion that would overrule all the former decisions of the State Supreme Court which declared the emancipation of all slaves by reason of residence north-west of the Ohio in virtue of the Northwest Ordinance of 1787. Their assumption was, Ryland told Bates, that Congress had no power to legislate on the subject of slavery in the territories and that all enactments to that effect were void. For his part, Ryland intended to write a counter opinion.[32]

Bates had some grounds for his suspicion that "this intended judicial decision was part and parcel of the bargain for a fusion of the Whigs and the Soft-Democracy." The Chief Justice, Napton, was the co-author of the resolutions of 1848 which had as their basic assumption the doctrine of Calhoun that Congress had no power to legislate on the subject of slavery in the territories, an opinion with which Judge Birch was in enthusiastic agreement. Both judges also heartily concurred in the belief that the removal of Senator Benton from the political scene was highly desirable. During the summer of 1850, Napton had noted that the north had already taken possession of the territory acquired from Mexico by forming governments for them which excluded slavery. If this result had been achieved "by the natural order of events, the south would have acquiesced." But it was done by the north and now both north and south regarded it as "a point of honor upon which we split." "The persistence of the North," he continued, "is regarded as a proof of her fixed and settled purpose, not only to prevent the increase of slave territory but gradually to undermine and ultimately to destroy the institution itself." [33] This, Napton prophesied, will be resisted, being a clear violation of the Constitution. The judge was ready to do his part to preserve that document intact.

In January, 1851, Henry Sheffie Geyer, a native of Maryland who had come to Missouri while it was still a territory, and a Whig who was distinguished for his knowledge of the law, was elected United States Senator from Missouri. He owed his election to the fact that the anti-Benton Democrats could not secure enough votes for their own candidate, Colonel Stringfellow. Sixteen of them switched to Geyer as the lesser of two evils after he had come out against the power of Congress over slavery in the territories, asserting that California had been admitted into the Union unconstitutionally. All the Whigs voted for him, but some twenty of them were secretly hostile to him and what Bates called "his black and white" doctrine.[34]

But "the heretical politico-legal opinion"—again Bates' phrase

17

—was not given and the bargain never received "the weight of judicial authority," if such had been the judges' intention. The alliance between the Whigs and the anti-Benton Democrats proved to be of a most temporary character and, in the reorganization of the State Supreme Court in 1851, both Judge Napton and Judge Birch were retired to private life. In the conferences of the judges that took place at this time, Napton was merely for overruling the decisions on the question of complete emancipation by residence in free states or territories. Birch wished to go further and declare the Missouri Compromise void, a position Napton did not think necessary to a disposition of the case. Ryland hesitated, but finally agreed to concur with Napton in this move to prevent "the undermining and ultimate destruction of slavery in the states." Napton was to write the opinion. But the composing of it had to be deferred "on account of the absence of Haggard's Reports which were not then in the State Library" and which Napton had to order from Philadelphia. While he was waiting for the volume, he and Judge Birch were superseded, "the whole Benton vote of the State" being cast against them.[35]

The case was now to be heard before a reorganized State Supreme Court. There had been three sets of candidates for the three vacancies. Hamilton R. Gamble, who was elected Chief Justice, had run as a Whig; Ryland, the candidate of the Benton Democrats, won on his ticket; and William Scott, upon whom, we are told, "nature had bestowed . . . a vigorous intellect" but "withheld all the graces of person," was chosen from the anti-Benton group.[36] On April 10, 1852, a divided court gave a decision in favor of Mrs. Emerson, reversing the decision of the lower court. Judge Scott, with whom Judge Napton had frequently conferred on the subject and between whom there was complete agreement,[37] wrote the opinion in which Judge Ryland concurred. The Chief Justice, Gamble, dissented.[38]

The firms that had argued the case in the lower court argued it in the Supreme Court. Norris, of Garland and Norris, appeared for Mrs. Emerson. In reviewing the prior decisions of the court on the effect of the Ordinance of 1787 and the Missouri Compromise of 1820, which he summed up as "once free, always free," Norris admitted that this dictum had been unquestioned. However, he regarded it as highly questionable. In the first place, he pointed out, the Ordinance no longer had any binding power, as the Supreme Court of the United States had decided in Strader vs. Graham among other cases.[39] Secondly, the laws of Illinois were of purely local effect and no recognition need be shown them, nor was it expedient to do so. Thirdly, the Missouri Compromise was also of local effect and applied only to the territory of which it was part of the organic law. Hall, of Field and Hall, spoke for the Scotts. His argument, in substance, was that the law of Missouri had consistently granted extraterritorial effect in slavery cases to the constitution of Illinois and to the pertinent section of the Missouri Compromise Act of 1820, declaring slaves brought into either free. He buttressed his argument with the precedents Norris had found questionable.[40]

Judge Scott's opinion had much in common with Norris's argument. In general, he declared that the sovereign State of Missouri would no longer extend recognition to the emancipating statutes of her sister commonwealths and the Federal government. "Cases of this kind," he asserted, "are not strangers in our courts. Persons have been frequently here adjudged to be entitled to their freedom on the ground that their masters held them in slavery in territories or States in which that situation was prohibited. From the first case decided in our courts, it might be inferred that this result was brought about by a presumed assent of the master. . . . But subsequent cases base the right 'to exact the forfeiture of emancipation,' as they term it, on the ground it would seem, that it is the duty of the courts of this State to carry into effect the constitution and laws of other States and Territories, regardless of the rights, the policy or the institutions of the people of this State. Every State has the right of determining how far, in a spirit of comity, it will respect the laws of other states. . . . The respect allowed them will depend altogether on their conformity to the policy of our institutions." In revoking the extension of comity which Missouri had shown to the laws of other States in freedom cases, Scott pointed out that "Times now are not what they were when the former decisions on this subject were made. Since then not only individuals but States have been possessed with a dark and fell spirit in relation to slavery, whose gratification is sought in the pursuit of measures, whose inevitable consequence must be the overthrow and destruction of our government." Missouri would not gratify this spirit.[41]

Chief Justice Gamble, in his dissent, reasoned that slaves were more than property, for slaves could acquire rights by the acts of their masters. One of these was the right to enforce freedom.

19

Emancipation, he continued, was regulated by statute and, when the requirements were fulfilled, the slave was free. His status was to be judged, if it were questioned, by the laws of the State in which he had become free. Removal from Missouri to Illinois was, in Gamble's eyes, virtual emancipation. He regarded the whole matter as settled law and, while the furor aroused by the abolitionists was to be deplored, the judicial mind should remain calm in the excitement. He reviewed the Missouri cases in point and concluded that the judgment of the lower court should be sustained.[42]

Benton had lost the State of Missouri on the issue which had played such a large, if indirect, part in the decision of the State Supreme Court in the case of Dred Scott. He was returned to the scene of his life's activities as a Congressman from St. Louis and he fully intended to carry the issue to the capitol. Dred's St. Louis friends determined to follow the same strategy—to appeal from the State to the nation. Having lost in the State, they would try the Federal courts.

NOTES

1. Bryan, "The Blow Family."
2. Chauncey R. Barns (ed.), *The Commonwealth of Missouri, A Centennial Record* (St. Louis: Bryan, Brand and Co., 1877), pp. 738-740.
3. Bryan, "The Blow Family."
4. Memoir of Judge Samuel Treat, Treat Papers, Missouri Historical Society, St. Louis, Mo.
5. John C. Calhoun to Treat, Treat Papers, Missouri Historical Society, St. Louis, Mo.
6. John Wilson to Thomas Shackelford, Jan. 13, 1866, Slavery Folder, Missouri Historical Society, St. Louis, Mo.
7. William E. Smith, *The Francis Preston Blair Family in Politics* (New York: Macmillan Co., 1933), I, p. 158, 2, p. 232.
8. St. Louis *Evening News*, April 3, 1857. Why Mrs. Emerson refused to allow Dred to purchase his freedom can only be conjectured. She may have thought it was against her daughter's interests for whom she was acting, having herself only a life interest in the estate. She may have thought, since the slaves were not mentioned specifically in her husband's will, that she could not. She may not have believed in freeing Negroes, either because the lot of the freedman was not a happy one or because she believed in slavery. At this time her father was prominent in pro-slavery circles, having been elected vice-president of a committee "for the protection of slave property against the evil designs of abolitionists and others" (J. Thomas Scharf, *History of St. Louis City and County* (Philadelphia: Louis Everts and Co., 1883) I, p. 185). Her first lawyer was an ardent pro-slavery man, George Goode. The Sanfords were relatively large slave-holders ("John F. A. Sanford," Files, Probate Court, St. Louis). There was always the danger of damages, once the suit was started.
9. Dred Scott Collection. Cf. Appendix A.
10. William Van N. Bay, *Reminiscences of the Bench and Bar of Missouri* (St. Louis: F. H. Thomas and Co., 1878), p. 569.

11. Thomas H. Benton, *Thirty Years' View* (New York: D. Appleton and Co., 1865), II, p. 697.

12. Dred Scott Collection.

13. William Hyde and Howard L. Conard (eds.), *Encyclopedia of the History of St. Louis*, I, p. 588.

14. Dred Scott Collection.

15. William Van N. Bay, *Reminiscences of the Bench and Bar of Missouri*, pp. 298-303.

16. Dred Scott Collection.

17. *Ibid.*

18. Horace White, *The Life of Lyman Trumbull* (Boston: Houghton Mifflin Co., 1913), p. 11.

19. John Livingston, *Portraits of Eminent Americans Now Living* (New York: Cornish, Lamport and Co., 1853), II, pp. 657-664.

20. John C. Fitzpatrick (ed.), *Autobiography of Martin Van Buren* (Washington: Government Printing Office, 1920), p. 438.

21. Dred Scott Collection.

22. Bay, *Reminiscences,* pp. 165-171.

23. Dred Scott Collection.

24. *Ibid.* Bryan, "The Blow Family."

25. "Emerson vs. Dred Scott," 11 Missouri Supreme Court Reports 413.

26. Eugene I. McCormac, *James K. Polk* (Berkeley: University of California Press, 1922), pp. 635-638; John J. Crittenden to John M. Clayton, Feb. 2, 1849, cited in Charles Warren, *The Supreme Court in United States History*, 2nd edition, (Boston: Little, Brown and Co.), II, p. 216.

27. Benjamin C. Merkel, "The Slavery Issue and the Political Decline of Thomas Hart Benton," *Missouri Historical Review*, 38 (October 1933-July 1934), pp. 388-407; William E. Smith, *The Francis Preston Blair Family in Politics*, I, pp. 251-257, John F. Darby, *Personal Recollections* (St. Louis: G. I. Jones and Co., 1880), pp. 183-185. An interesting analysis of the political situation in Missouri at this time is contained in a letter, dated June 6, 1849, of James B. Bowlin to Howell Cobb: "I send you by this mail a speech of Colonel Benton on slavery in general and Calhoun in particular. We are in a terrible political snarl, and God only knows how it is to terminate. The issue has sprung up, as you will perceive, by Calhoun's taking our State into his bailiwick alongside South Carolina and Virginia. A few of his agents smuggled through the Legislature a set of extreme resolutions, not from any practical effect they were likely to have, but to head Benton. On his part he goes almost to the length of the other extreme, as you will see. . . . The active leaders against Benton are his old foes. . . . They do not meet him, but bay him with meetings at a distance and scatter as old Bullion comes lumbering after them" (Ulrich B. Phillips [ed.], *The Correspondence of Robert Toombs, Alexander H. Stephens, and Howell Cobb*, Washington: Annual Report of the American Historical Association for . . . 1911, 1913, II, pp. 159-160).

28. Dred Scott Collection.

29. "Alexander Sanford" and "John F. A. Sanford," Files, Probate Court, St. Louis. Benammi S. Garland first appeared in the papers of the Scott case on August 13, 1844 when he went bond for Colonel Sanford who had been appointed administrator of Emerson's estate in Missouri. His name is not mentioned in the city directories of St. Louis but he was nominated for County Recorder on the American ticket (St. Louis *Daily New Era*, July 8, 1847). Whether he was related to Sanford's lawyer in the Scott case, Hugh A. Garland, is not clear, though he seems to have been responsible for hiring his namesake to try the case for Sanford ("John F. A. Sanford," Files, Probate Court, St. Louis).

30. Dred Scott Collection. From the court's instructions it is evident that Mrs. Emerson had pleaded that she had acted as her daughter's agent in hiring the

Scotts to the Russells. The question raised by Norris is the essential point in the matter of comity; cf. below, Chapter 10.

31. Bay, *Reminiscences*, p. 276.

32. Edward Bates, Diary, October 24th, 1850, Missouri Historical Society, St. Louis, Mo.

33. William B. Napton, Diary, August, 1850, Missouri Historical Society, St. Louis, Mo.

34. Edward Bates, Diary, October 26, 1850. Geyer was later counsel for Sanford in the Supreme Court.

35. William B. Napton, Diary, p. 224 (1857). Napton was interested in applying the doctrine of Lord Stowell in the case of the Slave Grace to the Scott case and that is why he sent for Haggard's Reports in which the Slave Grace opinion was published. Cf., below, Chapter 9, pp. 147-148; also, Richard R. Stenberg, "Some Political Aspects of the Dred Scott Case," *Mississippi Valley Historical Review*, 19 (1933), pp. 571-577.

36. A. J. D. Stewart, *The History of the Bench and Bar of Missouri* (St. Louis: Legal Publishing Co., 1898), p. 210. North T. Gentry, *The Bench and Bar of Boone County, Missouri* (Columbia: Published by the Author, 1916), p. 120.

37. William B. Napton, Diary, p. 223 (1857).

38. "Scott vs. Emerson," 15 Missouri Supreme Court Reports 413.

39. 10 Howard 82.

40. 15 Missouri Supreme Court Reports 579-582. The questions here raised by counsel and judges will be discussed in subsequent chapters.

41. *Ibid.* 582-587.

42. *Ibid.* 587-590.

3

APPEAL TO THE NATION

THE CROWDED CONDITION OF THE COURTHOUSE IN ST. LOUIS FORCED
Federal Judge Robert Wells, a Virginian who had come to Missouri by way of Ohio in 1820,[1] to hold the circuit court of November, 1853, in a small back room on the second floor of the Papin
Building on North Main Street, a situation the grand jury found
little to its own liking and unbecoming the dignity of the court.[2]
There, on November 2, Scott, as a citizen of Missouri, filed a
declaration in trespass, alleging that John F. A. Sanford, a citizen
of New York, had, on the previous January 1, assaulted him, his
wife, and his two children. For this collective indignity, Scott
asked nine thousand dollars in damages.[3] A new Scott case was
started.

Roswell Field was now Scott's lawyer. He was a native of Vermont who, after some years residence in St. Louis, had achieved
the reputation of being one of the ablest lawyers in the city. He
was not related to Scott's former counsel, A. P. Field.[4] After the
decision in the Missouri Supreme Court, adverse to the Scotts,
Edmund La Beaume, Peter E. Blow's brother-in-law and Dred's
employer in 1848, had asked Field's advice on how to get the case
into the Federal courts. Field, under the impression that the Scott
family had been sold to Sanford, whose legal residence was now
in New York City, recommended that suit be instituted in the
United States District Court on the grounds of diversity of citizenship. Not only did Field give his advice but he also undertook
the case.[5]

Sanford, Mrs. Emerson's brother, was named the defendant.
Mrs. Emerson, now resident in Springfield, Massachusetts, there
had met and married Dr. Calvin C. Chaffee, a politician of Abolitionist and Know-Nothing affiliations.[6] By her marriage, according to the laws of Missouri,[7] she could no longer act in any
capacity in regard to her first husband's estate, which had been
left in trust for her daughter, Henrietta Emerson. As a matter of
fact, her duties, so far as Emerson's Missouri possessions were con-

cerned, had, since the death of her father, who had been named administrator in Missouri, and her departure for the east, completely devolved on her brother, whose St. Louis agent, Benammi Garland, saw to most of the details connected with Sanford's interests there.[8] A summons was issued, which Sanford, who was in St. Louis at the time, being involved in another suit springing from that perennial source of litigation in the city, land grants, personally accepted.[9]

On November 16, Sanford swore out a plea to the jurisdiction of the court which, however, was not filed till the following April 7. On April 14, Field, who had, in his handling of the case, the assistance of a deeply interested fellow Vermonter, Abra Crane, a young lawyer in his office,[10] replied to Sanford's plea. Hugh A. Garland answered for his client. The matter was argued on April 24 before Judge Wells. The court, "not being sufficiently advised, took time to consider thereof" and, on the next day, sustained Scott's right to sue in a court of the United States.[11]

Sanford's plea to the jurisdiction of the court, like all the issues involved in this case, became the subject of much discussion. In itself it was peculiar. To get the case into the Federal courts, Scott's lawyers relied on diversity of citizenship. They affirmed that Scott was a citizen of Missouri. The whole matter in controversy up to this point had been the freedom of Scott and his family. If they were not free, it was idle to discuss their citizenship. The plaintiff's lawyers bypassed this vital question. On the other hand, the defendant's lawyers did not plead the Scotts' servitude but the alleged fact that Scott was "a negro of African descent, whose ancestors were of pure African blood, and who were brought into this country and sold as slaves." [12]

Wells decided to sustain Scott's answer to this plea, which, in substance, admitted the allegations contained in it and denied their relevance. Granted that Scott was such a person as was described, a Negro of pure African descent whose ancestors had been brought to this country and sold as slaves, such circumstances did not prejudice his citizenship, at least to such an extent that he would not be entitled to sue in a Federal court. The judge made his decision on the principle that citizenship, to give the court jurisdiction, meant only residence and the capability of owning property, an opinion that could scarcely be called common and generally acceptable, at this time, in the courts of the United States.[13]

24

On May 4, 1854, Garland filed the defendant's plea in his own defense. He now told the court that Sanford was not guilty of the alleged assault, because the Scotts were his slaves. Sanford had only "gently laid his hands on them, as the defendant had a right to do." On the same day, Field and Garland drew up an agreed statement of facts which related, in some detail, the legally pertinent wanderings of the Scotts when they were in Dr. Emerson's possession. The case came to trial on May 15. Field and Crane appeared for the Scotts; Garland continued for Sanford.[14] The trial was anything but sensational in itself and neither locally nor nationally was there any general interest in it.[15] Field read the agreed statement of facts to the jury; there was no further evidence. He then asked the court to instruct the jury that the agreed-upon facts should lead to a finding for the plaintiff. Wells declined and instructed the jury for the defendant. That body, thereupon, gave the following verdict: "As to the first issue [the assault], not guilty. As to the second issue, that the plaintiff was a negro slave and the property of the defendant. As to the third issue, that Harriet, his wife, and Eliza and Lizzie, his daughters, were negro slaves and the property of the defendant." [16] Wells, who later assured Montgomery Blair that he had wished the law had been on Dred's side, his feelings being "deeply interested in favor of the poor fellow," [17] gave judgment for the defendant with costs. Field moved for a new trial but was refused. The case was then taken, on a writ of error, to the Supreme Court of the United States. This time the bond was signed by Dred as principal, Taylor Blow going security. Pending the decision of the Supreme Court, the earlier case was continued, by common consent, in the St. Louis Circuit Court. The St. Louis *Herald*, three days later, after a brief summary of the case, ended its account on a hopeful note: "Dred is, of course, poor and without any powerful friends. But no doubt he will find at the bar of the Supreme Court some able and generous advocate, who will do all he can to establish his right to go free." [18]

Dred, now about to become a national figure and to assume legendary proportions, was left largely to his own devices. He supported himself by doing chores, one of which was the general care of his lawyer's office.[19] Field had taken the case because he felt sorry for Dred and because he, and other lawyers, saw in it a chance to settle a "much vexed" question, whether the removal of a slave to Illinois or Minnesota Territory worked "absolute emancipation," so that, even if the slave returned to slave territory, his servile condition did not revive—the very question that had concerned Judge Napton and the question which Judge Scott thought he had settled.[20] With a living reminder almost daily about him, Field took steps to push Dred's case at Washington, his resolution being enthusiastically seconded by his assistant, Abra Crane.[21] What was needed was an "able and generous advocate" who would appear before the Supreme Court in Dred's interest. Apart from the potential political implications of the case, there were other difficulties, not the least of which were financial. But Montgomery Blair, who, along with his family, had taken a decided stand on the issues involved, had left St. Louis the previous year to practice law in Washington.[22] Field thought Blair might be prevailed upon to take the case himself or to get some one to take it. On December 24, 1854, he wrote Blair, explaining the circumstances of the case and his interest in it. There was no money in the case, Field told him. While Dred had made enough interest with his friends to get the case to the Supreme Court, "neither he nor they have the means of paying counsel fees." But, Field continued, the cause of humanity would be greatly served "if you or any other lawyer in Washington would bring it [the case] up and get a hearing and a decision." At any rate, the question of the effect of the removal from and subsequent return to slave territory on a slave's status would be settled "by the highest court in the nation." [23]

Blair did not answer immediately, for he was in California, where he had gone to settle the estate of his brother, James, who had amassed a considerable fortune there as a pilot in the gold-rush days.[24] On his return, he sought the advice of his father, Francis P. Blair, who was soon to throw in his lot with the young Republican Party, and of Gamaliel Bailey, the veteran abolitionist editor of the *New Era*. Blair told Bailey that he would give his services gratis, if Bailey would guarantee the necessary court costs. The elder Blair and Bailey agreed as to the value of taking the case and the latter agreed to finance it, and so Blair wrote Field on December 30 that he would appear for the Scotts.[25]

Field, acknowledging Blair's acceptance, expressed satisfaction "that the case of Dred strikes you, as it struck me, as interesting enough to call for gratuitous assistance from our profession." He explained the case to Blair, as he saw it, at considerable length. After the decision by the Missouri Supreme Court, he related,

26

Edmund La Beaume had appealed to him for advice and he had recommended that suit be instituted in the Federal circuit court on the grounds of diversity of citizenship, a proceeding that, in Field's eyes, was certainly regular, "supposing Dred had any capacity to sue in the United States Court." Garland, acting for Sanford, had challenged that supposition, he went on, pleading that the court could not take jurisdiction over the case because Dred was not a citizen, being a Negro of pure African descent, a plea that Judge Wells would not sustain. "You will not," Field wrote, "fail to see the importance of the question involved here. If in fact, as Judge Wells had decided, a black man may sue his master in the Federal courts, the right of *trial by jury* is still left to the slave in an action at common law which, if brought in the Federal Courts, may be enforced in the judgment throughout the Union. And this jurisdiction, if it exists at all, exists by force of the constitution that no act of Congress may impair." Field, apparently, saw in the recognition of the capacity of a Negro to sue in a Federal court an opportunity to make the provisions of the recent Fugitive Slave Law, which denied jury trial to allegedly runaway slaves and entrusted their disposition to a Federal commissioner and a summary process, of no effect. He was also afraid that this possibility would be "a strong argument against allowing black men to sue as citizens."

There were many decisions, he continued, which declared that a Negro was not a citizen within the meaning of the privileges and immunities clause of the Constitution,[26] but Judge Wells had not found these to be in point, deciding that any one born in the United States and capable of holding property had the capacity to sue in the Federal courts. Field did not suppose that the question of Negro citizenship would arise from the writ of error by which the Scott case had been taken to the Supreme Court; nevertheless, he pointed out to Blair that it was "very desireable . . . to obtain the opinion of the Court upon it."

He then took up what he regarded as the "principal question presented by the agreed case." Judge Wells had decided that the Scotts were still slaves because their master's right to them had not been extinguished by their residence in free territory but merely had been made inoperative, being dormant and reviving when the Scotts returned to Missouri, a slave State. In so reasoning, Wells said that he was following the opinions of Lord Stowell and Justice Story.[27] In Field's estimation, there was "much plausi-

27

bility in the idea when applied to a case arising merely under the clause called the Missouri Compromise; but the Illinois Constitution is more stringent in its terms." That document, according to Field, emancipated slaves brought into the State. "Judge Wells," he told Blair, "parried that by saying the provision [of the Illinois Constitution] was *penal,* and could not be enforced beyond the limits of Illinois." [28]

Blair should feel easy, Field went on, about the case of Strader vs. Graham; it was not in the way. There, the Supreme Court had merely decided that questions of status were not such as to lie within its jurisdiction if they came to it from State courts; the Scott case was from a Federal court.[29] In closing this long and rather discursive letter, Field mentioned that the record of the case in the District Court had been printed at St. Louis and sent "to many in the eastern states," where, as had happened to the case itself in Missouri, it had not attracted any attention. He would enclose a copy in his letter, he promised Blair, if he could obtain one from Edmund La Beaume. The efforts of Dred's friends to obtain publicity and financial and other assistance for their client were not, at this time, too successful.[30]

Because of a crowded docket, the Supreme Court did not take up the Scotts' case for over a year. Justice John McLean, the most militant anti-slavery man on the bench, had noticed it, seen its political implications, and written about it to a friend, John Teesdale, an Ohio editor.[31] Apart from this, the case apparently did not cause a ripple. Montgomery Blair, in the meantime, was occupied with another case in which Sanford was again the defendant, the suit which involved his claim to a large tract of land in St. Charles County, Missouri, and in which Sanford was much more interested than in that which involved Dred and his family. Like the Scott case, it had been heard in St. Louis by the Federal District Court in 1854 and the court had taken jurisdiction over it on the same grounds that it had acted in the Scott case, diversity of citizenship. Judge Wells had instructed the jury that the law was in Sanford's favor and they had so decided. The defendants had carried the case on a writ of error to the Supreme Court and employed Blair to fight their case for them in Washington where, like the Scott case, it had to wait its turn.[32]

1. Bay, *Reminiscences*, pp. 540-542. Wells, who had been Attorney General of Missouri from 1826 to 1836, was a slave-holder most of his life but had become convinced "that the institution was a stumbling block in the progress of his state, and at a very early time had advocated a gradual system of emancipation" (Bay, *Reminiscences*, p. 540).

2. *Tri-Weekly Missouri Republican*, April 3, 1854.

3. "Dred Scott vs. John F. A. Sandford" [sic], Records, Supreme Court of the United States. In his declaration, Dred charged that Sanford, "with force and arms assaulted the plaintiff, and without law or right held him as a slave, and imprisoned him for the space of six hours and more, and then and there did threaten to beat the plaintiff, and to hold him imprisoned and restrained of his liberty, so that by means of such threats the plaintiff was put in fear and could not attend to his business, and thereby lost great gains and profits . . ." The same type of attack, allegedly, was made on Harriet and the girls.

4. Bay, *Reminiscences*, pp. 236-241; Edmund P. Walsh, "The Story of an Old Clerk," *Glimpses of the Past*, 1 (July, 1934), p. 67.

5. Edmund Chauvette La Beaume, the third son of Louis de Tarteron de la Beaume and Suzanne Chauvette du Breuil, was born in 1820 (Ms. in the possession of Mr. Louis La Beaume, St. Louis, Mo.). He became a lawyer and an early member of the American Party in St. Louis (St. Louis *Daily New Era*, April 6, 1846), was active in St. Louis in support of Taylor for the presidency (*ibid.*, April 20, 1848), and died in San Antonio, Texas, on May 15, 1858 (*Daily Missouri Democrat*, May 31, 1858). At the time of his death, he was not a slave-owner ("Edmund La Beaume," Files, Probate Court, St. Louis). Why he took such an interest in the Scott case is problematic. He may have been acting for the Blows, a close-knit family, who, at the departure of Drake from St. Louis, may have entrusted the case to another relative by marriage. He may, as a lawyer of conservative background and party affiliations, have been interested in seeing the questions raised by the Scott case laid to rest. If the motives of La Beaume could be ascertained, a great deal of the mystery about the Scott case would be cleared up. Roswell M. Field to Montgomery Blair, Jan. 7, 1855, Blair Papers, Library of Congress. On the matter of the sale of the Scott family, cf., below, notes 7-8.

6. Mrs. Emerson married Chaffee on Nov. 21, 1850 (Records, City Clerk's Office, Springfield, Mass.). On Chaffee, see *Biographical Dictionary of the American Congress: 1774-1927* (69 Congress, 2 Session, House Document 783, Washington, United States Printing Office, 1928), p. 798.

7. By virtue of an act of the General Assembly of Missouri, passed March 3, 1845, "No married woman shall be a guardian or curator of the estate of a minor; and if any woman, after her appointment, marry, the marriage shall operate as a revocation of her appointment; but a married woman may be the guardian of the person of a minor. . . ." By an act passed by the same body on March 26, 1845, ". . . no married woman shall be executrix or administratrix. . . . If any executrix or administratrix marry, her husband shall not thereby acquire any interest in the effects of her testator or intestate, nor shall the administration thereby devolve upon him, but the marriage shall extinguish her powers and her letters be revoked. . . . If there be more than one executor or administrator of an estate, and the letters of part of them be revoked or surrendered, or a part die, those who remain shall discharge all duties required by law respecting the estate" (William C. Jones (ed.), *The Revised Statutes of the State of Missouri* (St. Louis: J. W. Dougherty, 1845), pp. 63, 67, 69, 549). These laws were operative in Missouri till 1919. Cf. Charles H. Hardin (ed.), *The Revised Statutes of the State of Missouri* (Jefferson City: James Lusk, 1856), I, p. 825, and *Missouri Revised Statutes Annotated* 42 (1919).

8. "Alexander Sanford" and "John F. A. Sanford," Files, Probate Court, St.

Louis. Among the papers of John Sanford there is a bill from Benammi Garland, "To ten years service attending to Dred Scott's case, suing for freedom of self and family, employing counsel, attending to hires and collecting same at the request of Mr. Sanford from November 1846 to January 1857—$300." This amount was allowed Garland by the estate. This confusing situation has led some writers to postulate some sort of legal transaction by which Mrs. Chaffee transferred ownership to her brother. There is no evidence that such a sale took place and there was no need for one.

9. Dred Scott Collection. The other suit, in which Sanford was interested was an action of ejectment brought by Sanford "to recover . . . a certain tract of land, containing 750 arpens more or less," which had come to him from his father-in-law, Pierre Chouteau, Jr. Cf. "Sebastian Willot, John McDonald, and Joseph Hunn v. John F. A. Sandford" [sic], 19 Howard 79-82. In both the cases in which Sanford was the defendant at the December Term, 1856, of the Supreme Court, his name was misspelled. It was also misspelled in the District Court, where, for example, in the Scott case, the summons was issued against "John F. A. Sandford" by the clerk, Benjamin F. Hickman (Dred Scott Collection). The correct spelling of his name will be used except for direct quotations.

10. John F. Lee to Mary Louise Dalton, Feb. 15, 1907 (Dred Scott Collection). According to this letter, Crane, who had died a year or so before, told Lee that Dred, who had the chore of cleaning Field's office at this time, told him his story and that Crane, seeing that there were grounds for a suit for freedom, brought suit and did practically all the work in the case. Also, according to Crane, Dred was not particularly interested in the suit and was practically free. That Crane was very active in Dred's interest is clear. According to the writer in *Frank Leslie's Illustrated Newspaper* for June 27, 1857, Crane's "indefatigable industry to serve Dred had 'become a proverb.'" That he was the only person interested is not accurate. According to Lee, Crane drank heavily. Time may also have obscured the details. Crane was born in Wolcott, Vermont in 1834 and did not arrive in St. Louis till 1856 ("Abra Nelson Crane—A Memorial," St. Louis Bar Association, 1906).

11. Dred Scott Collection.

12. "Dred Scott vs. John F. A. Sandford" [sic], Records, United States Supreme Court.

13. Roswell Field to Montgomery Blair, Jan. 7, 1855 (Blair Papers, Library of Congress); Dred Scott Collection. For a discussion of citizenship, cf., below, Chapter 8.

14. Dred Scott Collection.

15. Thomas C. Reynolds, the United States District Attorney at the time of the case and later Governor of Missouri, stated, in an interview, that the Scott case created no stir at all when it was in the State courts and the Federal district court (Ms., Dred Scott Collection). A survey of the St. Louis papers from 1846 to 1856 revealed only one mention of the case (St. Louis *Herald*, May 18, 1854).

16. Dred Scott Collection.

17. Robert Wells to Montgomery Blair, Feb. 12, 1856, Blair Papers, Library of Congress.

18. Dred Scott Collection; St. Louis *Herald*, May 18, 1854.

19. *Frank Leslie's Illustrated Newspaper*, June 27, 1857; John F. Lee to Mary Louise Dalton, Feb. 15, 1907 (Dred Scott Collection).

20. Roswell Field to Montgomery Blair, Dec. 24, 1854 (Blair Papers, Library of Congress). For Napton and Scott, cf., above, Chapter 2, pp. 17-20.

21. Cf., above, note 10.

22. William E. Smith, *The Francis Preston Blair Family in Politics* (New York: The Macmillan Co., 1933), I, p. 185.

23. Roswell Field to Montgomery Blair, Dec. 24, 1854 (Blair Papers, Library of Congress). The Blows, at this time, were sufficiently well off to have financed the

suit. The two lawyers, La Beaume and Crane, would have found it a burden. Field himself could have met the costs. At this point in the history of the case, there apparently were limits to the lengths the Blows were willing to go for Dred. Governor Reynolds stated that "Scott's case was backed by people interested in testing the question . . . whether a slave taken into the Northwest territory became free, and when brought back to a slave-holding State, if he still remained free." Reynolds added that there was very little reason for testing the question, as very few slaves came back. He did not remember the names of the backers. They were not known as abolitionists, the Governor stated, because there was no such party in Missouri then (Ms., Dred Scott Collection).

24. *National Intelligencer,* Dec. 24, 1856; Smith, *The Francis Preston Blair Family in Politics,* I, pp. 209-210.

25. Gamaliel Bailey to Lyman Trumbull, May 12, 1857 (Lyman Trumbull Papers, Library of Congress); William E. Smith, *The Francis Preston Blair Family in Politics,* I, pp. 385-386; Roswell Field to Montgomery Blair, Jan. 7, 1855 (Blair Papers, Library of Congress).

26. "The citizens of each state shall be entitled to all privileges and immunities of citizens in the several states," Article Four, section 2, paragraph 1.

27. Cf., below, Chapter 10, pp. 146-151.

28. Cf., below, Chapter 4, p. 36.

29. 10 Howard 82; cf., below, Chapter 10, pp. 147-149.

30. Roswell Field to Montgomery Blair, Jan. 7, 1855 (Blair Papers, Library of Congress).

31. John McLean to John Teesdale, November 2, 1855 (*Bibliotheca Sacra,* 56, 1899, p. 737).

32. "Sebastian Willot et al., Plaintiffs in Error, vs. John F. A. Sandford" (Records, United States Supreme Court). Sanford's lack of interest in the Scott case is frequently mentioned. Cf. *Missouri Daily Republican,* March 22, 1857; New York *Courier and Enquirer,* Dec. 18, 1856.

4

BEFORE THE HIGHEST TRIBUNAL

BLAIR SENT A COPY OF HIS BRIEF FOR THE SCOTTS TO JUDGE WELLS for criticism on January 31, 1856, but he had to appear in court without the judge's advice.[1] The Supreme Court of the United States heard the case for the first time on February 11, 1856. It was to the old courtroom on the ground floor of the Senate wing that Blair betook himself that day, making his entrance from the circular enclosure under the rotunda, dark, damp and cellarlike, through a hall, into a rather plain, moderately sized room, which Benjamin Latrobe had dignified with a masonry vault supported by square columns. It was lighted by windows immediately behind the seats of the judges, an arrangement that made it difficult for the spectators to see the justices' faces, once they were seated.

The judges entered "without any flourish of parade . . . in their black silk gowns . . . ranked according to the dates of their respective commissions." At the head of the procession there walked "with firm and steady step . . . a tall, thin, man, slightly bent with the weight of years, of pale complexion, and features somewhat attenuated and careworn, but lighted up with that benignant expression which is indicative at once of a gentle temper and a kindly heart," Taney, the Chief Justice whom Jackson had appointed in 1836.[2] He sat in the center of the bench. On his right was John McLean, of Ohio, now in his seventy-first year, who had been on the bench since 1829, having been elevated to that post when Jackson found him an uncooperative Postmaster General. On Taney's left was James Moore Wayne, of Georgia, who had been appointed to his position by Jackson in 1835, after he had given the General loyal support in the House of Representatives. Next to McLean was John Catron, a homespun man from Tennessee, whose appointment to the bench, in 1837, was one of Jackson's last acts as President. On Wayne's right sat Peter Vivian Daniel, Virginia aristocrat, who owed his position to Van Buren. Next to Catron was Samuel Nelson, of New York, a veteran State judge, who had been appointed to the Supreme Court by Tyler.

Daniel was flanked by Robert Cooper Grier, of Pennsylvania, college professor, farmer, lawyer, judge, who had come to the court in 1846 through Polk. At the far side of the right end of the bench was Benjamin Robbins Curtis, of Massachusetts, an appointee of Fillmore, who, with his fellow junior on the left, John Archibald Campbell, of Alabama, a nominee of Pierce, were the only two justices on the bench to be born in the nineteenth century.

It was not before complete strangers that Blair was to plead the case of Dred Scott and his family. In the old days of "King Andrew," Taney, McLean, Wayne, Catron had once been household names in the Blair family, only less familiar than those of Benton and Jackson himself. For many years, though, they had all gone their own ways and how widely they had separated would soon be made clear.

At this trial, Blair appeared alone for the Scotts.[3] Speaking in the high, thin voice that was characteristic of himself and his father, he first addressed himself to the question of citizenship, arguing in support of Judge Wells' decision on Scott's demurrer upholding the citizenship of free Negroes, at least in so far as to enable them to sue in the courts of the United States. Blair first analysed a case that had appeared before the Supreme Court of Kentucky in 1822, that of Amy vs. Smith. He found that the opinion of the majority, "that to be a citizen, it is necessary that he [the person so claiming] should be entitled to the enjoyment of those privileges and immunities upon the same terms upon which they are conferred upon other citizens, and unless he be so entitled, he cannot, in the proper sense of the term, be a citizen," [4] displayed "no research, logic or learning." Its pronouncement in 1822 was merely one of the results of the bitter struggle over the admission of Missouri into the Union and the agitation of the Negro question.[5]

He adopted the reasoning of Judge Mills, who had dissented. According to Blair, Mills first disposed of "the absurd test of citizenship" set up by Chief Justice Boyle, who had spoken for the majority, by showing that such a definition of citizenship would exclude many who were acknowledged to be citizens by all. It would, for example, Mills had pointed out, exclude all naturalised citizens who were, by the Constitution, ineligible for the Presidency. Blair made his own Mills' distinction between political functions and civil rights, stressing the fact that the qualifications required for electors, representatives, jurors and witnesses were tests of fitness, not of citizenship. Stipulations as to age, property, sex, religious belief, or the lack of it, Blair continued, paraphrasing Mills, determined capability for office and did not affect citizenship. In concluding his analysis of Mills' opinion, Blair declared, "It appears . . . that the essence of citizenship is the right of protection of life and liberty, to acquire and enjoy property and equal taxation. Suffrage is not an absolute right of citizenship." These rights free Negroes had and, so, were citizens.[6]

This statement of Judge Mills on the constituent parts of citizenship, Blair continued, was fully sustained by the opinion of Judge Washington in Corfield vs. Coryell.[7] The same doctrine was held and applied to the precise point under discussion in the Scott case, the citizenship of free Negroes, by Judge Gaston, of the North Carolina Supreme Court, in the State vs. Manuel.[8]

Blair rejected the argument against Negro citizenship drawn from the Federal immigration laws, which limited the right to become citizens to alien whites, as not being *in pari materia*. It confused, he said, emancipation with naturalisation, two legal processes Judge Gaston had said it would be "a dangerous mistake to confound." To remove the disabilities of alienage, a function of the Federal government, was not the same as removing the incapacity of slavery, a matter which depended wholly upon the internal regulations of a State. Naturalisation, Blair continued, was not restricted to whites by the Constitution. As a matter of fact, he pointed out, it had been extended repeatedly to Indians and free Negroes. Blair then cited numerous treaties with various Indian tribes, the treaty of 1803, by which Louisiana had been acquired, the Adams-Onís Treaty of 1819, by which Florida was secured for the United States, and the Treaty of Guadalupe-Hidalgo of 1847 in which California and New Mexico were ceded to the Union. In the three last-mentioned treaties provision had been made that the inhabitants of the ceded lands should become citizens of the United States, and among these inhabitants were many free Negroes.

Blair then challenged the defense. That citizenship was acquired by birth, he stated, was a well-settled common law principle. "If there be limitations," he contended, "on a principle adopted in the United States, which is of universal application in the mother country, it is for those who insist on the limitation to show affirmatively that such limitations have been established here." He felt sure that it could not be proved that free Negroes were not citizens in the limited sense for which he and Judge Mills contended.[9] Dred Scott, he admitted, was not eligible to office, he was not a voter, "and therefore is not a citizen entitled to all the privileges secured by the fourth article [of the United States Constitution]; but that he is a *quasi* citizen, or citizen in the sense of the term which enables him to acquire and hold property under the States and the United States is universally admitted; and it would seem to follow, necessarily, that all the incidents to these acknowledged rights of person and property, or all the rights necessary to maintain them, and which are allowed to others in the same circumstances . . . attached also to these persons." [10] Free Negroes could sue and be sued in the State courts. What was more, "suits have heretofore been maintained in the courts of the United States, without question—an instance of which is the suit of Legrand vs. Darnell [sic] . . . brought by the present Chief Justice of the Supreme Court in which the defendant is described in the bill as a Negro." [11] The whole purpose of the provision of the Constitution, he concluded, which gave Federal courts jurisdiction over cases which arose between the citizens of different States was to facilitate justice and good will. How, he asked, was this end furthered by excluding free Negroes?

Blair next considered "whether Dred and his family, or either of them, was emancipated by being taken to Illinois and to that part of Louisiana Territory lying north of thirty-six degrees thirty minutes, and being detained there in the manner described in the agreed case." [12] Reserving for separate treatment the validity of the eighth section of the Missouri Compromise Act, on which the freedom of Harriet Scott and the younger daughter, Lizzie, depended, Blair made a special plea for Eliza, the older daughter, arguing that, since she was born on board ship on the Mississippi River north of the Missouri line, the presumption was that she was born in Illinois, "if such presumption is, for any reason, more favorable to her freedom than the supposition that she was born in the Territory." [13] To free Eliza, Blair cited both sections of the sixth article of the Illinois Constitution, first that "neither slavery nor involuntary servitude shall be introduced into this State otherwise than for the punishment of crime whereof the party shall be duly convicted"; secondly, "that no person bound to labor in any other State shall be hired to labor in this State, except within the tract reserved for the Salt Works near Shawneetown, nor even at that place for a longer period than one year at a time; nor shall it be allowed there after the year one thousand eight hundred and twenty-five. Any violation of this article shall effect the emancipation of such person from his obligation to service." He buttressed his argument with two cases—one, Spotts vs. Gillaspie, in which the Virginia Court of Appeals had decided that a child, born in Pennsylvania after slavery had been abolished there, was free in Virginia as well as Pennsylvania, though born of a mother who was still a slave; the other, Commonwealth vs. Holloway, in which the child of a fugitive slave, born in Pennsylvania, was held to be free by that State's Supreme Court.[14] As for the younger daughter, Blair pointed out that she would be free if her mother were at the time of her birth.

He next turned his attention to the case of Strader vs. Graham,[15] in which the Supreme Court of the United States had said that there was "nothing in the Constitution of the United States that can control the law of Kentucky upon this subject [the status of persons domiciled within the State]; and the condition of the Negroes, therefore, as to freedom or slavery after their return, depended altogether upon the laws of that State, and could not be influenced by the laws of Ohio. It was exclusively in the power of Kentucky to determine for itself whether their employment in another State should or should not make them free on their return." According to Blair, this decision had force "only upon questions arising upon a local law of real property, or on the construction of the statutes of a State . . . and then only when such exposition is settled and fixed by the decisions of the State courts, whereas, in this case, no such statute or local law is invoked."

This led Blair to a consideration of comity. Judge Scott, of the Missouri Supreme Court, had refused to recognize the liberating effects of the sixth section of the Illinois Constitution and the eighth section of the Missouri Compromise Act in Missouri, in substance a refusal to extend comity to the laws of that State and Territory in this matter. On the contrary, Scott had held that, by returning to Missouri, Dred Scott had caused his master's right in him, suspended while he was in Illinois and the Minnesota Territory, to revive. To support his position the Missouri judge had relied, to some extent, on the reasoning of Lord Stowell in the case of the slave Grace.[16] Stowell could hold for such a suspension of dominion in the case cited, Blair contended, because there was no statute law at all on slavery in England. The theory, however, was not tenable in the Scott case because, by the Constitution of Illinois and the Missouri Compromise Act, ownership became non-existent. While Judge Scott had cited the slave Grace case and also, in passing, the Massachusetts case of Commonwealth vs. Aves,[17] Blair held that he had really decided the fate of the Scotts on the principles laid down by Justice Story in his *Conflict of Laws*. But, Blair charged, Judge Scott could find support for his decision only by severing the statement of the doctrine "from that portion of the section referred to which pointed to the mode of ascertaining and giving application to its principles." Granted that courts of justice did not presume the adoption by their own government of laws prejudicial to its own policy and interests, Story's teaching on the subject, Blair held that it was not the function of judges to decide what was prejudicial and what was not. The comity of the State, not of the courts of the State, was to be ascertained and administered and it was to be found in the statutes, customs and precedents of the State, not in the reasoning and will of Judge Scott.[18]

Having completed his plea for the citizenship of free Negroes, in so far as to enable them to sue in the Federal courts, and having finished his critique of the arguments of Judges Scott and Wells on the nature and extra-territorial effect of the Illinois Constitution and the Missouri Compromise Act, Blair next considered the effect on the Scotts' status of their residence in the Minnesota Territory alone. To get the Supreme Court of the United States to hear the case, the first point had to be established. His contention that the Illinois Constitution had effect beyond its own boundaries, if accepted by the judges, would establish Dred's claim to freedom and, possibly, Eliza's. To secure the freedom of the whole family, Blair would have to depend on the effect of the eighth section of the Missouri Compromise Act. But to have effect, the act had to be valid and its validity depended on the power of Congress, under the Constitution, to pass it.

The Blairs had no doubts about the power of Congress to exclude slavery from the territories. They had all supported Van Buren in his annoyance campaign of 1848 and had never wavered in their devotion to the slogan, "Free soil, free speech, free labor and free men." The whole family had collaborated in 1850 on an "Address to the Democracy of Missouri" which had urged the prohibition of slavery in New Mexico and California and which had expatiated on the virtues of Senator Benton. Congress, the address asserted, had the power to pass prohibitory legislation and it was proper to use it. In the Blairs' opinion, and in that of the thirty-five Democrats of Missouri who signed it with them, "domestic slavery is pernicious to the prosperity of a community." Since the policy of prohibition was traditional in the United States, "the only question ought to be, and every friend of humanity ought to resolve to make it the only question, whether it would be wise and beneficial to the people who are to occupy those vast domains . . . to prohibit the introduction of domestic slavery there." The pride of the southern States, the Blairs and their associates charged, so skillfully played on by Calhoun whose ambition was at the root of the whole slavery agitation, was the only obstacle to the reasonable settlement of the whole problem.[19]

Montgomery Blair argued along the same lines in the Supreme Court. He first called attention to the crucial character of the issue, saying, "This is a question of more importance, perhaps, than any which was ever submitted to this court; and the decision of the court is looked for with a degree of interest by the country which seldom attends its proceedings. It is, indeed, the great question of our day and times, and is, substantially, the issue on which the great political divisions among men is founded in all times and countries. It is in form here a question on the construction of a few words in our fundamental law. But it is in the principle involved that shapes the conclusions of political men and parties, rather than the force or meaning of the language which constitutes properly the legal question." After this portentous introduction, Blair stated that the issue was "whether Congress has the power to prohibit slavery in the Territories; or, which is the same thing, whether the Constitution carries slavery into the Territories." He was aware, he continued, that there were some who supposed that an intermediate position might be maintained, but "the argument in support of what is known as squatter sovereignty" seemed to him "wholly *ad captandum,* and not to rest upon any basis recognised by the court." Having disposed, in this summary fashion, of Douglas and his theory, Blair, following on this point the views of his family and Benton, argued for the power of Congress to exclude slavery from the territories.

He first laid down some general principles. As there was for Blair no middle ground between the prohibition of slavery in the territories and the constitutional enforcement of slavery on them, between Wilmot and Calhoun, so, too, there was for him a "natural division among men wherever born . . . into those who sympathise with power and dread the people . . . and those who dread tyranny and fear the people less. . . . The power party naturally associates itself with property interests and institutions which create political privileges. The other naturally allies itself with the advocates of personal rights and opposes privileges. The contest going on under the issue here presented is but one phase of this ever-continued and ever-varying strife." Slavery vested political power in the few by the monopoly of the soil, wealth and knowledge it caused, Blair declared. The sense of inequality and privilege it created lay at the bottom of the contest then raging in the country, the outcome of which involved the fate of the whole continent. Were, Blair asked, the unsettled lands of the country to be filled with communities characterized by privilege? [20]

Such was not the intention of the framers of the Constitution, he continued. The prohibition of the slave trade proved "conclusively" that the policy of the founding fathers was against the extension of slavery, a conclusion that was strengthened by "the expressive silence of the Constitution on the subject of slavery." Congress had the power to prevent slavery from entering the national domain from the territorial provision of the Constitution, Blair went on, because that section dealt not only with the territory as land to be disposed of but also as land to be governed. Such, he contended, was the opinion of the Supreme Court in the Insurance Companies and Gratiot cases; [21] so Congress had always acted. It was for the opponents of Congressional power to point out "the express restrictive provisions of the Constitution on the legislative power" by which the exercise of such power was inhibited. So far, Blair said mistakenly, no such restraint had been cited but appeal had been made only to the spirit of that document. [22]

After Blair had concluded his argument that his clients, the Scotts, were free by reason of their residence on free soil and that a decision to that effect by the Supreme Court of the United States was due them because they were citizens of the body civil, if not politic, Senator Geyer, of Missouri, who owed his position in Washington to that unholy alliance between pro-slavery Democrats and the Whigs in Missouri which Edward Bates had found so deplorable, rose to speak for the defendant. His views on the questions involved were almost as well known as Blair's. An adverse decision a year before in a case which he had argued before the court had rather soured the cold, austere Senator. In his irritation he had announced that he had "no confidence in a court that will allow a man [Catron] who is always half drunk to write out so absurd a decision and let it go to the world as the opinion of the court." Perhaps he felt that he could convince the Court more easily on the citizenship of Negroes, the power of Congress over slavery in the territories, and the position of a sovereign State in the matter of extending comity to a sister State than he had concerning the superiority of certain land titles in Missouri.[23] On all these questions he held and, probably, expounded the southern viewpoint in a way that should have pleased the coalition that had sent him to the Senate.[24]

On the day following the argument of the case, Judge Wells wrote to Blair from Jefferson City, forwarding his opinion of Blair's brief. The problem of the right of a free Negro to sue in the Federal courts had been on his mind and he had a new slant on it. It had been urged in the district court, he told Blair, that the allowing of such suits "may be viewed as a privilege extended or attempted to be extended to Negroes against the feelings or policy of the people of the Slave States." But, Wells reasoned, if free Negroes could not sue in the courts of the United States, they could not be sued there. This would amount to according them an exemption that white citizens did not enjoy. He pointed out that aliens could sue in the Federal courts and that, consequently, Negroes of British citizenship could go to law in them. After this rather novel discussion of citizenship, the judge told Blair that his brief was incomplete and, for that reason, unfair to him and his court. The legal status of the inhabitants of a State was a matter for that commonwealth to decide. The Supreme Court of Missouri had decided that the Scotts were slaves. The Supreme Court of the United States usually followed the interpretations of State supreme courts of their own laws. The case of Strader vs. Graham was in point and Blair should consider it carefully. It was on this ground that he had decided against Scott in the lower court, though, in doing so, he had acted against his own feelings.[25]

A week after the case had been heard, James Harvey, a confidant of Judge McLean, wrote a dispatch from Washington to the New York *Tribune* which informed the widely scattered readers of that paper that the case would be decided against Scott on the "pretext" that his return to Missouri restored his servile status.

By this means the Court would "evade" the real issue, the power of Congress over slavery in the territories, and "prevent" the delivery of dissenting opinions which would sustain the constitutionality of the Missouri Compromise which had been repealed almost two years before. But, Harvey assured his *Tribune* audience, "an effort will be made to get a positive decree of some sort, and, in that event, there is some hope of aid from the Southern members of the court." [26] McLean, whom Duff Green twenty-five years before had discovered to aspire "to the first honor," was about to disregard that worthy's advice and attempt to bring the bench "in collision with a popular election." [27] A rousing dissent on the question of the extension of slavery in the territories and the power of Congress to inhibit it would make an excellent pre-convention impression on the delegates to the Republican Convention to be held in Philadelphia in May, 1856. It was about the only way a justice of the highest court in the country could appear before the electorate without shocking that susceptible body's convictions on judicial propriety. McLean's friends thought that the opportunity presented by the Scott case should not be wasted and were loath to see the Court settle the question of the Scotts' freedom by a denial of its own jurisdiction over the matter.

On April 7, the Court held consultations on the case. The next day, Judge Curtis wrote, as was his custom, a rather full letter to his uncle and patron, the scholarly George Ticknor. After discussing some French law books, in which his uncle was interested, and the beauties of the Washington spring, he told his uncle, "The court will not decide the question of the Missouri Compromise line—a majority of the judges being of the opinion that it is not necessary to do so. (This is confidential)." The capital was agog over the coming election, he told Ticknor, "and upon this everything done or omitted . . . depends. Judge McLean hopes, I think, to be a candidate for the office. He would be a good President, but I am not willing to have a judge in that most trying position of being a candidate for this great office." [28] The efforts of McLean's friends had not been successful so far.

On the same day, Harvey supplied the *Tribune* with the quite accurate information that the Court was evenly divided on the question, whether the plea in abatement to the jurisdiction of the lower court was before it and, consequently, whether the Court could consider the citizenship of free Negroes, the subject matter of the plea. Justice Nelson, Harvey said, was the undecided mem-

41

ber.[29] *Tribune* readers of April 10 were told that the Court would decide against Scott but that Justice McLean would confound those "who are prepared to repudiate the judgments of Southern Courts and the practices of Southern States" in his dissent.[30]

The consultations of the Court were repeated and protracted. The bone of contention was the disposition to be made of the plea in abatement and the question it contained, the citizenship of free Negroes. Taney and Curtis argued with great earnestness that it was a proper subject for consideration. Wayne was of the same opinion and Daniel informed his brethren that he intended to give his opinion on the question presented by it. Nelson inclined to this view of the question. McLean, Catron, Grier and Campbell were opposed. The plea was not before the Court, in their opinion, and some of them denounced it as an astute attempt by some unscrupulous lawyers to catch an opinion on a mooted point which the facts of the case did not demand. When the matter was put to a vote, a bare majority favored a discussion of the citizenship of free Negroes in the opinion of the Court. After this vote and at the same consultation of the Court, before any judge was designated to write the opinion, Nelson, apparently still weak in his conviction that the subject should be treated and, perhaps, wary of bringing the bench "in collision with a popular election," moved a reargument of the questions which had divided the Court and the motion was carried. Nelson was asked to prepare an order, relative to the questions to be reargued, and, when it was reported to the judges, they adopted it.[31]

The case was to be reargued at the next term and two points were to be stressed. Could the Supreme Court take notice of the facts admitted in Scott's answer to Sanford's plea to the jurisdiction of the Court, after the latter had submitted to Judge Wells' ruling on the plea and had fought the case on its merits, in order to decide whether the lower court had jurisdiction over the matter? Granted that the Court could, was Scott a citizen of Missouri?[32] This decision of the Supreme Court to rehear the case annoyed Harvey thoroughly. There would be no dissent to publicise and the estimable virtues of Judge McLean would have to be made known in some other way. He entertained his readers with a snarl or two at what he chose to regard as the essential duplicity of his candidate's associates.[33]

Meanwhile, the Justice was busy receiving and writing letters. One of the first to be received was from Judge Hornblower, retired Chief Justice of New Jersey, who wrote on May 13 that he was concerned about the Scott case, involving as it did the Missouri Compromise. His opinion on the question coincided with that McLean had expressed in a communication to the *National Intelligencer* in 1847, which had recently been reprinted at Newark. If only their opinion were to prevail, Hornblower told McLean, there would be no more trouble. The crisis, he continued, demonstrated the need of "a wise, patriotic, well balanced, experienced, firm, self-reliant statesman" and Hornblower was glad to see the public mind turning toward McLean. "You are on the spot," he told the Justice, "and as this is a purely political question, and partakes not at all of a judicial character, you may properly express your opinions and exercise your rightful influence in regard to it. The exigency demands that we overlook mere forms." [34]

McLean did not reply to this very flattering proposal. On June 2, a correspondent, John Allison, wrote to McLean that their mutual friend, Alexander C. Pennington, was anxious to know if he had received Hornblower's letter and, if he had, whether he intended to answer it. It was Pennington's opinion that much depended on a speedy answer. The letter presented McLean with a fine opportunity to place his views on Kansas before the country "in such a way as not to be at all obnoxious to any charge of impropriety." Allison appreciated the delicacy of McLean's position, but a statement from him on public affairs was urgently needed. [35]

On June 6th, McLean, whose friends had kept his hopes of reaching the presidency alive for years, replied to Hornblower from Cincinnati. The Scott case, he told the Jersey judge, was to be reargued and he could not properly say anything on it. But, he assured him, "I must express my gratification in knowing that you are satisfied with my views, already publicly avowed, as to the constitutional power of the General Government over the subject of Slavery in the Territories." In closing, he deplored the public indifference, manifested in all quarters, to the salutary principle of the Northwest Ordinance. Hornblower's letter and McLean's reply were promptly published in the Newark *Daily Advertiser* on June 14th and reprinted in the New York *Tribune* two days later. The latter paper thanked both the judges "for this timely and noble correspondence" and assured McLean that the whole weight of the Greeley organ would be behind him, if he managed to get the nomination at Philadelphia.[36]

On the same day that he had written Hornblower, McLean wrote a much fuller letter to the anxious Mr. Pennington. He already knew, McLean presumed, that the Missouri suit, to which Pennington had referred, was continued to the December Term. This, of course, effectively shut the justice's mouth; still, the latter felt that he had to express his gratification that Pennington agreed with him on the constitutional powers of Congress over slavery in the territories. He had been moved, he continued, by his correspondent's allusions to his native State, his adopted home and the Northwest Ordinance. He had always cherished New Jersey, though he had grown up in the west "under the congenial influences of that immortal ordinance which has wisely guaranteed liberty forever to that beautiful region; and which her millions of peaceful and patriotic people will never cease to reverence as the foundation of their progress, prosperity and power." As he had told Hornblower, he now told Pennington that he was pained by the growing hostility to the great measure of Jefferson. Though it had been the theme of eulogy with lawyers and statesmen of the highest eminence in all sections of the country, some, now, even questioned its constitutionality.

Events in Kansas, McLean went on, were equally deplorable. They were all "parts of that ill advised and mischievous measure, the repeal of the Missouri Compromise, which from the first I have earnestly deprecated." Kansas should be admitted as a State immediately. The justice closed with a gloomy prophecy, "No intelligent observer can fail to see that the tendency of our institutions is now rapidly downward, and all history and experience show that no free government with such tendencies was ever arrested in its declining career without a revolution, either by peaceful change of its policy and rulers, or by the bloody arbitrament of the sword." Let the people act, he urged.[37] Justice McLean's dissent was already a matter of record and these letters placed the judge before the Republican Convention, which was to assemble eleven days after they were written, as a candidate. The nomination, however, went to John C. Frémont, to the chagrin, among others, of Orville H. Browning, who assured McLean that the choice would have fallen on the judge if only his friends had held fast. All that could be done was to hope for 1860.[38]

Little attention was paid the Scott case while the country was

44

occupied in the business of assessing the merits of Buchanan, Frémont and Fillmore, the presidential candidates of the Democratic, Republican and American Parties.[39] Toward the end of June, Representative Campbell, a Republican from Ohio, rose in the House to ask Alexander Stephens why he and those who agreed with him that the Missouri Compromise was unconstitutional had never brought the question before the courts and so put an end to the agitation. Stephens replied, rather vaguely, "There is a case of that sort now before the Supreme Court." Campbell was not satisfied with this reference to the Scott case, in which Stephens was to manifest a much keener interest before the year was over, and asked Stephens again why he had never gone to law in the matter. Stephens answered that it was his first duty, as a legislator, to see that Congress repealed what he considered "that old political upas planted by Rufus King in 1820" which had grown up, flourished and sent "its poisonous exhalations throughout this country, till it came well nigh to extinguishing the life of the Republic in 1850." If Congress had not repealed it and he was, as a resident of a territory, personally affected by it, he might very well have fought its constitutionality in the courts.[40]

NOTES

1. Robert Wells to Montgomery Blair, Feb. 12, 1856 (Blair Papers, Library of Congress).
2. George Van Santvoord, *Sketches of the Lives and Judicial Services of the Chief Justices of the Supreme Court of the United States* (New York: Charles Scribner, 1854), pp. 460-462.
3. Washington *Daily Union,* March 19, 1857.
4. 1 Littell 326; cf., below, Chapter 8, p. 98.
5. "Argument of Montgomery Blair . . . for the Plaintiff in Error," Records, Supreme Court of the United States, December Term, 1856, No. 7, pp. 5-6. Hereafter cited as "Argument of Montgomery Blair." Blair filed two briefs. The one here cited is the earlier. It was filed Dec. 2, 1856.
6. "Argument of Montgomery Blair," p. 7.
7. 4 Washington Circuit Court Reports 371.
8. 4 Devereux and Battle 24; cf., below, Chapter 8, pp. 102-103.
9. "Argument of Montgomery Blair," p. 10.
10. *Ibid.,* p. 14.
11. 2 Peters 670; cf., below, Chapter 8, p. 99.
12. "Argument of Montgomery Blair," p. 16.
13. *Ibid.*
14. 6 Randolph 572; 2 Sergeant and Rawle 305.
15. 10 Howard 93; cf., below, Chapter 10, p. 151.
16. 2 Haggard 94; cf., below, Chapter 10, pp. 147-149.
17. 18 Pickering 194; cf., below, Chapter 10, pp. 149-150.
18. For a discussion of Story's influence, cf., below, Chapter 10, pp. 150-151.

45

19. Montgomery Blair [*et al.*], "Address to the Democracy of Missouri," Library of Congress.

20. "Argument of Montgomery Blair," pp. 26-28.

21. Insurance Companies vs. Canter, 1 Peters 542; United States vs. Gratiot, 14 Peters 527. Cf., below, Chapter 9, pp. 117-120.

22. Cf. the rather frequent use of the Fifth Amendment to the Constitution in this connection as discussed in Chapter 9, below.

23. John Magwin to Thomas Ewing, March 14, 1855 (Ewing Papers, Library of Congress).

24. Senator Geyer's brief, if he filed one, is not among the records of the Supreme Court. He and Blair were the only two lawyers at this hearing; cf. Washington *Daily Union,* March 19, 1857.

25. Robert Wells to Montgomery Blair, Feb. 12, 1856 (Blair Papers, Library of Congress).

26. New York *Tribune,* Feb. 18, 1856.

27. Duff Green to John McLean, Sept. 5, 1829 (Duff Green Letter Book, Library of Congress).

28. Benjamin R. Curtis (ed.), *A Memoir of Benjamin R. Curtis* (Boston: Little, Brown and Co., 1879), I, pp. 179-180.

29. New York *Tribune,* April 8, 1856.

30. *Ibid.,* April 10, 1856.

31. John A. Campbell to George T. Curtis, Oct. 18, 1879 (Copy of Mr. Charles Warren, Campbell Papers).

32. 20 Wallace, x-xi, remarks of Judge Campbell on the death of Judge Curtis; "Dred Scott vs. Sandford," Records, Supreme Court of the United States. John A. Campbell to George T. Curtis, Oct. 18, 1879 (Campbell Papers, Copy of Charles Warren).

33. New York *Tribune,* May 14, 1856. That the author of these dispatches was James Harvey has been proved by Jeter A. Isley. See his, *Horace Greeley and the Republican Party, 1853-1861* (Princeton: Princeton University Press, 1947), p. 226.

34. New York *Tribune,* June 16, 1856.

35. McLean Papers, Library of Congress.

36. New York *Tribune,* June 16, 1856.

37. McLean to A. C. Pennington, June 6, 1856 (McLean Papers, Library of Congress).

38. Orville H. Browning to McLean, March 23, 1857 (McLean Papers, Library of Congress).

39. Warren, *The Supreme Court in United States History,* I, p. 285.

40. *Congressional Globe,* 34 Cong., 1 sess., Appendix, pp. 725-726.

5

THE CASE REARGUED

THE CASE CAME UP FOR REARGUMENT ON DECEMBER 15, 1856. In the November election, James Buchanan had been chosen President and he and the Democratic Party were still congratulating themselves on having saved the Union and laid to rest the distracting question of the extension of slavery into the territories. According to President Pierce, the election had condemned geographical parties. He did not hesitate to call the Missouri Compromise unconstitutional.[1] Their wishful thinking ignored their own divided feelings on the question, the showing the young Republican Party had made at the polls, and the potentialities for political disaster of the journeyings, years before, of Dred Scott and his family.

Some members of the winning party thought they saw in the case a way to make security doubly sure. On the day the second argument commenced, Alexander Stephens, who, in 1848, had tabled the Clayton Compromise in the House of Representatives because, as a matter of principle, he was opposed to referring political questions to the court, wrote to his brother, Linton, that he had "been urging all the influences I could bring to bear upon the Supreme Court to get them to postpone no longer the case on the Missouri Restriction before them, but to decide it. They take it up to-day. If they decide, as I have reason to believe they will . . . ," the restriction would be declared unconstitutional and the question would not only be dead but buried.[2]

Montgomery Blair opened for the Scotts before "a superior audience." He intimated that he had had some difficulty in obtaining the help of associate counsel. Senator Geyer was joined in this rehearing of the case by Reverdy Johnson, of Maryland, late Attorney General of the United States, the leading forensic orator of his day, and a close personal friend of the Chief Justice. Blair, doubtful of his ability to handle two such titans of the law alone, had looked, first, to the south for assistance. Senator Badger, of North Carolina, who believed firmly in the power of Congress to legislate for the territories, had given the question of helping Blair some thought, but declined. Senator Fessenden, of Maine, had refused because the time for preparation was too short. Blair did secure, however, "the great ability and learning of Mr. Curtis, of Boston, to maintain the constitutionality of the power exerted by Congress" in the Missouri Compromise Act on which the freedom of the Scotts depended.[3]

George Ticknor Curtis was the brother of Justice Curtis and, like him, he had been a devoted follower of Daniel Webster, adhering to him in 1850 when many thought the god-like Daniel had betrayed the north in supporting the compromise measures of that year. In 1852, Curtis had accepted appointment as United States Commissioner in Boston, the office set up by the draconian Fugitive Slave Act of 1850 for the more effective return of runaway slaves. This, added to the fact that his brother, the judge, had upheld the constitutionality of the act and urged its enforcement on various grand juries, had made the name of Curtis anything but popular in certain Bostonian circles.[4]

For three hours Blair argued the questions that the Court had ordered, following, in the question of the citizenship of free Negroes, the line of argument he had previously used, distinguishing between civil and political rights, and contending that free Negroes were citizens in the sense that they enjoyed the former. He barely touched the constitutional question.[5]

Senator Geyer replied for Sanford, beginning on the 15th and closing the next day. He began by arguing the highly technical point involved in the first question the Court wished to rehear, the right the Supreme Court had to consider the facts alleged in the plea against the jurisdiction of the lower court after Sanford had submitted to the decision of that court on the question and passed on to the merits of the case.[6] Concluding that the Supreme Court could, Geyer discussed the citizenship of Negroes. Scott, he said, was a Negro who was born a slave. Whether he was free or not, he could not be a citizen of the United States. To be a citizen of the United States, a person had to be a citizen of the State in which he resided. To be a citizen of the United States, a person had to be born such or naturalized. All persons born in the United States were not its citizens. Indians were not and neither, in general, were persons of color. Geyer cited numerous cases which had decided that Negroes were not citizens to the extent of being entitled to all the privileges and immunities guaranteed to United

States citizens by the Constitution. Free Negroes were not born citizens of the United States. They could not be naturalized. They did not become citizens by manumission. So, they were not and the lower court erred in taking jurisdiction on the ground that Scott was a citizen of Missouri and, consequently, of the United States.

But, if the Court were not persuaded of the non-citizenship of Negroes and decided that the lower court had had jurisdiction, the agreed facts, Geyer continued, did not entitle any of the Scotts to their freedom. The Illinois Constitution and the Missouri Compromise Act prohibited slavery, but the clauses by which they did so did not change the condition of the slave brought into territory subject to either. The slave was free merely because there was no law to restrain him. On his return to a slave State, he remained a slave unless an act of virtual emancipation had taken place. Temporary sojourn, such as Dr. Emerson had intended and had taken place, was not such an act. The fate of the Scotts depended on the laws of Missouri and by those laws the Scotts were slaves and it was these laws that must determine the decision of the courts of the United States.

But, Geyer continued, a claim to freedom by reason of residence at Fort Snelling was useless. "Slavery," he declared, "existed by law in all the territory ceded by France to the United States, and Congress has not the constitutional power to repeal that law, or abolish or prohibit slavery within any part of that territory." The Senator conceded that Congress had the power to institute municipal governments for the territories but he denied that such power was "supreme, universal and unlimited power over the persons and property of the inhabitants." Congress had no authority to abolish slavery, "or to interfere with the local law of property in any form." [7]

Geyer contended that the power conferred by the territorial provision of the Constitution was merely one to dispose of and make rules and regulations for the lands and other property of the United States. "The subject of the power," he said, "is property and the property only of the United States, not of the inhabitants of the States or Territories." The power to organize a municipal government for a district "and more especially an unlimited power to legislate in all cases whatsoever over the inhabitants of a Territory and their property" could not be deduced from the clause of the Constitution under discussion. He then denied that the power of Congress to legislate for the government of acquired territory could be claimed as inevitable consequence of the right to acquire such lands. "The power of acquisition," he said, "is raised by implication and carries with it no incidents. . . . When territory is acquired, the power of acquisition as to that territory is exhausted." [8]

In Geyer's opinion, the source of the power which enabled Congress to institute temporary governments over the territories resulted from the fact that such districts were within the jurisdiction of the United States, but outside the jurisdiction of any particular State. It was a power that arose from necessity and which was limited by the necessity from which it arose. It was limited to the erection of temporary governments and was not an absolute power over persons and property. In the concrete, Geyer declared that "To change the law of property, to emancipate slaves, to abolish slavery where by law it exists, to confiscate property, or divest vested rights, cannot be necessary or proper to the institution of a temporary government." When the Senator had finished, the Court adjourned.[9]

On the following day, December 17, Reverdy Johnson spoke for Sanford. "With expressions and manners of supercilious disdain, which cannot be counterfeited by any man outside the ranks of the born-slaveholders and aristocrats," wrote James S. Pike, Johnson denied that Negroes were citizens. According to the same authority, Johnson sneered at the noble language of Lord Mansfield in the Somerset Case. While he did not go all the way with Calhoun and assert that the Constitution carried slavery into the territories, he did deny the constitutionality of the Missouri Compromise, aligning himself with Madison in his doubts on the validity of the measure.[10] A more equable critic, his opponent in this case, George T. Curtis, found Johnson's speech "a forcible presentation of the southern view of our Constitution, in respect to the relation of slavery to the territories and of the territories to the nation." [11]

The next day, Blair spoke for another two hours in rebuttal on the subjects of jurisdiction, citizenship and comity. He was followed by Curtis, who spoke for an hour on the constitutionality of the Missouri Compromise.[12] He informed the Court that the sole purpose of his argument was to discover whether or not the Constitution conferred upon Congress power to legislate for the territories and that he approached the question in a purely

50

juridical manner. In so doing, he hoped, perhaps vainly, "to eradicate from the public mind those feelings which in one part of the country lead to a claim of the power in order that it might be exercised always in one way, and in another part of the country lead to a denial of the power in order that its exercise in any way be prevented." As a jurist, he continued, he believed that Congress had full power to prohibit the introduction of slavery in the territories. As a citizen, he could see circumstances that would make the exercise of that power unjust.

The question, he asserted, could only be solved by an historical inquiry into the origins of the phrase of the Constitution which concerned territorial government, the fourth section, the third article. The Congress of the Confederation, which had no power from the Articles to do so, passed the Ordinance of 1787. Both facts were known in the Constitutional Convention—that Congress had no power and that Congress had acted. The Convention remedied this defect by the second section of the third article. "It was one of those fortunate achievements of the pen," Curtis said, "by which a man of great experience and legislative tact [Gouverneur Morris], sitting as if in the centre of men's minds, and combining their thoughts and purposes into a single sentence, engraves the needed provision upon the record by a single stroke, and leaves it to do its office through all coming time."

The power conferred on Congress by this sentence, "The Congress shall have power to dispose of and make all needful rules and regulations respecting the Territory or other property belonging to the United States," was a power to legislate, a plenary power "embracing all the subjects of legislation of which any full legislative power can take cognizance." But, like all power in the United States, it was restricted by the Constitution with respect to certain great public and private rights. Among these restrictions Curtis enumerated those contained in the document itself and in the first ten amendments, including that by which no man could "be deprived of life, liberty, or property without due process of law."

A priori, Curtis said, it was to be expected that the convention created the power he had described. *A posteriori,* Congress, in its earliest acts concerning territories, legislated as if it had the power. Curtis cited the act receiving the cession of North Carolina, the re-enactment of the Ordinance of 1787, the legislation on the slave trade in the Mississippi and Orleans Territories. The subject, he pointed out, had been regulated both prohibitively and permissively.

Curtis concluded that he had established the existence of the power to legislate for the territories. The expediency of its use was for Congress to decide, not for the judges. He closed, committing the case to the Court.[13]

Judge Catron, apparently impressed by an argument Senator Geyer had used to prove that Dr. Emerson had no permanent residence in free territory, the fact that he was an army officer acting under orders, tore a piece of foolscap in half and sent a hasty note to Jefferson Davis, then the Secretary of War, inquiring, "Is there anything in the rules and articles of war, allowing, or prohibiting, the carrying of servants—(Slaves if you please) into the Indian Country north of Missouri?" The Secretary replied with more formality, on December 20th, that there was no special provision on the question. However, he continued, "officers of the Army being, by law, allowed servants have always been in the habit of taking them to the Indian country, when their duties required their presence there, whether they were white men, free blacks, or slaves, and the officer has been paid by the government the amount allowed for their services in each case." Apparently there had been many slaves in the frontier posts on free soil, retained there at the expense of the United States.[14]

While the Court was, supposedly, considering the case, the press, particularly in the north, was misleading public opinion with garbled accounts of the case and groundless speculations on the decision of the judges. Blair felt the need of clearing the air, in some degree, and sent a long letter to the editor of the *National Intelligencer*, explaining his connection with the case and denying that it had any political implications. Specifically, it had not been brought to the Supreme Court to influence the previous presidential election. He had taken the case, Blair wrote, out of *noblesse oblige*, at the request of Roswell Field, "a distinguished lawyer in Missouri, and one who never during the fifteen years that I have known him, manifested any interest in politics." In taking the Scott case, Blair felt that he had done what any other high-minded southern gentleman would have done if his charity had been appealed to.[15]

Along with New Year's greetings, Alexander Stephens sent his brother, Linton, a copy of Curtis's speech before the court which he found "chaste, elegant, forensic, but . . . not . . . convincing."

The case, in Stephens' estimation, *"the great case,"* was not yet decided and he felt "a deep solicitude as to how it will be." From what he heard, *"sub rosa,* it will be according to my own opinions on every point, as abstract political questions. The restriction of 1820 will be held to be unconstitutional. The judges are all writing out their opinions, I believe, *seriatim.* The Chief Justice will give an elaborate one." This, Stephens pointed out, would destroy Douglas and his Squatter Sovereignty.[16] Stephens' information, from under whatever rose he got it, was not accurate at the moment, but it was a remarkably clear prophecy of what the Court and the Chief Justice did do when Justice Wayne, a fellow Georgian with Stephens, later assumed control of the strategy of the judges. The embarrassment of Douglas by the decision and the difficulties into which he was thrown by it were clearly foreseen and, apparently, desired at this time by at least one outstanding member of the southern faction of the Democratic Party.

Montgomery Blair had much better information as to the state of the case. Writing to Van Buren to thank him for his congratulations on his arguments, he promised to send the ex-president the opinion "of your old friend Taney, if he gives one." It seemed to be the impression of the more knowing in Washington that the Court would decide against Scott and the power of Congress in the territories, he continued. But he was assured that the Court had not as yet held a conference on the case, in which he had been correctly assured. He feared, he told Van Buren, that the result would be as predicted and was inclined to think that the decision would be influenced by outside pressure on the judges.[17]

The day after Blair wrote to Van Buren, Catron answered a letter he had received from his old friend, Buchanan. The decision of the Court was of considerable importance to the successful candidate, who was resting at Wheatlands, his country home, before going to Washington to assume office. His problem, as he saw it, was to reunite the country by means of a reunited Democratic Party. A Supreme Court decision on the question at issue would provide the basis for an attempt to restore harmony among the factions which were disrupting the party and the nation. His immediate task was to determine what he was to say about sectional strife in his inaugural address. When was the Court going to decide the question, he had asked Catron in his letter of February 3rd. Would it be before March 4th? Catron replied that it rested with the Chief Justice to move in the matter and, so far, he had said nothing to Catron on the Scott case. The circumstances surrounding the first hearing of the case had made Taney "more wary than usual." The fact that, as Catron put it, "all our opinions were published in the *New York Tribune* the next day," after the judges' consultations, "a gross breach of confidence, as the information could only come from a judge who was present," had gravely concerned Taney. The tragic death of Judge Daniel's young wife, who was burned to death before his eyes, had caused delay. But Catron felt that Buchanan ought to know whether and when the case was likely to be decided and promised to find out and inform him in several days. With this assurance and the request that Buchanan give some thought to Cave Johnson's recommendation of Governor Aaron Brown, of Tennessee, for the office of Postmaster General in his cabinet, Catron closed.[18]

On February 10th, Catron told Buchanan, in a confidential letter, that the Scott case would be decided on the 15th. But the decision would be no help to Buchanan in preparing his inaugural. Some of the judges would not touch the question of the power of Congress over the territories. Others might, but it was Catron's opinion that the decision would settle nothing. It would not be announced till the end of the month.

Catron then gave Buchanan the benefit of his views on the question of the power of Congress. That body had the power from the Constitution, specifically from article four, section three. The Supreme Court, two years before, in the case of Cross vs. Harrison, had held so. This "was done on deliberation and at the instance of Campbell and myself." To hold that no power existed to govern the territories, he continued, after a practice of sixty-eight years, would shock all the substantial lawyers of the country and "subject the court to the ridicule that the Nicholson letter received." "Of course," he went on, "the securities contained in the Constitution limit the power. This, however, does not settle the contested question." He then outlined an argument on the effect of the restrictions imposed on Congress in legislating for the territory purchased from France in 1803 by the treaty of acquisition, particularly by the third article, which guaranteed that the inhabitants of the territory then purchased would be maintained and protected in the free enjoyment of their liberty, property, and the religion they professed. In Catron's reading of this article, it meant that all the inhabitants of all the ceded territory were to be protected in their property, of whatever descrip-

54

tion, during the whole period from the date of acquisition until the region was admitted as a State into the Union. "As to the original inhabitants," he asked, "and their descendants, can it be otherwise?" And was it not a fair and true construction, he continued, "that where the filling of vacant country was contemplated before new states could be admitted," Congress intended to place the immigrants on an equal footing with the original inhabitants? If this were so, in Catron's opinion the treaty settled the controversy. By this time it was eleven o'clock and Catron had to hurry off to court.[19]

On Saturday, February 14, the judges met, for the first time, to consult on their disposal of the case. After the case had been thoroughly aired at several meetings, a majority of the judges, consisting of McLean, Catron, Grier, Campbell, and Nelson, decided that the question of Negro citizenship was not before the Court and that an opinion on the merits had to be given.[20] After further discussion it was agreed that the case could be satisfactorily decided without giving an opinion on the constitutionality of the Missouri Compromise and Judge Nelson was selected to write the opinion of the Court upon the merits of the final judgment of the circuit court, that the Scotts were not free, in which a majority of the judges agreed. But the two judges who dissented from this solution of the case which confirmed the servitude of the Scotts, McLean and Curtis, expressed their determination to include in their opinions both the troublesome points: the citizenship of Negroes and the constitutionality of the Missouri Compromise. A number of the other judges felt that both these points were in the case and could be legitimately considered, but that they were not absolutely necessary to a disposition of the case. In view of the action of the dissentients, all, except Nelson and Grier, felt compelled to express their opinions, at least on the validity of the Missouri Compromise and the power of Congress in the territories. The two exceptions refused to commit themselves.[21]

At this juncture, Judge Wayne, quite abruptly, moved that the Chief Justice should write an opinion on all the questions as the opinion of the Court. The case, he pointed out, had created public interest and expectation. It had been argued twice and the impression existed that the questions argued—citizenship, the power of Congress in the territories over slavery, and the effect of removal and return on the status of a slave—would all be treated in the

55

opinion of the Court. The Court would fail in its duty if it did not satisfy the expectations of the country. Other members of the Court shared Wayne's views on their duty to the country and his proposal received the assent of a majority.[22] Judge Nelson was not present at this meeting of the Court.[23] James Harvey's hopes of the previous year, that with "aid from the Southern members of the court" a full decision would be obtained, was about to be realised and Alexander Stephens' prophecy that the restriction of 1820 would be declared unconstitutional, that the judges would feel called upon to give opinions *seriatim,* the Chief Justice elaborately discussing all the points presented by counsel, was about to be fulfilled.

The faithful Catron wrote to Buchanan on February 19th that the case had been under discussion and that the newly elected President could "safely say" in his inaugural address "That the question involving the constitutionality of the Missouri Compromise line is presented to the appropriate tribunal to decide; to wit, to the Supreme Court of the United States. It is due to its high and independent character to suppose that it will decide and settle a controversy which has so long and seriously agitated the country, and which *must* ultimately be decided by the Supreme Court. And until the case now before it (on two arguments) presenting the direct question, is disposed of, I would deem it improper to express any opinion on the subject." He informed Buchanan that the majority of the Court had been "forced up to this point by two dissentients." He urged him to drop Judge Grier, still uncommitted, a line, telling him "how necessary it is—and how good the opportunity is to settle the agitation by an affirmative decision of the Supreme Court, the one way or the other." Catron felt that Grier should not occupy "so doubtful a ground as the outside issue—that admitting the constitutionality of the Missouri Compromise line of 1820, still, as no domicile was acquired by the Negro at Fort Snelling, and he returned to Missouri, he was not free." Grier had no doubt that the Missouri Compromise was unconstitutional, Catron told Buchanan, but he had been persuaded "to take the smooth handle for the sake of repose."[24]

Buchanan wrote to Grier. The judge received the letter on the 23rd and answered it the same day. On receiving the letter, Grier had shown it "in confidence to our mutual friends, Judge Wayne and the Chief Justice." All three had agreed, he told Buchanan,

56

in the President-elect's views "as to the desireableness of having an expression of the opinion of the court on this troublesome question." With the concurrence of Taney and Wayne, Grier then gave Buchanan a history of the case "with the probable result." A majority of the Court had decided that the question of citizenship was not before it and the case had been committed to Judge Nelson to write an opinion affirming the opinion of Judge Wells in the District Court. "But," he continued, "it appeared that our brothers who dissented from the majority, especially Justice McLean, were determined to come out with a long and labored dissent, including their opinions and arguments on both the troublesome points, although not necessary to a decision of the case." The judges who differed on these points from McLean and Curtis and who believed that both these points were in the case and could be legitimately considered, but from which they had deliberately abstained, then felt the need of expressing their views. Grier was anxious lest the line of latitude should mark the line of division of the Court and was afraid that the opinion of the Court would lose much of its effect because all the judges who agreed on the result were from south of the Mason and Dixon line. To make matters worse, they all differed in their reasons for coming to the same conclusion. After conversation with the Chief Justice, Grier told Buchanan, he had decided to concur with him. Wayne and he would do all in their power to get Daniel, Campbell and Catron to do likewise. The result of this agreement would be "that, if the question must be met, there will be an opinion of the court on it, if possible, without the contradictory views which would weaken its force." But Grier feared that "some rather extreme views may be thrown out by some of our southern brethren." However, there would be at least six who would hold the Missouri Compromise line to be invalid. Nelson's position was still doubtful.

The opinion of the Court, he went on, would not be delivered before March 6th. He promised Buchanan that Taney, Wayne and he would "not let any others of our brethren know anything about *the cause of our anxiety* to produce this result." This procedure was contrary to usual practice, but the Chief Justice, Wayne and he thought it due Buchanan to tell him "in candor and confidence" the real state of the matter.[25]

Grier was not aware that Buchanan had written to him at Catron's instigation. Catron was not aware that Grier no longer

57

needed prodding. On the same day that Grier was unburdening himself to Buchanan, Catron answered a letter he had received from Wheatlands. He told the President-elect that his whole anxiety was to have the opinion delivered before March 3rd. Most of the judges were ready or nearly so. One day would be sufficient to finish the opinions of five of them. The two dissentients, McLean and Curtis, were fully ready. Unaware of the fact that, for a change, Judge Grier was about to exert pressure on him, Catron told Buchanan that he wanted Grier speeded. "I think what you wish may be accomplished," he told Buchanan in closing.[26]

On March 3rd, Buchanan arrived in Washington and went to the National Hotel. He had his speech with him. Sometime during the hours before the ceremony began, he inserted a clause "in regard to the question then pending in the Supreme Court." [27] The next morning, he and the out-going President, Franklin Pierce, drove down Pennsylvania Avenue to the Capitol and both mounted to the platform prepared there. The two friends met a third, Roger Brooke Taney, the Chief Justice, who was to administer the oath of office. Some remarks were exchanged. The ceremony took place. Buchanan then addressed the crowd. After congratulating the country on the peaceful settlement of the question of domestic slavery in the territories by the "simple rule that the will of the majority shall govern," he continued that the "difference of opinion . . . in regard to the point of time when the people of a territory shall decide this question for themselves" was "happily a matter of but little practical importance. Besides, it is a judicial question which legitimately belongs to the Supreme Court of the United States before whom it is now pending, and will, it is understood, be speedily and finally settled." To their decision, "whatever this may be," Buchanan pledged himself "in common with all good citizens" to submit. It had always been his "individual opinion that, under the Kansas-Nebraska Act, the appropriate period will be when the number of actual residents in the Territory shall justify the formation of a Constitution with a view to its admission as a State into the Union." It was the duty of the government, he went on, to secure to every resident of a territory the free and independent expression of his opinion by his vote. Once this was accomplished, nothing could be "fairer than to leave the people of a Territory free from all foreign interference to decide their own destiny for themselves, subject only to the Constitution of the United States." The whole territorial ques-

58

tion, then, would be settled "upon the principle of popular sovereignty," everything "of a practical nature" would have been decided and no other question would remain "for adjustment." [28]

The function over, the crowd departed, some to prepare for the inaugural ball, Taney home to finish writing his opinion to which the President, "in common with all good citizens," would submit.

NOTES

1. James D. Richardson, *A Compilation of the Messages and Papers of the Presidents* (Washington, D. C.: Government Printing Office, 1897), 5, pp. 398-401.

2. Richard M. Johnston and William H. Browne, *Life of Alexander H. Stephens* (Philadelphia: J. B. Lippincott and Co., 1878), p. 316.

3. New York *Tribune,* Dec. 17, 1856.

4. Carl R. Fish, "George Ticknor Curtis," *Dictionary of American Biography,* IV, 613-614; Curtis, *Memoir,* I, 122-136; II, 172-190.

5. New York *Tribune,* Dec. 16, 1856. In a supplementary brief, filed Jan. 9, 1857, Blair did go into the question of congressional power at some length. He argued that Congress had the power to legislate from the territorial provision of the Constitution, that it had acted as if it had the power and that, by the admission of the opponents of use of the power, the whole question was one of the extent of the power not of its existence. In brief, he urged, that the question was not a judicial but a legislative one. Cf. "Additional Brief of M. Blair for the Appellant," Records, Supreme Court of the United States, December Term, 1856, No. 7.

6. This question is a highly technical legal one and beyond the province of a historian. It was decided on non-partisan grounds. Taney and Curtis were both of the opinion that the plea and the question contained in it were before the court.

7. "Argument of George S. Geyer, of Counsel for the Defendant," Records, Supreme Court of the United States, December Term, 1856, No. 7, p. 10.

8. *Ibid.,* p. 11.

9. *Ibid.,* p. 12; New York *Tribune,* Dec. 17, 1856.

10. New York *Tribune,* Dec. 17, 1856; cf., below, Chapter 9, pp. 116-117, for Madison's opinion.

11. Bernard C. Steiner, *The Life of Reverdy Johnson* (Baltimore: Norman, Remington Co., 1914), p. 38, citing the proceedings of the bench and bar at Johnson's death. If Johnson filed a brief, it is no longer in the records of the Supreme Court.

12. New York *Tribune,* Dec. 19, 1856.

13. George T. Curtis, *Constitutional History of the United States* (New York: Harper and Brothers, 1889), II, pp. 499-517.

14. John Catron to Jefferson Davis, Dec. 17, 1856; Davis to Catron, Dec. 20, 1856 (Records, War Department, National Archives).

15. *National Intelligencer,* Dec. 24, 1856.

16. Johnston and Browne, *Life of Alexander H. Stephens,* p. 318.

17. Montgomery Blair to Martin Van Buren, Feb. 5, 1857 (Van Buren Papers, Library of Congress).

18. Philip Auchampaugh, "James Buchanan, The Court and the Dred Scott Case," *Tennessee Historical Magazine,* IX (January, 1926), p. 234.

19. *Ibid.,* p. 235.

20. John Catron to Samuel Treat, May 31, 1857, Treat Papers, Missouri Historical Society, St. Louis, Mo. Catron says that Campbell, Grier, Nelson, McLean and Curtis, as well as himself, held that the question of the plea and the issue involved in it were not before the court. He is wrong about Curtis. John A. Campbell to

George T. Curtis, October 18, 1879, Papers of Charles Warren. Campbell says that the plea was decided to be no part of the case, the Chief Justice, Wayne, Daniel and Curtis being the minority on this question.

21. Robert Grier to James Buchanan, Feb. 23, 1857 (Philip Auchampaugh, "James Buchanan, the Court and the Dred Scott Case," p. 238). McLean discussed the citizenship of Negroes though he was of the opinion it was not in the case. See 19 Howard 531-532.

22. John A. Campbell to Samuel Tyler, Nov. 24, 1870 (Samuel Tyler, *Memoir of Roger Brooke Taney* (Baltimore: John Murphy and Co., 1872), pp. 382-384).

23. Samuel Nelson to Samuel Tyler, May 31, 1871 (Tyler, *Memoir*, p. 385). Nelson had read and substantiated Campbell's letter to Tyler.

24. Philip Auchampaugh, "James Buchanan, the Court and the Dred Scott Case," p. 236.

25. *Ibid.*, p. 238.

26. *Ibid.*

27. Steiner, *Life of Roger Brooke Taney*, p. 341.

28. Richardson, *A Compilation of the Messages and Papers of the Presidents*, V, pp. 431-432.

6

THE "MAJORITY" OPINION

On March 6, 1857, the nine judges again filed into their basement courtroom. Leading the way, as usual, was the Chief Justice, Roger Brooke Taney, of Maryland, born almost eighty years before on the "good landed estate" of his family in Calvert County. Of the planter class and bred to the law, Taney had early and easily entered politics, first as a Federalist, then, after its dubious behavior in the War of 1812 had made that party a nullity, as a supporter of Andrew Jackson.[1] By birth and training he was no great friend of corporate wealth and, under Jackson's aegis, he had gone on to become the pliant tool or avenging angel, depending on the way the individual viewed the issue, who removed the government deposits from the Second Bank of the United States. For this he had been twice rejected by the massed Whiggery of the Senate, once for the Secretaryship of the Treasury and the second time for an associate justiceship on the bench over which he now presided. In his early days as Chief Justice, by his opinion in the famous Charles River Bridge case,[2] he had, in the mistaken judgment of Daniel Webster, "completely overturned . . . one great provision of the Constitution," the contract clause, succeeding at the same time in disgusting the conservative Chancellor Kent and reducing Justice Story to a state of humiliation and "subdued confidence."[3] Many years before, he had manumitted the slaves he inherited and, while he was no enthusiastic supporter of the institution of slavery, he was, on the other hand, no friend to some of the groups that could be found in the anti-slavery movement.[4] He was unacquisitive to the point of carelessness. A defender of the Court was soon to say of him, "he is old, very old. The infirmities of age have bowed his venerable form. Earth has no further object of ambition for him; and when he shall sink into his grave after a long career of high office in our country, I trust that I do not rudely or improperly invade the sanctity of private life in saying that he will leave behind him, in the scanty heritage that shall be left for his family, the noblest evidence that he died, as he had lived, a being honorable to the earth from which he sprang, and worthy of the heaven to which he aspired." [5] After the other justices were seated, Taney began to speak in a low voice.[6] The case, he remarked, due to differences in opinion among the members of the Court, had been argued twice. These questions of the highest importance having been deliberately considered, he would now, Taney said, "proceed to deliver its [the Court's] opinion." [7] The record presented two leading questions. Did the Federal District Court in St. Louis have jurisdiction over the case or not? If it had, was its judgment erroneous or not? Taney then briefly outlined the history of the case. The basis for the suit in the Federal courts was that Scott and Sanford were citizens of different States. This the defendant had denied, alleging that Scott could not be a citizen of Missouri because he was a Negro. The court had sustained the denial and the case had gone over to the merits. A verdict and judgment had been given for the defendant and the plaintiff had sued out a writ of error to the Supreme Court.

Was the plea to the jurisdiction of the lower court before the appellate court, Taney asked? It was argued that the plea was a closed issue. In the lower court the judgment on the plea had been in Scott's favor and it was to be presumed that he did not want it reversed or revised. By pleading to the merits, Sanford had admitted the court's jurisdiction. Those who so argue, Taney said, have forgotten that the courts of the United States differ in the matter of jurisdiction from the common law courts of England and from those State courts which have adopted common law rules. The latter were presumed to have jurisdiction unless the contrary was proved. In the Federal courts, the suitor must show that his case was within the jurisdiction of the court. The record coming from the lower court must also show that his case was within the jurisdiction of the lower court. In the present instance, Taney specified, it must demonstrate that Scott and Sanford were citizens of different States. Citizenship was asserted and denied. The facts alleged to sustain the demurrer were admitted by the plaintiff. Consequently, the plea, the denial, and the judgment of the lower court on the plea were before the Supreme Court, being part of the judicial proceedings of the circuit court and recorded as such. A writ of error brought the whole record before the appellate court which must decide if the facts stated in the plea were sufficient to show that the plaintiff was entitled to sue as a citizen in the courts of the United States. "This is certainly a very serious question, and one that now for the first time has been brought for a decision before the court. But it is brought here by those who have a right to bring it, and it is our duty to meet it and decide it," the Chief Justice said.

Taney then addressed himself to the question of the citizenship of free Negroes. He phrased the question: "Can a Negro, whose ancestors were imported into this country, and sold as slaves, become a member of the political community formed and brought into existence by the Constitution of the United States, and as such become entitled to all the rights, and privileges, and immunities, guaranteed by that instrument to the citizen?" One of these rights, he continued, was the privilege of suing in a court of the United States in the cases specified by the Constitution. Observing that the plea applied only to that class of persons whose ancestors were Negroes of the African race who were imported into this country and sold and held as slaves, he rephrased the question: "The only matter in issue before the court, therefore, is whether the descendants of such slaves, when they shall be emancipated, or who are born of parents who had become free before their birth, are citizens of a State, in the sense in which the word citizen is used in the Constitution of the United States."

The Chief Justice then distinguished free Negroes from Indians who could be naturalised by act of Congress. He next distinguished them from those who composed the body politic which was designated in the Constitution as "the people of the United States" or, synonymously, "citizens." Free Negroes were not members of either group. Consequently, they could claim none of the rights and privileges which the Constitution guaranteed to citizens of the United States. Not only were free Negroes not citizens, but, at the time the Constitution was adopted, "they were considered as a subordinate and inferior class of being . . . and had no rights or privileges but such as those who held the power and the government might choose to grant them." The justice or injustice, policy or impolicy, of these laws, Taney said, was a matter which those who formed the sovereignty and drew up the Constitution had decided. The Court but interpreted the document they framed according to its true intent and meaning.[8]

It was necessary, he continued, to differentiate the citizenship which a State may confer within its own limits and the rights of citizenship accruing to a citizen of the Union. From the fact that a State had accorded the rights of citizenship to a person, it did not follow that the person was a citizen of the United States. State citizenship gave no rights or privileges in other States beyond those secured by the law of nations and the comity of states. Finally, he said, no State, since the adoption of the Constitution, could "introduce a new member into the political community created by the Constitution of the United States." [9]

The principle, basic to the discussion, Taney continued, was that every person who was a citizen of a State at the time of the adoption of the Constitution became a citizen of the United States. Who, then, were citizens of States at that period? Were free Negroes? Taney argued that the inferior condition of the Negro for at least a century before 1787, as demonstrated in English and American law and practice, indicated that this class of people was not intended to be embraced by the general clauses of the Declaration of Independence or the Constitution when those documents spoke of "the people of the United States." The slave trade and fugitive slave provisions of the latter document pointed the same way. Laws passed by the several States after the promulgation of the Declaration and, in some, after the adoption of the Constitution, supported the contention that free Negroes were not regarded as members of the body politic at that time. Stating that there was no need to discuss the situation in the slave-holding States, the precise point at issue having been settled by the courts of those commonwealths where the question had arisen, Taney turned his attention to the discriminatory legislation of Massachusetts, Connecticut, New Hampshire, and Rhode Island.[10] These laws, Taney argued, buttressing his inference with a citation from Chancellor Kent,[11] all showed the inferior condition of the Negro at the time of the adoption of the Constitution. "It cannot be supposed," he remarked, "that they intended to secure to them [free Negroes] rights, and privileges, and rank in the new political body throughout the Union which every one of them denied within the limits of its own dominion." [12]

The power of naturalisation, the Chief Justice continued, confided exclusively to Congress, was confined in its exercise to foreigners. The naturalisation law of 1790 was a gloss on the constitutional term, "citizen of the United States." The right of adoption was there confined "to aliens being free white persons." [13] The militia law of 1792 directed the enrollment of white males only; that of 1813 distinguished between citizens of the United States and persons of color, native to the United States.[14] The congressionally drawn charter of the District of Columbia drew the same line.[15] These were the opinions of Attorneys General Wirt and Cushing.[16]

Taney, who had been the attorney in the case of Legrand vs. Darnall, one in which a free Negro whom Taney had represented had gotten a verdict and judgment in a Federal court, now considered this rather embarrassing precedent. It was not in point, he said. Legrand had not contested Darnall's citizenship so that there was nothing on the record to show African descent on the part of the latter.[17] The Chief Justice concluded by pointing out that such was the law: free Negroes were not citizens of the United States. There was a constitutional way to change it available to those so disposed. But, till it was changed, it was clear that the lower court had had no jurisdiction and the judgment on the plea in abatement was erroneous.

Having disposed of the jurisdiction of the lower court on one ground, Taney approached the same question from another. "We are aware," Taney said, "that doubts are entertained by some of the members of the court, whether the plea in abatement is legally before the court upon this writ of error; but if that plea is regarded as waived or out of the case upon any other ground, yet the question as to the jurisdiction of the Circuit Court is presented on the face of the bill of exception itself, taken by the plaintiff at the trial, for he admits that he and his wife were born slaves. . . ." [18] His alleged citizenship, the Chief Justice said, depended on his freedom. Being a free Negro, he could not sue. *A fortiori*, if he were a slave, he could not sue. The question of jurisdiction must be studied from this angle.

Before entering this part of the case, Taney noticed an objection to the authority of the Court to decide it. It was contended that the Supreme Court could go no further, after having declared that the circuit court had no jurisdiction on one score, and that, if it did, everything else that was said was *obiter dictum*. The Chief Justice said that this argument was founded on a failure to distinguish a writ of error to a Federal court from one to a State court. In the former, the whole record was before the Supreme Court for examination and decision. The correction of one error did not prevent the appellate court from correcting "any other material errors that may have been committed in the inferior court." [19] As a matter of fact, he asserted, such was the daily practice of the Court. Silence would but lead to misconstruction or future controversy. This was especially the case, Taney added, where erroneous judgments concern the points most stressed by counsel. The eloquence of Blair and Curtis, Geyer and Johnson was not to be ignored, and Roswell Field was to have all the answers he desired.

After recounting the various wanderings of Scott and his family through Illinois and the Minnesota Territory, Taney asked two questions. Were the Scotts free by reason of their stay in the territory? If they were not, was Dred himself free by reason of his sojourn in Illinois? Taking up the first question, the Chief Justice stated that Scott's counsel had based the argument in favor of the freedom of the whole family chiefly on the eighth section of the Missouri Compromise Act of 1820, the section which prohibited slavery north of the line thirty-six degrees, thirty minutes, in the Louisiana Territory. Did Congress have power to pass this act? Counsel had argued to the possession of such power by Congress from the fact that the Constitution gave that body the power "to dispose of and make all needful rules and regulations respecting the territory or other property belonging to the United States." [20]

This provision, the Chief Justice declared, had no bearing on the present controversy, the general power of the national legislature in the territories of the United States. "It was," he said, "a special provision for a known and particular territory, and to meet a present emergency, and nothing more." [21] Taney then proceeded to prove this assertion from the historical circumstances under which the provision was written and from the wording of the article itself.

According to Taney, the chief problem that the States had to meet and solve from the very commencement of the Revolution was the disposal of the large, unsettled territories which were included in the chartered limits of some of them. The States which were not so amply dowered, of which Maryland was a leader, argued that such lands would owe their preservation to the efforts of all the States. If "the common sword and the common purse" wrested them from Great Britain, it was only just that the benefit that accrued should be similarly common. As a result of this agitation, Congress passed resolutions, urging the cession of such lands on those who possessed them. The owner States ceded the territories. The principal objects of these acts of surrender were to promote unity and to obtain money, which could be realised from a sale of the lands. With the land, Taney admitted, went sovereignty as well as ownership. But, he continued, the nature of the government to which they were ceded must be considered. It was a government which, under its then organic law, the Articles of Confederation, had no power to accept the cessions. The Chief Justice described the Articles and the government they created as "little more than a Congress of ambassadors, authorized to represent separate nations in matters in which they had a common concern." [22] While the general government had no power to act in the matter of the surrendered territory, the States which composed the alliance, as independent sovereignties, had a clear right, not only to accept the lands, but also to exercise absolute dominion over them. The only limits to their power were those laid down in the acts of cession. Consequently, in passing the Ordinance of 1787, Congress had acted with unquestioned right. But the validity of its action did not rest on any authority given by the Articles of Confederation but on the power the States, of which the members of Congress were delegates, possessed as independent sovereignties.

But, Taney continued, these States were about to surrender a portion of their sovereignty to a new government, then in the process of formation, a government that was to be endowed with carefully limited powers. Some provision was necessary to give this new government the power to carry out the objects for which the territory had been ceded. The lands had to be sold to pay the common debt. Citizens of the United States, migrating to the territory, must be protected in their rights of person and property. The new government should be authorized to accept the confidently expected cessions of North Carolina and Georgia. Title to the property and military stores, belonging to the old Confederation and actually in the territory, must be vested in the new government. As a result of all these considerations, Taney concluded, we have the provision in the Constitution alluded to by counsel.

The very language of the clause in question substantiated the historical account he had just given, he continued. The clause spoke, not of any territory, nor of territories, but of *the* territory of the United States, that is, the territory they then possessed. The words, "dispose of," "needful rules and regulations," did not indicate, either from their meaning or from the common usage of statesmen, supreme legislative power. The territory described in the provision was equated to other property which, by its nature, was movable or personal. The concluding words of the clause, that "nothing in the Constitution shall be so construed as to prejudice any claims of the United States, or of any particular state," was convincing proof, Taney said, of the construction he had given to the whole provision. They meant that neither the other States, who had ceded their lands, nor North Carolina and Georgia, who had not, surrendered any claims both may have had to the lands possessed by those two States. In addition, the words "rules and regulations" were ordinarily used in the Constitution to refer to some particular power. To interpret them, in this section, as an unlimited grant of power over territories which the country might acquire later was to see in them a sense alien to the document in general. If a parallel to the passage under discussion were to be sought, it could be found in that clause by which the new government took over all the financial obligations of the old.[23] On the one hand, the new nation had no right to the property of the old Confederation; on the other, it was not liable for that government's obligations and engagements. Both clauses referred to a present emergency as did that which ratified the treaties of the old government.[24]

The conclusions that flowed from this elaborate argument were that the power exercised by the old Congress of the Confederation over the Northwest Territory furnished no precedent for the exercise of a similar power by the Federal government over territories acquired since the adoption of the Constitution and that the power, if any, that the latter did have in the territories was not derived from the provision in the Constitution which concerned the territory of the United States. The Chief Justice then evolved his theory of the origin of congressional power in the territories acquired since 1787. He first considered the case of the American and Ocean Insurance Companies vs. Canter which had arisen in Florida Territory, a domain acquired by purchase in 1819. It had been argued that the decision of Chief Justice Marshall in this case was convincing precedent that congressional power in the territories stemmed from the constitutional provision. Taney said that between his line of argument and that of Marshall only the appearance of conflict could be created and that by the old device of citing words out of their context. He quoted text and context: "In the meantime Florida continues to be a Territory of the United States, governed by that clause of the Constitution which empowers Congress to make all needful rules and regulations respecting the territory or other property of the United States. Perhaps the power of governing Territory belonging to the United States . . . may result necessarily from the facts that it is not within the jurisdiction of any particular State, and is within the power and jurisdiction of the United States. The right to govern may be the inevitable consequence of the right to acquire territory. Whichever may be the source from which the power is derived, the possession of it is unquestionable." [25] The Chief Justice removed the whole problem from the realm of hypothesis where Marshall had left it. "The power," he declared, "stands firmly on the latter alternative put by the court—that is, as 'the inevitable consequence of the right to acquire territory.' " [26]

It was evident, Taney continued, that the Court, in deciding the Insurance Companies Case, had not intended to settle the question of the source of congressional power in the territories. Justice Johnson had heard the case in the circuit court. It was his opinion that the constitutional provision on the territory of the United States did not pertain to territory acquired since the adoption of the Constitution, but only to territory within the limits of the country in 1787. Yet he felt no need to dissent from the opinion of the Court because that body regarded the source of congressional power as an open question. The further statement that Congress, in legislating for a territory, exercised the combined powers of a State and the Federal government [27] related to the establishment of judicial tribunals, as the Court plainly stated. "And we are satisfied," Taney concluded, "that no one who reads attentively the page in Peter's Reports to which we have referred, can suppose that the attention of the court was drawn for a moment to the question now before this court, or that it meant in that case to say that Congress had a right to prohibit a citizen of the United States from taking any property which he lawfully held into a Territory of the United States." [28]

The right to govern depended on the right to acquire. Taney now addressed himself to the basic question of the right to acquire. Where was that given to the Federal government in the Constitution? Granted that there was a right to acquire territory outside the original limits of the United States, Taney pointed out that the next question would be what powers Congress may exercise over the person and property of a citizen of the United States who resided in such territory.

The power to admit new States being clearly granted in the Constitution,[29] the territorial limits of the Union could be enlarged for this purpose. But Taney could see no other reason for extending them. The United States could not acquire territory and hold it as a colonial empire. The power to admit new States implied the power to acquire the territory out of which they were to be formed. This territory might or might not be fit for immediate admission into the Union. This was for Congress to decide, because the function of determining what was within the limits of the United States was a political one. The judiciary but administered the laws in such regions and maintained in them both the authority of the government and the personal and property rights of individuals there, such rights being secured by the Constitution. Since the Constitution did not define the powers which the government had over persons and property in the territories, the Court must look to the general provisions of that document to give its decision. Clearly, citizens of the United States, resident in such territories, were not to be ruled as mere colonists. It was equally obvious that the territory which had been acquired was intended for the benefit of the people of the several States. The general government was "their trustee, acting for them, and charged with the duty of promoting the interests of the whole people of the Union in the exercise of the powers specifically granted." [30]

Taney then applied these principles to the territory purchased from France in 1803. That great land mass, when it was acquired, Taney pointed out, was not in a condition to be admitted into the Union. It was necessary to care for it. It was the duty of the government to pass laws to preserve it, laws that would enable all the people, whose representative the government was, to reap the benefit of its acquisition. It was the duty of the government to see that it became populated so that it could become a State or States. The form of government adopted for the territory was within the discretion of Congress. Congress, however, had to act within the framework to which it owed its own existence, the Constitution, and Congress could not infringe "upon the rights of persons or the rights of property of the citizen" who went there to live.[31] These rights were clearly defined in the Constitution. Congress, when it legislated for a territory, could not assume despotic powers. It could not establish a religion in the territory,

70

abridge freedom of speech, deny the right of petition. The rights of property had been guarded with equal care, Taney continued. They were united with personal rights and placed on the same ground by the Fifth Amendment to the Constitution, which provided that no person should be deprived of life, liberty, or property without due process of law. "And," he stated, "an act of Congress which deprives a citizen of the United States of his liberty or property, merely because he came himself or brought his property into a particular territory of the United States, and who had committed no offence against the laws, could hardly be dignified with the name of due process of law." [32] There was no difference between property in a slave and other property; the Constitution made none. On the contrary, it affirmed the right of the master in his slave. Consequently, the Chief Justice concluded, the eighth section of the Missouri Compromise Act of 1820, which did so deprive a citizen of his property, was void. The Scotts, then, were not free in virtue of that provision and, again, had no right to sue in a Federal court.

Was Dred Scott himself free by reason of his stay in Illinois, Taney asked? The principle, first enunciated in the case of Strader vs. Graham, was clear, he replied.[33] The status of slaves who had been taken to free States or territories and who had afterwards returned depended on the law of the State where they resided when they brought suit. State courts interpreted State laws and the Supreme Court had no jurisdiction to revise the judgment of a State court on this question. Taney conceded that there had been some dispute on the law governing these cases in Missouri. But, after a careful consideration, he continued, "we are satisfied . . . that it is now firmly settled by the decisions of the highest court in the State, that Scott and his family on their return were not free, but were, by the laws of Missouri, the property of the defendant; and that the Circuit Court of the United States had no jurisdiction, when, by the laws of the State, the plaintiff was a slave, and not a citizen." [34]

Before pronouncing judgment, Taney criticised the way in which the case had been brought to the Supreme Court. Scott, he said, had brought a similar action in the Missouri courts. The case had gone to the State Supreme Court, where it had been decided that none of the Scotts were entitled to their freedom. "If," Taney continued, "the plaintiff supposed that this judgment of the Supreme Court of the State was erroneous, and that this court had jurisdiction to revise and reverse it, the only mode by which he could legally bring it before this court was by writ of error directed to the Supreme Court of the State, requiring it to transmit the record to this court." If this had been done, the writ must have been dismissed for want of jurisdiction in the Supreme Court, Taney said, the case of Strader vs. Graham being directly in point. "But," Taney went on, "the plaintiff did not pursue the mode prescribed by law for bringing the judgment of a State court before this court for revision. . . ." Scott had allowed his case to be remanded to an inferior State court, where it was being continued, pending the judgment of the United States Supreme Court. While the case was yet open, Scott had gone into the Circuit Court of the United States and had brought to the Supreme Court "the same case from the Circuit Court, which the law would not have permitted him to bring directly from the State court. And if this court takes jurisdiction in this form, the result, so far as the rights of the respective parties are concerned, is in every respect substantially the same as if it had in open violation of law entertained jurisdiction over the judgment of the State court upon a writ of error. . . . It would ill become this court to sanction such an attempt to evade the law. . . ." He then gave the judgment of the Court. Since Scott was not a citizen, being a Negro slave, the Circuit Court had erred in taking jurisdiction and could give no judgment. "Its judgment for the defendant must, consequently, be reversed, and a mandate issued, directing the suit to be dismissed for lack of jurisdiction," he said.[35]

It had taken the Chief Justice about two hours to read his opinion, in which he had covered all the points argued by counsel and covered them all from the viewpoint of jurisdiction.[36] Scott could not sue in the courts of the United States, he said in substance, because free Negroes could not sue in them. Those who had become free since 1787 were not "citizens of a State, in the sense in which the word is used in the Constitution of the United States," because the Federal government had not made them such and a State government could not. Those who were free in 1787 were not members of the body politic at that time and had not been included in the general clauses of the Declaration of Independence or the Constitution.[37] Scott could not sue in the courts of the United States, he went on, because he and his family were slaves. The Scott family was not entitled to its freedom by reason of the eighth section of the Missouri Compromise Act of 1820, because that part of the act was an invasion of the rights of property protected against Federal interference by the due process clause of the Fifth Amendment to the Constitution.[38] Dred himself was not free in virtue of his residence in Illinois, because State courts were the sole judges of status when such a question arose within their limits and the Supreme Court of Missouri had declared Dred to be a slave.[39] Free he could not sue, slave he could not sue, so the judgment of the lower court must be reversed and the case dismissed for lack of jurisdiction.

Judge Nelson read his opinion next. He was described by the *Tribune* as "a New York Democrat of the perishing school" and had been a lawyer and judge of considerable ability and experience before President Tyler appointed him to the Supreme Court. Fourteen years as a justice on the Supreme Court of New York, the last seven as its Chief Justice, added to a deep knowledge of the technicalities of common and admiralty law, had made his selection by Tyler eminently fitting and he had been confirmed with no delay by a Senate that had shown itself anything but amenable to the leading of Harrison's successor.[40] He read the opinion that he had written when it had been decided that he was to speak for the Court.[41]

Using the plural pronoun, a survival of that earlier phase of the case, he remarked, "in the view we have taken of the case, it will not be necessary to pass upon the question" raised by the plea in abatement, the citizenship of Negroes.[42] From a review of the case on its merits, he found that the judgment of the circuit court should be affirmed. The status of the Scott family was to be determined by the laws of Missouri. She was a sovereign State, Nelson said, and whether she extended comity to a sister State was for her to determine. Justice Story and Chancellor Kent agreed on this.[43] The doctrine of Huberus that personal qualities accompanied a person wherever he went depended on the acquisition of a permanent domicile. This Scott did not have. In addition, Huberus conceded that a foreign government gave effect to the laws of domicile of a State only in so far as they were not inconsistent with their own.[44] The case was governed by the law laid down in the case of Strader vs. Graham which made each State the final judge of the question of the status of slaves who had sojourned in free territory and then returned within her limits. The Missouri Compromise Act and the Northwest Ordinance had no more extra-territorial effect than had the Constitution of Illinois. On the basis of these principles the circuit court had to follow the law of Missouri.[45]

What was the law of that commonwealth on this subject, Nelson asked? In his review of Missouri precedents on the condition of slaves who had lived in free territory and then returned to the State, Nelson found only two cases which were contrary to the decision of the State Supreme Court in the Scott case. In all the other cases which had been brought forward, there was missing the requisite note of permanence of domicile.[46] The decision, he continued, was in line with other border State decisions on the subject and with English precedents. In his opinion the judgment of the lower court should be affirmed, that is, that the Scotts were slaves.[47]

John Catron, of Tennessee, followed Nelson. He had served under Jackson in the War of 1812 and, on his return, had studied law. From 1824 to 1834, he served on the Supreme Court of his State, the last three years as Chief Justice. Two years after the court was abolished, he was elevated to the Supreme Court by Jackson, whose heir-apparent, Van Buren, he had actively supported in the preceding election.[48] He was a friend of long standing of President Buchanan, whose interests he served to such an extent that a harsh critic dubbed him Buchanan's "wire puller." [49] He opened with the statement that he was of the opinion that Sanford had waived the plea in abatement when he consented to a trial of the case on its merits and that, consequently, he would not consider the questions raised in the plea. Catron then passed on to the question of Scott's status by reason of his stay at Fort Armstrong, Illinois. On this point he found himself in complete agreement with Judge Nelson. It was a matter for the Missouri Courts, the judiciary of a sovereign State, to decide.

He then asked: Were the Scotts free in virtue of their residence at Fort Snelling, in the Wisconsin Territory? That, he said, depended on the validity of the eighth section of the Missouri Compromise Act of 1820, which, in turn, depended on the power of Congress to pass that act. The territorial provision of the Constitution, Catron declared, gave Congress the power to legislate for the territories. By the treaty of 1763 the territory west of the mountains had passed to the English Crown. By the treaty of 1783, it had passed to the United States. Virginia, which surely had jurisdiction over this domain, had ceded the territory to Congress. This act of cession was incorporated in the Constitution. On

74

this doctrine Congress had acted for sixty years. For nearly twenty years Catron himself had worked on the same theory and, he said, "it is asking much of a judge who has been exercising jurisdiction, from the western Missouri line to the Rocky Mountains, and, on this understanding of the Constitution, inflicting the extreme penalty of death for crimes committed where the direct legislation of Congress was the only rule, to agree that he had been all the while acting in mistake, and as an usurper." [50]

Congress, then, had the power under the Constitution to legislate for the territories, but that body was always bound by the acts of cession which were treaties. The same condition applied to the territory acquired by the Louisiana Purchase, Catron affirmed. He then repeated in more detail the argument he had outlined earlier to Buchanan and from the delivery of which Grier, evidently, had not dissuaded him.[51] By article three of the treaty with France, by which Louisiana was acquired, "the inhabitants of the ceded territory shall be incorporated in the Union of the United States, and admitted as soon as possible, according to the principles of the Federal Constitution, to the enjoyment of all rights, advantages, and immunities, of citizens of the United States; and, in the meantime, they shall be maintained and protected in the free enjoyment of their liberty, property, and the religion which they profess." [52] This protection was to be extended to the inhabitants of Louisiana and to all immigrants to that region till it achieved statehood. In view of this guarantee, Congress could not draw a line, destructive of property rights, at any point in the territory acquired by the treaty of 1803. Such action would be tantamount to a repeal of the third article of that document and Congress had no power to do this. If it could, Catron argued, Congress could also repeal the acts of cession it made with North Carolina and Georgia, which were also treaties, and prohibit slavery in the States of Tennessee, Mississippi and Alabama, which had been formed from lands ceded by the former States.

But even apart from considerations drawn from the treaty, Catron continued, the Missouri Compromise line violated the equality of privileges and immunities guaranteed to the citizens of all the states by the Constitution. By that document the States were made equals in political rights and equals in the right to participate in the common property of the "States United." The line of thirty-six degrees, thirty minutes, violated this equality and was void. For these reasons Catron concurred with his brother judges that Scott was "a slave, and was so when this suit was brought." [53]

The Court now adjourned. The other judges would be heard on the morrow.[54]

NOTES

1. Carl B. Swisher, *Roger B. Taney* (New York: The Macmillan Co., 1935), pp. 119-131.

2. 11 Peters 420.

3. William W. Story, *Life and Letters of Joseph Story* (London: John Chapman, 1851), II, pp. 269, 270, 277.

4. Joseph A. Walter to the Editor, *The Century Illustrated Monthly Magazine*, XXVI (May 1883-October 1883), pp. 957-958; Courtenay De Kalb, *op. cit.*, p. 958. Roger B. Taney to Samuel Nott, August 19, 1857 (Proceedings of the Massachusetts Historical Society, XII (1871-1873), pp. 445-447).

5. Speech of Judah P. Benjamin, *Congressional Globe*, 35 Cong., 1 Sess., pp. 1070-1071.

6. New York *Tribune*, March 7, 1857.

7. The opinions of the judges herein analysed are those printed in 19 Howard 393-633. There is no substantial difference between those delivered in the court-room and those later printed. Cf. Curtis, *Memoir*, I, 212-232 for a discussion on this point between Taney and Curtis. Taney spoke of his opinion as that of the court at 19 Howard 400. His opinion runs from page 399 to page 454.

8. 19 Howard 403-405.

9. *Ibid.* 406.

10. *Ibid.* 413-416.

11. James Kent, *Commentaries on American Law* (New York: Published by William Kent, 1854), II, p. 258, note b.

12. 19 Howard 416. For a discussion of citizenship, cf., below, Chapter 8.

13. Richard Peters (ed.), *The Public Statutes at Large of the United States of America* (Boston: Little, Brown and Co., 1856), I, p. 103.

14. *Debates and Proceedings in the Congress of the United States*, 2 Congress (Washington: Gales and Seaton, 1849), p. 1092.

15. *Ibid.*, 12 Congress, 2 Session, 1318.

16. Benjamin F. Hall (ed.), *Official Opinions of the Attorneys General of the United States* (Washington: Published by Robert Farnham, 1852), I, 506-509; C. C. Andrews (ed.), *Official Opinions of the Attorneys General of the United States* (Washington: W. H. and O. H. Morrison, 1871), VIII, 751-752.

17. 2 Peters 664-670; 19 Howard 423-426.

18. 19 Howard 427.

19. *Ibid.* 428. Willoughby (Westel W. Willoughby, *The Constitutional Law of the United States* (New York: Baker, Voorhis and Company, 1929, 2nd ed.), I, pp. 27-28) regards this question, the consideration of the merits of the case after the jurisdiction of the lower Federal court had been denied, as "a very fine one." He cites with approval Corwin's defence of Taney's action in which Corwin points out that the Chief Justice carefully canvassed all the points involved from the jurisdictional aspect. Cf. Edward S. Corwin, *The Doctrine of Judicial Review . . . and Other Essays* (Princeton: Princeton University Press, 1914), pp. 129-157. Both Corwin and Hagen (Horace H. Hagen, "The Dred Scott Decision," *Georgetown Law Journal*, XV [1926], pp. 95-114) reject the contention that Taney's remarks, subsequent to his denial of the jurisdiction of the lower court, were *obiter dicta*. As Hagen points out, it was only on the argument that Scott was still a slave that a majority on the jurisdictional point was obtained. On the right of the court to vest its de-

cision on two or more grounds, although any one of them would be sufficient to dispose of the case, see the cases cited, from Hagen, by Willoughby (*op. cit.*, p. 27). All these, however, are subsequent to the Scott case.

20. Article 4, Section 3, Paragraph 2.
21. 19 Howard 432.
22. *Ibid.* 434.
23. Article 6, Section 1, Paragraph 1.
24. *Ibid.*, Paragraph 2.
25. 1 Peters 542.
26. 19 Howard 443.
27. 1 Peters 546.
28. 19 Howard 446.
29. Article 4, Section 3, Paragraph 1.
30. 19 Howard 448.
31. *Ibid.* 449.
32. *Ibid.* 450.
33. 10 Howard 182.
34. 19 Howard 453.
35. 19 Howard 454.
36. *National Intelligencer*, March 7, 1857.
37. Cf., above, pp. 63-65, and note 20.
38. Cf. above, pp. 70-71.
39. Cf., above, p. 71. This argument would also include Eliza's claim to freedom by reason of her birth in Illinois waters.
40. *National Intelligencer*, March 7, 1857; New York *Daily Tribune*, March 17, 1857; Warren, *The Supreme Court in United States History*, II, p. 119.
41. Cf., above, Chapter 5, p. 55.
42. 19 Howard 458. Nelson's opinion runs from page 457 to page 469 of 19 Howard.
43. Joseph Story, *Commentaries on the Conflict of Laws, Foreign and Domestic* (Boston: Little, Brown and Co., 1852), 29, 33-38; James Kent, *Commentaries on American Law*, II, p. 457.
44. Ulricus Huberus, *"De Conflictu Legum Diversarum in Diversis Imperiis"* (Friedrich Von Savigny, *A Treatise on the Conflict of Laws* (Translated by William Guthrie), Edinburgh, T. and T. Clark, 1880), pp. 508-516). Savigny reprinted the eight pages of Huber on this subject from the latter's *Praelectionum Juris Civilis*, 3 vols. (Lipsiae, 1725) because of the rarity of the work.
45. 19 Howard 465.
46. Nelson did not cite the two cases.
47. 19 Howard 467-469.
48. Livingston, *Portraits of Eminent Americans Now Living*, II, pp. 805-812, which is largely a letter from Catron to the author.
49. Smith, *The Francis Preston Blair Family in Politics*, I, p. 638, citing a letter of Andrew Jackson Donelson to his son. Catron's opinion runs from page 518 to page 529 of 19 Howard.
50. 19 Howard 522-523.
51. Cf., above, Chapter 5, pp. 54-55.
52. William Malloy (ed.), *Treaties, Conventions, International Acts, Protocols and Agreements between the United States of America and Other Powers* (Washington: Government Printing Office, 1910), I, pp. 508-509.
53. 19 Howard 529.
54. *National Intelligencer*, March 7, 1857.

7

DISSENTING AND OTHER VOICES

ON MARCH 7TH, THE TWO DISSENTIENTS, MCLEAN AND CURTIS, READ their opinions. They were followed by Daniel, Grier, Campbell and Wayne.[1] John McLean, whose father, a Revolutionary veteran, took his family from New Jersey to what is now West Virginia, then to Kentucky, finally settling in Warren County, Ohio, had a typically American early history. His education was largely his own doing. He worked to hire tutors for himself. At eighteen he was indentured to the clerk of the Hamilton County Court which sat at Cincinnati. There he read law under Arthur St. Clair and was admitted to the bar in 1807. A turn at newspaper work on the *Western Star* at Lebanon, Ohio, preceded his election to Congress as a War Democrat. Re-elected in 1814, he resigned two years later to become a member of the Supreme Court of Ohio. In 1822, Monroe made him Commissioner of the Land Office. In the following year he became Postmaster General, to which office he was reappointed by President Adams. Jackson placed him on the Supreme Court in 1829.[2] From this time forward he was periodically regarded as highly available presidential timber by certain politicians. Thad Stevens, an ex-Federalist in search of a party, considered McLean very favorably for the head of the Anti-Masonic ticket in 1831. The Free Democracy in 1848 and the Whigs in 1852 had both thought of him. In 1856, certain powers in the new Republican Party, particularly his old admirer, Stevens, thought him a safe candidate, much more acceptable to the Native Americans than either Seward or Frémont. His chances in 1860 were to appeal not only to Stevens but also to Lyman Trumbull and Abraham Lincoln. He had long been an outspoken free soiler and, by marriage to the daughter of Israel Ludlow, was connected with abolitionist circles.[3]

The question involved in the plea in abatement, the citizenship of free Negroes, was not before the Court, Judge McLean affirmed. Neither side had any ground for complaint. The defendant, Sanford, had won on the merits. Scott had won on the demur-

78

rer. McLean regarded it "as rather a sharp practice" for the Court to look at the record and, finding that the circuit court had no jurisdiction, move that the case be dismissed.[4] The pleadings did not show lack of jurisdiction and such a lack must be very clear before the court could decide to dismiss. However, the Ohio judge went on, the plea in abatement was radically defective. There was nothing in it to prevent Scott from suing in the Federal courts. To say that he was a Negro did not show that he was not a citizen of Missouri. A citizen need not be a voter, the justice said, a ground no one would controvert. Having been born here, the Scotts did not need to be naturalized. The most general meaning of the word citizen, he said, was freeman. If a man were free and lived in a different state from the defendant, he was a citizen of the United States and could sue in the Federal courts. That was all that was required by the Constitution.

Having completed his views on the plea in abatement and the question involved in it, which he did not regard as before the Court, McLean reduced the issues involved in the case to six headings. They were the local nature of slavery, the relation of the Federal government to slavery in the States, the power of Congress over slavery in the territories, the effect of taking slaves into a State or territory where slavery was prohibited, the effect on such slaves of a return to slave territory, the binding force of the decisions of the Missouri Supreme Court.[5] On the first question, McLean argued that slavery was a municipal institution founded on and bounded by territorial laws, citing in support of this position the decision of the Supreme Court in the case of Prigg vs. Pennsylvania and the opinion of Lord Mansfield in Somerset's case.[6] From the law as laid down in these two cases, McLean declared that slavery, to exist, had to have behind it the authority of positive law. It made no difference how it was introduced. It was immaterial that few, if any, instances of the establishment of slavery by statutory enactment were on record. McLean cited the opinion of Judge Mills, of Kentucky, in the case of Rankin vs. Lydia, with which he was in full accord. This was that slavery existed by positive law of a municipal character and had no foundation in the law of nature or common law, written or unwritten.[7]

The relation of the Federal government to slavery in the States next engaged his attention. The slave trade provision of the Constitution, in his opinion, clearly indicated that slavery was a State, not a national, institution and its regulation was to be left to the individual commonwealths.[8] As regarded the power of Congress over slavery in the territories, it was McLean's opinion that the constitutional provision on the territories gave Congress full authority. The power to make all needful rules and regulations, he contended, was a power to legislate, for the only way that Congress could pass rules and regulations was by legislation. The word territory, as used in the provisions, was not synonymous with land. The power to dispose of the land was expressly given and, in addition, there was given the power to make all needful rules and regulations. Both were complete in themselves. Otherwise, there would be useless verbiage in the Constitution. There was also, he continued, no lack of precision in Marshall's language in the Insurance Companies Case. While it was true that the source of congressional power in the territories was not there defined, it was clearly stated that the power was unquestioned, McLean said, occupying ground already taken by Taney.[9] Reverting to textual criticism again, McLean found, by consulting Worcester's *Dictionary,* that the word territory had three meanings: land, country, district of country. The word, "other," might give the impression that the word, as used in this section of the Constitution, meant land. This, however, was not its exclusive meaning; it could also mean government.

But, no matter what the word meant, he continued, Congress had the power to organize a temporary government in the territories. Was this power one of unlimited discretion, as Marshall had said in the Insurance Companies Case where he affirmed that Congress possessed the combined powers of a State and the Federal government in legislating for the territories? [10] It was not absolutely unlimited, he answered, for Congress could not make a man a slave. It was limited to means appropriate to its constitutional object, the making of new States, another position taken by Taney.[11] With his next step the Justice and the Chief Justice parted company. If Congress, McLean went on, should deem the institution of slavery injurious in a public way to a territory, it could prohibit it. This was not unfair. The south had only one quarter of the whole population residing within its borders and yet was possessed of much more fertile soil than the north. If slavery were not prohibited in a territory, fifty to one hundred northerners would be prevented from emigrating to it. A restriction on slavery would deter about one southerner from going to the same place. Passing from these considerations to those more properly legal, McLean then returned to the familiar argument that moved from the right to acquire to the right to govern. But he still felt that the constitutional provision on territories gave ample power for legislation. Still the right was unquestioned; Congress could act. McLean held that there was no difference between the Northwest Ordinance and the Missouri Compromise Act, because the acts of cession of the various States did not put the territory then acquired by the United States on a different footing from territory acquired later. Congress, he concluded, using its own discretion, can establish a territorial government and the Court cannot control that discretion.[12]

On the general question of comity, a question he had broken down into two, McLean declared that the effect of taking slaves into free territory emancipated the slaves completely. In this respect the United States differed from England, where slavery was only unauthorized. The slave was property by State law alone and Congress had no power to make him property. The slave owner could not carry his State law with him when he went into free territory. What the majority of the Court said, that a slave was property like any other property, made no difference. Anything that the majority said, which had no bearing on the question of jurisdiction, was beside the point and of no authority. For his part, McLean asserted, a slave was not a mere chattel, for "he bears the impress of his Maker, and is amenable to the laws of God and man, and he is destined to an endless existence." [13] According to the laws of Missouri, he continued, slaves brought into free territory were thereby freed. The decision of the State Supreme Court in the Scott case overruled a thirty-year-old exchange of comity. In so acting, that court had not held that the law had been misconstrued but had held that the law, due to existing circumstances, would no longer be recognized. To this McLean could not assent. It was his opinion that a statute was required to effect such a change. A judicial opinion did not suffice. For the Missouri Supreme Court to hold that the Scotts' status reattached when they returned to a slave State was not consonant with the respect due the State of Illinois. In addition, to bring the Scotts within the reach of Lord Stowell's decision in the case of the Slave Grace, their return must have been voluntary and the agreed statement of facts in the record only said "removed." [14] Strader vs. Graham was a pure case of jurisdiction and anything that was said in the opinion besides that point was *obiter dictum*.[15] On this final point, the binding power of the decision of the Missouri Supreme Court in the case, McLean pointed out that the rule laid down in the case of Pease vs. Peck was that the Supreme Court of the United States was bound only by a consistent line of decision by a State court.[16] The decision of the Missouri Supreme Court in the Scott case did not rejoice in that quality. He concluded by saying that it was his opinion that the judgment of the court below should be reversed.[17]

Benjamin Robbins Curtis was, in many ways, the antithesis of Taney. He was Massachusetts born and bred. After completing his study of the law under Judge Story, he became, from 1840 on, a strong supporter of the fortunes and principles of Daniel Webster, incurring considerable odium in his native state because of his continued adherence, after the Compromise of 1850, to that, in the eyes of some, fallen idol. In 1851 he had attacked the coalition of Free Soilers and Democrats that had made the anti-slavery extremists, Boutwell and Sumner, governor and senator.[18] Like Webster, he was a strong unionist and feared, as he wrote his uncle, George Ticknor, another outbreak of excitement in the north that would result in the formation of a purely sectional party to which "the wisest and the best men" could not belong and whose success would be very dangerous to the country.[19]

In opening, the Justice announced that he dissociated himself from the opinion of the Chief Justice and from the judgment of the majority of the Court, a careful distinction of which the Curtis family always made much.[20] Turning to the first question, Curtis asked himself whether the plea in abatement were before the Supreme Court or not. It was, he answered. According to the twenty-second section of the Judiciary Act of 1789, there was to be no reversal on a writ of error in the Supreme Court, for error in ruling on any plea in abatement, other than on a plea to the jurisdiction of the court. Circuit courts were not the final judges of their own jurisdiction in civil cases. Their records, coming on a writ of error, were to be inspected by the higher court. If the court below had no jurisdiction, the judgment must be reversed and the case remanded to the court, from which it came, to be dismissed. Sanford, in pleading to the merits, did not waive the benefit of his plea to the jurisdiction. Such a waiver should include his consent and this he did not give. Any error, no matter which way the decision on the plea went, could be examined in the Supreme Court. If the judgment on the plea went against the plaintiff (Scott), the case being thereby dismissed, the plaintiff could swear out a writ of error at once. If, on the other hand, it went against the defendant, the latter had to plead over to the merits and wait for a final judgment. Then he could swear out his writ of error. The Supreme Court could give its judgment on the error involved, if it appeared on the record. "Upon a writ of error," Curtis quoted from the Bank of the United States vs. Smith, "the whole record is open for inspection." [21]

The Justice then turned to the question at issue. The plea, he pointed out, did not show that Scott was a slave and, by the laws of pleading, no inference could be drawn to that effect.[22] The question was solely concerned with the citizenship of Negroes. Curtis then asked himself the same question Taney had; who were citizens of the United States at the time of the adoption of the Constitution? This, he said, was to ask who were citizens of the United States under the Articles of Confederation. They were, he replied, the citizens of the several States, because citizenship, at that time, was purely a State matter over which the Congress of the Confederation had no control. The question then resolved itself, Curtis continued, into an enquiry as to whether or not free Negroes of the class described in the plea, those of African descent whose ancestors had been brought to this country and sold as slaves, were citizens of any State at the time of the adoption of the Constitution? Curtis stated that, in 1787, all free, native-born inhabitants were citizens in New Hampshire, Massachusetts, New York, New Jersey and North Carolina.[23] In some, all the male inhabitants of that description voted. No discrimination having been made, it followed that Negroes, who were free and native-born, were citizens of those five States if they were living in them at the time of the adoption of the Constitution. This conclusion, Curtis argued, was strongly supported by the history of article four of the Articles of Confederation.[24] This stated that the free inhabitants of one State were entitled to the privileges and immunities of citizens in all the other States. On June 25, 1778, the South Carolina delegation moved that the word, "white," be inserted before the words, free inhabitants. The proposal was voted down by a vote of eight to two. The Constitution did not deprive any one of citizenship if he already possessed it. Curtis then announced that it was his opinion that, "under the Constitution of the United States, every free person born on the soil of a State, who is a citizen of that State by force of its Constitution and laws, is also a citizen of the United States." [25]

The Justice proceeded to establish this doctrine of the unicity of citizenship. By the Constitution, citizenship may be acquired by birth.[26] From this fact, one of four inferences that could be drawn must be true. Curtis rejected the conclusions that the Constitution itself described what native-born persons were to be citizens of the United States, that the Constitution had empowered Congress to say which free persons, born in a State, should be citizens, and that all free persons born within a State are citizens of the United States. The proper inference, he contended, was that which he had already stated as his own opinion, that it was left to each State to determine what free-born persons, native to it, should be its citizens and, thereby, citizens of the United States. Birth on the soil created citizenship. The States had the right to confer it. The only power, in this matter, conferred on the national government was that by which the disabilities of alienage were removed. Curtis substantiated this contention by pointing to the limited nature of the Federal government, in which all powers that had not been expressly granted to the Federal government were reserved to the States, by arguing that the privileges and immunities clause of the Constitution guaranteed to the citizens of each State the benefits of general citizenship, and by citing the fact that the franchise, the highest attribute of citizenship, had been left in the hands of the States. Curtis concluded, after rebutting several objections to his position, that the circuit court had been correct in sustaining the demurrer, because free Negroes were citizens of the United States by reason of their citizenship in individual States and, so, could sue in the Federal courts.

At this point, Curtis continued, he must dissent from what he deemed an unwarranted assumption of authority on the part of the majority of the court in examining the validity of the Missouri Compromise Act. They had decided that the circuit court had no jurisdiction. The only course open to them, in his opinion, was to dismiss the case. Curtis, however, was convinced that his position was different. He had held that the circuit court had jurisdiction. As a consequence, he was bound to consider the merits of the case to see if the judgment of the lower court were correct.

Curtis first considered the effect of Dred's residence in Illinois on his status. Depending on its expressed will, the intention of a State not recognizing the institution of slavery could have, in his opinion, three effects. It could work the absolute dissolution of the bond between master and slave. Such, Curtis said, was the intent of French law on the subject. It could refuse the master all aid in exercising his right of dominion, while in its boundaries, and could prevent any such act of dominion the master himself or his agents should attempt. This, Curtis stated, was the law of England and Massachusetts. It could distinguish the case. If the master entered its limits with the intention of remaining there, the bond was broken. If his sojourn was but temporary, no change in the master-slave relationship was effected. Such, the Justice said, was the law of Prussia. The intent of the act of 1820, the Missouri Compromise, and that of the act of 1836, by which Congress organized the Wisconsin Territory, were the same as the law of France and had the same effect, the relationship becoming simply nonexistent, Curtis declared. Did the State of Missouri recognize such an effect in these congressional acts, he asked? By international law, he replied, every State, in the absence of positive law to the contrary, must be presumed to allow such effects. The function of the judges of a State was to ascertain its will and follow it, for the comity they were extending was not that of the court but of the State. They would find their answer in the statutory or customary law of the State. They were not to look to political considerations for the answer. What, then, was the will of Missouri, as expressed in its statutory or customary law, in regard to the extension of comity to the law of other commonwealths in matters of status? There was no statutory law, Curtis pointed out. The customary law was the common law, introduced into the State by statute in 1816. The common law adopted the law of nations to its full extent and held it to be part of the law of the land. What was the international law on the change of status effected, not only by the law of Illinois, but by the law of the Wisconsin Territory? Commentators on international law, Curtis stated, were in general agreement that status was to be determined by the law which "next previously" had rightly operated and fixed such status. But this was to hold only in case of residence, not of sojourn. Did, Curtis asked, Dr. Emerson have a domicile at Fort Snelling? A military officer could have one. The presumption is that Emerson did have. However, he went on, it was not necessary to determine this point. In the United States, an attempt to decide a case solely by reference to the technicalities of the law of domicile was often inconsistent with sound principles. The Scott case would be such an attempt.

Domicile, in the technical sense, being put to one side, Curtis asked how any one could say that Emerson and Scott did not fall under the laws of Congress, assuming their validity? The fact that Dred and Harriet were married in the Minnesota Territory, with the consent of their master, was the equivalent of saying that they had made a contract there, a contract of marriage which, by international law, was valid everywhere, if it were valid at the place of contract. To declare Scott a slave in Missouri would be to impair a valid contract. Curtis characterized the opinion of the Supreme Court of Missouri in the Scott case as in conflict with its own previous decisions, with the great weight of judicial authority in the slave States, and with the fundamental principles of international law. In any event, he concluded, the Supreme Court of the United States was not bound to accept the last decision of a State supreme court as a binding rule.

His whole argument to this point, Curtis continued, depended on the validity of the eighth section of the Missouri Compromise Act. Was that section constitutional? The source of congressional power in the territories was the right to acquire new territory and the constitutional provision for such domain. The organization set up by the Northwest Ordinance could not have continued under the new form of government whose fundamental law was the Constitution, unless it had been provided for in some way. This fact must have been clear to the framers of the Constitution. Curtis then reviewed the history of the provision under discussion as it made its way through the Convention of 1787. Randolph introduced a resolution on the admission of new States. Madison, noting that there was no provision looking to the preparation of these future States before they were admitted into the Union, moved a resolution to that effect. Gouverneur Morris worded it as it stands today. That Congress had some power over the territories, all agreed. If, Curtis queried, necessity forced the admission of an implied power by which the territories were to be governed, why did gentlemen balk at liberally construing an express grant? A grossly inadequate provision on the territories was not likely in view of the circumstances in which it was composed.

The word, "territory," in the provision meant, according to Curtis, the ceded tracts and similar tracts, to be acquired later, with their essential qualities and incidents. The founding fathers, he asserted, were building for posterity and they must have considered the possibility that the United States would expand beyond the limits which, in 1787, bounded it. Consequently, the wording of the constitutional provision on the territories contained nothing which restricted it to territory possessed when the Constitution was adopted. Granted that there had been doubts as to the constitutionality of the acquisition of territory outside the original limits of the country, this question must be regarded as settled by the actions of every department of the government which had acquired new territory by four different treaties under four different administrations. Rules and regulations meant laws and their needfulness was at the discretion of Congress, Curtis went on, pointing out that slavery was no exception to this power; up to 1848, Congress had regulated that institution, in one way or another, fourteen times.[27]

Curtis then noticed Taney's argument that the power of Congress in the territories was inhibited by the Fifth Amendment to the Constitution in the matter of slavery where its exercise would amount to a deprivation of property without due process of law. His answer to this argument was that property in a slave was not the same as other property. Such a right existed only by positive law of a municipal character and these laws differed from State to State; other laws of property did not. If it were conceded that property rights in slaves were the same as other property rights, all sorts of legal anomalies would result. He next addressed himself to a consideration of the argument drawn from the third article of the treaty with France by which the Louisiana Territory was acquired. Curtis more than doubted that a treaty with a foreign nation could deprive Congress of any part of the legislative power conferred on it by the people to such an extent that it could not legislate as it was authorized to do by the Constitution. He conceded that the Constitution did make treaties part of our municipal law, but, Curtis argued, it assigned them no higher authority than other laws. It did not make them irrepealable. In the particular case at hand, he concluded, the stipulation appealed to was temporary and ceased to have any effect when the people of the Louisiana were incorporated into the Union. In his mind, Curtis ended, the Missouri Compromise Act was constitutional. Consequently, the judgment of the circuit court, holding that the Scotts were slaves, should be reversed and the cause remanded for a new trial.

87

Peter Vivian Daniel, of a prominent Virginia family, had been a protégé of Attorney General Randolph, whose daughter, Lucy, he had married. Before his appointment to the Supreme Court by Van Buren, whose close friend he continued to be, he had served as a legislator and member of the Privy Council in his native State. More immediately, he had been the judge of the United States District Court of Virginia.[28] Daniel was a deeply convinced exponent of the States Rights theory in government and of *laissez faire* in economics.[29] He spoke at some length and, apparently, from a rather full heart.[30]

Daniel found it difficult to imagine a more comprehensive case. In fact, it was so all-embracing that it aroused his suspicions. The question raised by the plea in abatement, the citizenship of free Negroes, was, in his opinion, before the Court. Daniel, like Taney, reminded his hearers that they were present at the sitting of a Federal court, not of a common law court. He cited many examples of the extent to which the requisite of jurisdiction had been enforced.[31] Canvassing citizenship from the angle of the law of nations, Daniel found that the African race had never been regarded as belonging to the family of nations. Its members were considered as subject to capture, purchase, commerce. They had been introduced into every section of the United States as "property in the strictest sense of the term," not as constituent members of the body politic.[32] A slave, Daniel said, was not a citizen. Did emancipation make him one? This, Daniel said, was tantamount to asking whether an individual by his own act, and his only, could make a citizen. Daniel went back to Rome for his answer, remarking that American slavery was much more akin to that institution than to medieval villenage. From his reading of ancient history, Daniel emerged with the finding that emancipation did not effect citizenship till the time of Justinian when the imperial *fiat,* being the sole expression of the sovereign power of the nation, made it do just that. Daniel contended that, if emancipation were to work citizenship, every American slave owner would be a potential Justinian. Apart from the dangerous social implications of such a doctrine, the Justice found that it ran counter to the naturalisation laws of the United States, which extended citizenship solely to free white aliens. Diversity of residence was not sufficient to give a Federal court jurisdiction. The Constitution spoke of citizens, not residents.

Daniel then undertook to discuss the merits of the questions involved in the case. He remarked that, "According to the view taken of the law, as applicable to the plea in abatement in this cause, the questions subsequently raised . . . might be passed by. . . . But these questions are intrinsically of primary interest and magnitude, and have been elaborately discussed in argument, and as with respect to them the opinions of a majority of the court, including my own, are perfectly coincident, to me it seems proper that they should be here fully considered and, so far as it is practicable for this court to accomplish such an end, finally put to rest." [33] After these prefatory sentences, Daniel turned to the question of the effect of Scott's residence in Illinois on his status. Vattel and Kent, he pointed out, were both in agreement on the perfect equality of States and the consequent incapacity on the part of one State to dictate to another on a matter of internal polity. [34] The decision in Somerset's case in no way impaired the force of this fundamental principle, since that decision was limited to the realm of England, as Lord Stowell had pointed out in the case of the Slave Grace. The laws of Illinois, then, did not free Dred when he brought suit in Missouri.

Did residence at Fort Snelling free him and his family? Daniel replied that it did not, because the same principle controlled this part of the case. The Missouri Compromise Act had no more extra-territorial effect than the Constitution of Illinois, granting that the act were valid. But it was not, Congress not having the power to pass that section of the act by which slavery was prohibited in the territory. The territorial provision of the Constitution gave no such power. It referred to the territory only as property. It gave Congress no authority over the personal and political rights of the citizens who emigrated to the territories. This property, to which the provision referred, was to be so administered by Congress, the trustee of the States, in such a way that the accruing benefits would be shared equally by all the States. From this principle, Daniel concluded that the constitutional clause, whatever its meaning, could not be interpreted in such a way as to prevent citizens of the United States who owned slaves, a type of property peculiarly protected by the Constitution, from enjoying the common patrimony. In concluding, he stated that the lower court had erred in sustaining Scott's reply to Sanford's plea in abatement. The decision should be reversed and the action abated.

Robert Cooper Grier did as he had told Buchanan he would

do. In a short opinion he expressed his concurrence with Judge Nelson on the point that he had elaborated, that the question of Dred's status was one for Missouri to decide. He also agreed with the Chief Justice that the sixth section of the Missouri Compromise Act was unconstitutional. Being a slave, Grier pointed out, Scott could not sue in a Federal court.[35]

John Archibald Campbell was a Georgian who, after admission to the bar by a special act of the legislature of that State at the early age of eighteen, emigrated to Alabama where he achieved distinction as a civil and common lawyer. Brought up under the influence of Calhoun, he was a strict constructionist of the Constitution, though he was no blind admirer of his father's friend. When Campbell met Calhoun in Washington, he found him to be "of interesting appearance and of an intense form of address." During their interview, Calhoun, to Campbell's annoyance, practiced a speech on him. Like Taney, he was a man of great personal kindliness toward Negroes and, on coming to the bench, had manumitted all his slaves.[36]

Although he concurred in the judgment pronounced by the Chief Justice, Campbell said, opening with the same distinction Curtis had made earlier, he felt that the importance of the case, public expectation, and his own sense of responsibility forced him to express his own opinion more in detail. He would not, he continued, discuss the question raised in the plea in abatement, the citizenship of Negroes because, in his judgment, the case was not affected by it. Campbell, accordingly, discussed the merits of the case. Scott's claim to freedom, he pointed out, depended on the effect his absence from Missouri in Illinois and the Minnesota Territory had upon his status, an effect to be determined by the laws of Missouri. The Justice took as his point of departure the truism that slavery was licit in Missouri. From this he passed on to another undisputed assertion, that a slave's removal from slave territory, without his master's consent, did not free him. Campbell then asked whether the removal of a slave, for the purpose of temporary residence, with the consent of and in the company of his master, both parties continuing their existing relations, effected emancipation in such a way that the slave was free on his return according to the laws, in this case, of Missouri? With this complicated query, the Judge occupied disputed ground. He retired to general principles before answering his own question. In general, he stated, status was determined by the law of the place of birth. Such an imprint, he added, was not indelible. A different status could be acquired by change of domicile, since every sovereign power determined such questions for itself within its own limits. But, he continued, neither Emerson nor Scott had acquired a domicile in Illinois or Minnesota. Scott's plea was based on the assumption that the laws governing status in these two places were irrevocably impressed on him by his stay in both of them and that these effects endured after his return to Missouri. This assumption was invalid. The proper question to be asked and answered was what were the effects of commorancy on the status of a slave. The French cases on this point, in which a sojourn worked emancipation, depended, for their liberating force, on positive charters. A survey of English precedents, a consideration of the role England had played in the slave trade, the fact that public slave auctions had been conducted in London for over a century, and the circumstance that, in 1772, there were 15,000 slaves in the United Kingdom caused Campbell to find that Lord Mansfield was not justified in his sweeping assertions in the Somerset Case.[37] The proper interpretation of English law on the status of slaves, actually within the realm, was that of Lord Stowell in the case of the Slave Grace and it was Campbell's opinion that the Scott case did not differ materially from that of the slave from Antigua. In fact, the basis of Scott's complaint on this score appeared to Campbell to be that the judiciary of Missouri did not denounce "as odious the Constitution and laws under which they have organized, and have not superseded them on their own private authority, for the purpose of applying the laws of Illinois, or those passed by Congress for Minnesota, in their stead."[38]

The Justice then canvassed the argument that Scott was free, and with him his whole family, because of the effect of the eighth section of the Missouri Compromise Act of 1820. Did it, he asked, provide grounds for pronouncing a judgment the Supreme Court of Missouri had refused to allow? It was settled doctrine, Campbell pointed out, that the Federal government could not touch slavery in the States. The power to prohibit it in the territories must rest on some condition peculiar to those regions. The territorial provision of the Constitution was not sufficient. Power to dispose of public lands and to organize a temporary government did not extend to power to interfere in internal polity. The exercise of such power was alien to the American tradition. It had more in common with the power claimed by the British Parliament and against which the colonies had rebelled. A survey of the early history of the United States, Campbell felt, would clarify the issue. By the American Revolution, thirteen sovereign States had come into existence. These States, due to the fact that some of them ceded large tracts of land to all for the common good, became jointly interested in the ceded territory. In the light of the jealous care with which these States resisted an external power invading internal concerns, it was hardly probable that a clause inserted in the Constitution to handle a definite problem, the disposal of the ceded lands in the interests of all, was intended by its authors, men of the Revolution, to be an assertion of a supreme authority, vested in Congress, over the territory then belonging to the United States or over that which it might subsequently acquire.

The fundamental error in the whole business, according to Campbell, was that men assumed that Congress had the power to do everything which was not expressly forbidden by the Constitution. This was to forget the nature of that document and its Tenth Amendment which limited the powers of the Federal government to those expressly granted to it. Congress had exceeded these powers in 1798 and 1800 in the matter of the Georgian lands, and in 1820 when it had tried to place restrictions on the state of Missouri, all actions which perverted the nature of the Union. An expedient had been arrived at in the eighth section of the Act of 1820 and its constitutionality was now before the Court. Campbell phrased the question, "Can Congress determine the condition and status of persons who inhabit the territories?" and answered that it could not.[39] The constitutional provision on the territories did not give this power, although, he admitted, it did confer certain powers on the Federal government. It was not necessary to a decision of the present case to ascertain the full scope of these powers. It was enough to decide whether the residuary sovereignty of the States or people had been invaded by the eighth section of the Act of 1820.

Campbell was of the opinion that it had been, and the reason for his answer was the nature of the Federal system. When the Federal government was founded, the judge from Alabama stated, the States were already organized bodies with distinct systems of municipal law in which were provisions for the determination of the status of the persons residing within their borders. These provisions were beyond the power of the Federal government to touch. While Congress could, to a certain extent, determine what should or should not be property, it really depended on the States to determine what was property. If the States said a thing was property, Congress must recognize it as such. This followed from the structure of these governments and their relations one to the other. The people had bestowed different powers on both and both were but agents and trustees of the people. Consequently, their acts were mutually obligatory. All this argument concluded to the assertion that a prescription by which the Federal government determined property, thereby endangering the social systems of one or more States, was repugnant to the nature of the Federal compact. He closed saying that the opinion of the circuit court was correct, Scott and his family were slaves and, being so, could not sue in the Federal courts.

Justice Wayne, like Judge Grier, was true to his agreement; he was brief. This "intelligent, prompt, good looking Georgian" had studied at Princeton and been initiated into the law by Judge Chauncey at New Haven.[40] Although he had been appointed to the bench by Jackson, he was considered by a competent critic one of "the most high toned Federalists" of his time.[41] He had recently enjoyed the distinction of a short, one-man presidential boom, which originated and ended with Senator Benton, who had urged Wayne as "all right and a *new candidate*." This recommendation aroused no enthusiasm in the elder Blair, who remarked to Van Buren, "Yes, *new* for nobody thought of him." [42]

Wayne concurred fully with the Chief Justice. Nothing belonging to the case, he said, had been omitted. The Court had not sought the case and, in its action on it, had but done its duty. The questions were such, he remarked, "that the peace and harmony of the country required the settlement of them by judicial opinion." He closed repeating his unqualified assent in the opinion of the Court.[43]

The judges, having stated the case for the north and the south, filed out. Their hearers, both in the courtroom and the nation— for their opinions were soon to be spread widely—were given the choice of adjusting themselves to the decision, provided they could find out just what had been decided, or of declaring the law, as pronounced by the judges, no law at all. This process would not require much time, for the judges had said nothing new. The arguments they had used had been the *loci communes* of congressional oratory for years. The conclusions they had reached had been arrived at before, both by the bench and by sectional spokesmen in and out of Congress.

1. *National Intelligencer,* March 9, 1857.
2. Francis P. Weisenburger, *The Life of John McLean* (Columbus: Ohio State University Press, 1937), pp. 1 66, 220.
3. White, *The Life of Lyman Trumbull,* pp. 103-105; Current, *Old Thad Stevens,* pp. 19, 103.
4. 19 Howard 531. McLean's opinion runs from page 529 to page 564.
5. 19 Howard 533-534.
6. 16 Peters 594; Thomas B. Howell (ed.), *A Complete Collection of State Trials* (London: T. C. Hansard, 1814), 20, p. 79; hereinafter referred to as 20 Howell.
7. 2 A. K. Marshall 467-479.
8. Article 1, Section 9, Paragraph 1: "The migration or importation of such persons as any of the states now existing shall think proper to admit, shall not be prohibited by the Congress prior to the year one thousand eight hundred and eight, but a tax or duty may be imposed on such importation, not exceeding ten dollars for each person."
9. Cf., above, Chapter 6, pp. 68-69.
10. 1 Peters 546.
11. Cf., above, Chapter 6, pp. 69-70.
12. 19 Howard 547.
13. *Ibid.* 550.
14. *Ibid.* 398.
15. 10 Howard 182.
16. 18 Howard 589. For Pease vs. Peck, see 18 Howard 595-601.
17. 19 Howard 564.
18. *Dictionary of American Biography,* IV, pp. 609-611.
19. Curtis, *Memoir,* I, p. 193.
20. *See* George T. Curtis, *Constitutional History of the United States,* II, pp. 270-272. Curtis's opinion runs from page 504 to page 633 of 19 Howard.
21. 19 Howard 566. Bank of United States vs. Smith, 11 Wheaton 171; "But the present case being brought here on a writ of error, the whole record is under the consideration of the court, and the defendant having the judgment of the court below in his favor may avail himself of all defects in the declaration, that are not deemed to be cured by the verdict." J. Thompson for court.
22. *Ibid.* 567-568.
23. *Ibid.* 572-574.
24. "The better to secure and perpetuate mutual friendship and intercourse among the people of the different states in this union, the free inhabitants of each of these states, paupers, vagabonds and fugitives from Justice excepted, shall be entitled to all privileges and immunities of free citizens in the several states. . . ."
25. 19 Howard 576.
26. "No person except a natural born citizen, or a citizen of the United States, at the time of the adoption of this Constitution, shall be eligible to the office of President. . . ." Article 2, Section 1, Paragraph 5.
27. 19 Howard 617-619.
28. *Dictionary of American Biography,* V, p. 69.
29. Swisher, *Roger B. Taney,* p. 68.
30. Daniel's opinion occupies pp. 469-492 of 19 Howard.
31. 19 Howard 473.

32. *Ibid.* 475.

33. *Ibid.* 482.

34. Emmerich de Vattel, *The Law of Nations* (Translation of the edition of 1758 by Charles G. Fenwick, Washington: Carnegie Institution, 1916), p. lxiii; Kent, *Commentaries,* I, pp. 21-22.

35. Grier's concurrence is on p. 469 of 19 Howard.

36. Henry G. Connor, *John Archibald Campbell* (Boston: Houghton Mifflin Company, 1920), pp. 263-264. Campbell's opinion runs from page 493 to page 518 of 19 Howard.

37. 20 Howell 81-82.

38. 19 Howard 500.

39. *Ibid.* 509. Campbell's opinion on the power Congress possessed in the territories had changed since 1848 in which year he had given his opinion on the subject to Calhoun at the latter's request. He said, "When you admit that Congress may form a government you concede the right to it to define what shall be property. . . . It may decide that persons shall or shall not be property. There is nothing about slave property that I know of that takes it from the sway of legislative authority. . . . I think Congress has the power to organize the inhabitants of a territory of the United States into a body politic, and to determine in what manner they shall be governed. As incident to this power, I think that Congress may decide what shall be held and . . . not be held as property." (John A. Campbell to John C. Calhoun, March 1, 1848, cited in Eugene I. McCormac, "Justice Campbell and the Dred Scott Decision," *Mississippi Valley Historical Review,* 19 (1933), pp. 565-571).

40. Cf., above, Chapter 5, p. 57; New York *Daily Tribune,* March 17, 1857.

41. Benjamin R. Curtis, *A Memoir of Benjamin Robbins Curtis,* I, p. 168.

42. Alexander A. Lawrence, *James Moore Wayne* (Chapel Hill: University of North Carolina Press, 1943), p. 150.

43. 19 Howard 454-455. Wayne's concurrence in the Chief Justice's opinion on the power Congress could exercise over slavery in the territories nettled Catron who regarded Wayne's position in the Scott case as contradicting his former stand in the case of Cross vs. Harrison. Cf., below, Chapter 9, p. 133, and note 77.

8

THE QUESTION OF CITIZENSHIP

THE QUESTION OF CITIZENSHIP, LIKE THE CLOSELY RELATED QUESTION of the nature of the Federal Union, was, in 1857, still a debated one. Of the five judges who explicitly treated the issue in the Scott case, only three—Taney, Wayne and Daniel—concluded that, as they construed the Constitution, free Negroes were not entitled to share in the benefits conferred on the citizens of States by Article Four (section two, paragraph one) of the Constitution and, consequently, could not bring suit in the Federal courts. What Nelson, Campbell, Grier, and Catron felt about the matter, they did not say. The question had become further involved by a technical point: Whether the plea in abatement was before the Court at all. As a result, the clarity of the issue and the Court's opinion on it suffered.[1]

The Constitution did not define the term, "citizen." By implication, it recognized a State citizenship when it declared that "The citizens of each state shall be entitled to all privileges and immunities of citizens in the several states." [2] A Federal citizenship was indicated by the requirement that the President be a natural-born citizen.[3] It was generally admitted that there was a distinction between State and Federal citizenship, but the relation of one to the other was still a matter of speculation. Curtis asserted that the source of Federal citizenship lay in citizenship in a State. Taney declared that it came from the national government, except for the descendants of those who became citizens at the time of the adoption of the Constitution.[4]

On the precise point at issue, the citizenship of free Negroes in so far as to enable them to sue in the Federal courts, confusion was doubly confounded, for the question could not be settled on its own merits. Lurking in men's minds when they considered the subject was the possibility that, if the benefits of the Federal courts were extended to Negroes, the recognition of their right to all the privileges and immunities of United States citizenship would follow, a conclusion that very few of the States, at that time, were prepared to accept. Many of them had discriminatory laws of one sort or another on their books.[5]

The problem had engaged Madison's attention in 1820. The exclusion of free Negroes from the State by the Constitution of Missouri, the last phase in the battle over the admission of that commonwealth, raised the question of the privileges and immunities of this section of the population. Explaining that he did not have a copy of the State constitution at hand, Madison told Monroe that he could form no definite opinion on the subject. He presumed that "a right in the States to inhibit the entrance of that description of colored people . . . would be as little disrelished by the States having no slaves as by the States retaining them." There was room, Madison continued, "for a more critical examination of the constitutional meaning of the term 'citizens' . . . " than had yet taken place, "and of the effect of the various civil disqualifications applied by the laws of the States to free people of color."[6]

A somewhat critical examination of the question took place the next year. The collector of the port at Norfolk, Virginia, proposed a difficulty to the Secretary of the Treasury, William H. Crawford. He wanted to know whether a free person of color was a citizen of the United States within the meaning of the acts to regulate foreign and coastal trade, at least to the extent of being able to command a vessel that put in at Virginia ports. Attorney General William Wirt was called upon by the Secretary for his opinion. Assuming that the term, "citizen of the United States," had the same meaning in both the Constitution and in the acts of Congress passed under the Constitution, Wirt took the former as his norm of judgment. A consideration of the Constitution, he said, made it "seem very manifest that no person is included in the description of citizen of the United States who has not the full rights of a citizen in the State of his residence." This doctrine, which was soon to appear in the decisions of State courts, was the basis for Wirt's reply to Crawford and, through him, to the Norfolk collector that free Negroes were not citizens of the United States, with the consequence that they suffered the disabilities of their position as non-citizens, whatever they might be.[7] According to Wirt, Federal citizenship came through State citizenship, the position later taken by Curtis. But Wirt's opinion, that disqualification in a State precluded the penalised person from the enjoyment of Federal citizenship, could only have meaning when the person involved was a resident of a State which discriminated against free Negroes. It would have no application to a free Negro from a State which recognised no civil or political distinctions between its Negro and its white inhabitants. The collector of the port at Norfolk would, logically, first have to find out in what State the free Negro captain lived and decide, on the basis of the laws of that State, whether he was a Federal citizen or not.

In 1822, the Supreme Court of Kentucky found it necessary to discuss the problem of the status of free Negroes. The court, through Chief Justice Boyle, Justice Owsley concurring, was of the opinion that the terms "citizen" and "subject" were not synonymous. Place of birth made a person a subject, but citizenship, as that word was used in the Constitution, meant something more than "those ordinary rights of personal security and property" extended to all.[8] Amy, the plaintiff, was not a citizen, for the presumption was against her. This presumption was founded, in the opinion of the court, in the circumstance that "Free Negroes and mulattoes are, almost everywhere, considered and treated as a degraded race of people; insomuch so, that, under the Constitution and laws of the United States, they cannot become citizens of the United States." [9] Boyle conceded that the States, before the adoption of the Constitution, could make any one a citizen. But the Federal naturalisation law, which excluded Negroes, "marked national sentiment," on the subject and gave grounds for the assumption that no State made persons of color citizens. Amy had not combatted this presumption with sufficient evidence.[10] Judge Benjamin Mills dissented from this opinion. Analysing the idea advanced by Wirt and adopted by the majority of the Kentucky judges, that citizenship in the United States was possessed only by those who enjoyed the fulness of privileges and immunities in their own states, Mills pointed out that, by this reasoning, only one-eighth of the population could claim citizenship. Logically, minors, women, all who could not vote by reason of property qualifications, as well as free Negroes, should be regarded as beyond the meaning of the term "citizen." He advanced the opinion, which he had already outlined in earlier decisions,[11] that the solution of the problem was to distinguish political from civil benefits and immunities. The possession of the latter constituted a man a citizen.[12]

The effects of the various disqualifications applied by the States to free Negroes, the subject that had concerned Madison, were being slowly formulated by the courts. The drift of judicial rea-soning on the subject, which was not alien to the current thought of the country at large, was toward the creation of a third class of residents in the United States, citizens, free Negroes and aliens. Men like Judge Mills, who tried to stay this current, had become, by 1822, figures of the past, the Missouri question having charged the atmosphere. When the case under discussion did not concern a Negro, some judges did not feel the need to distinguish between subjects and citizens. The Court of Appeals of Virginia decided in 1824 that all persons permanently residing in the Old Dominion at the time she declared herself independent of Great Britain, even though they were hostile to the new government, were mem-bers of the community and had to be considered as citizens. This was true despite the various acts of the Virginia Legislature from 1786 on which attempted to define the limits of the term.[13]

January, 1829, found the Supreme Court of the United States sitting in the case of Le Grand vs. Darnall, in which Chief Justice Taney, then State's Attorney for Maryland, had appeared for the mulatto, Darnall, and which Montgomery Blair had used as an *argumentum ad hominem* against Taney in his defense of the citizenship of free Negroes.[14] The point at issue was a decision of the Court of Appeals of Maryland which declared that "a devise of property, real or personal, by a master to his slave, entitles the slave to his freedom by necessary implication." [15] The Supreme Court, speaking through Justice Duval, entertained the same opinion, and Nicholas Darnall, the son of Bennett Darnall by one of his slaves, was vested with the title to his father's large land holdings in Anne Arundel County, Maryland. Taney had sub-mitted the case without argument, "stating that it had been brought up merely on account of its great importance to the appellee," Darnall.[16] The proceedings were friendly. Nicholas Darnall had sold his lands to Le Grand and the case was an effort to certify his title to them and to protect him in it against his father's brother. As Taney pointed out, the question of Negro citizenship did not appear on the record and was at no time called to the court's attention.[17]

When Taney came to Washington in 1831 to succeed John Berrien as Attorney General, he fell heir to a problem that had been the cause of considerable complaint on the part of the Brit-ish government. This was the question of the legality of the South Carolina laws respecting colored seamen. Berrien had regarded these laws, harsh and inequitable though they were, as a valid exercise of the police power of the State, analogous to quarantine laws. The citizenship of the seamen did not concern him.[18] The British Minister, Charles Vaughan, continued to raise the issue and Taney was asked for an opinion by the Secretary of State, Edward Livingston. In his reply, Taney stated that, since England extended no comity in the matter of slavery in general and since there was no express stipulation in our treaties with her on the matter, the problem was one for the individual States to handle.[19] The Attorney General evidently gave the question more thought. On June 9, 1832, he wrote to Livingston that he was sending him a supplement to his remarks on the South Carolina laws. On his return from the current session of the Maryland Court of Appeals, he hoped to have the benefit of the Secretary's ideas on the subject. He would then put the whole matter in proper form.[20] Unfortunately, he never did so, but, from the notes that he made on the question, Taney was, in 1832, of the same opinion as Chief Justice Boyle of Kentucky. "The African race has never been regarded as a portion of the people of this country and have never been considered as members of the body politic. In our most solemn and public acts where we speak of our people or our citizens they are never intended to be included and this is so well understood that it has not been deemed necessary to qualify general principles or stipulations made in general terms in cases where it is evident they were not intended to be embraced," he wrote Livingston. In this way, the Declaration of Independence, "drawn by a distinguished citizen of a slave holding state," was to be interpreted. A quarter of a century before the Dred Scott decision, Taney's mind on one point seems to have been clear.[21]

Justice Catron had given the question of Negro citizenship some thought in 1834 when he was the Chief Justice of Tennessee. He was concerned with the effect in that commonwealth of manumission by will. He found that the process was not of itself void. It communicated an imperfect right to freedom to the slave, a right which, to become perfect, required the assent of the State. He regarded manumission as "adopting into the body politic a new member." [22] This he considered a vastly important measure in any community "and especially in ours where . . . the free negro's vote at the polls is of as high value as that of any man." This reflection and the fact that where slaves were numerous free Negroes were "a very dangerous and most objectionable population," degraded as they were by their color and condition, were the reasons why the consent of the government to the act of manumission was imperative. Such an act, he continued, being as high an act of sovereignty as naturalisation, could not be left to an individual's pleasure.[23] Free Negroes, as Catron read the law of Tennessee, were citizens, though to what degree he did not say. He did say that, in reality, the free Negro, whether resident in the north or the south, was "a degraded outcast, and his fancied freedom a delusion." [24]

While Catron was reviewing the question of the citizenship of free Negroes in Tennessee and arriving at the conclusion that they were citizens of some sort, Chief Justice Daggett, of Connecticut, was considering the constitutionality of a statute, passed by the State in the preceding year, 1833, which restricted the education of free Negroes, who were not inhabitants of the State, within its borders. In the lower court, when the case first appeared before him, Daggett instructed the jury that free Negroes were not citizens of the United States in the sense of the privileges and immunities clause of the Constitution. Therefore, the law which discriminated against non-resident free Negroes in Connecticut was not void on that score.[25] To his mind, "it would be a perversion of terms to say that slaves, free blacks, or Indians, were citizens, within the meaning of that term, as used in the Constitution." [26] When the case came before the Supreme Court of Errors, Justices Williams, Bissell, and Church waived the constitutional question and reversed Daggett's decision in the lower court because of an error in the judgment.[27]

Three years later, Chief Justice Gibson of Pennsylvania was called upon to decide an election case which involved the right of a free Negro, named Fogg, to vote. His vote had been challenged by, among others, one Hobbs on the grounds that Fogg was not a citizen within the meaning of that term as it was used in the constitutions of Pennsylvania and the United States.[28] Gibson reversed the decision of the lower court which had been in favor of the free Negro, Fogg. He summed up the position of those who held for the citizenship of free Negroes, saying, "Now the argument of those who assert the claim of the colored population is, that a Negro is a man; and, when not held to involuntary service, that he is free; consequently that he is a free man; and if a free man in the common acceptation of the term, then a free man in every acceptation of it." [29] This sentence, Gibson maintained, comprised the whole argument for Negro citizenship, "which, however elaborated, perpetually gets back to the point from which it started." [30] Gibson pointed out what appeared to him to be the weak link in this chain of reasoning. Freedom, he said, only meant exemption from involuntary service. An inhabitant, who was not a servant or a slave, could very well be no free man with respect to government. The status of Negroes, at the time of the adoption of the Constitution, was indeed a depressed one. The privileges and immunities clause of that document was not a shield to the free Negro but, rather, an insuperable obstacle to his political freedom. Gibson formulated the problem that was troubling the legal minds of the country; "It is to be remembered that citizenship, as well as freedom, is a constitutional qualification; and how could it be conferred so as to overbear the laws imposing countless disabilities on him in other states, is a problem of difficult solution." [31] In view of the fact that "no colored race was party to our compact," Gibson decided that Fogg had no right to vote.[32]

The question arose again in Tennessee in 1838 when the constitutionality of a State statute which prohibited vagrant free Negroes from residing for more than twenty days in the commonwealth was challenged as a violation of the privileges and immunities of a citizen of the United States. Attorney General Thomas, for the State, argued like Wirt that a citizen was a person who had all the privileges and immunities of the highest class in society. There might be in a State, he admitted, a class of people with limited privileges and immunities who might be called citizens. But, not being entitled to all the benefits enjoyed by those possessed of citizenship in its fullest sense, they did not fall under the protection of the constitutional provision.[33] This reasoning found favor with Judge Green. Free Negroes, he decided, were never entitled to all the privileges and immunities of citizenship in any of the States and, consequently, were not included under the term citizen in the Constitution. The statute was valid.[34]

During the same year, 1838, there came before Chief Justice Ruffin, of North Carolina, and his two associates, Judges Joseph Daniel and William Gaston, the case of The State vs. William Manuel.[35] Manuel, a free Negro, could not pay a fine for an assault. There was on the statute books of the State a law, passed in 1831, which provided that free Negroes, in Manuel's position, were to be hired out and their wages used to pay their fines. The

102

constitutionality of this statute was challenged by the defendant's counsel as in conflict with the State's bankruptcy laws and the bill of rights. In particular, it was argued that this law deprived Manuel of the benefits of due process of law which were guaranteed to all citizens of the State.[36]

Judge Gaston, speaking for the court in an opinion which was to be given wide publicity, especially in the north, started with the premise, which he held to be the law of the State, that all human beings within the boundaries of North Carolina fell into two categories, aliens and citizens. Slaves, manumitted in North Carolina, became free men and, if they had been born within the State, were citizens of it, a position Chief Justice Gibson had regarded as untenable when the dual nature of government in the United States was considered. According to the law of North Carolina, Gaston explained, the term "citizen" was "precisely analogous to the term *subject* in the common law, and the change of phrase has entirely resulted from the change of government." [37] This legal theory, which was the same as that of the Virginia judges in the earlier case cited above, Barzizas v. Hopkins and Hodgson,[38] did not save Manuel, because Gaston found the law complained of constitutional. Its enunciation by a southern judge, however, did provide ammunition for northern publicists.

A similar case, concerning the constitutionality of a statute which forbade free Negroes from carrying firearms without a license, was decided in North Carolina in 1840 in favor of the statute. Judge Nash, who had succeeded Gaston, was not as sure as he had been that free Negroes were citizens. "Free persons of color in this State," he said, enunciating the theory first laid down by Wirt in 1821, "are not to be considered as citizens, in the largest sense of the term, or if they are, they occupy such a position in society as justifies the legislature in adopting a course of policy in its acts peculiar to them—so that they do not violate those great principles of justice, which lie at the foundation of all law." [39] Nash, like Gibson of Pennsylvania, feared that, if this law were declared void, all discriminatory legislation concerning free Negroes would fall to the ground, a serious invasion of the legislature's prerogative.[40]

In January, 1843, the question was aired in Congress when Robert Winthrop, of Massachusetts, reported to the House of Representatives on the question of the imprisonment of free colored seamen who put in at certain southern ports, notably Charleston,

Savannah, Mobile, and New Orleans. The Commerce Committee, of which Winthrop was chairman, had gone into the matter at the request of some one hundred and fifty citizens of the Bay State, among whom were Abbott Lawrence, James S. Amory, Caleb Loring, Benjamin R. Curtis—the Justice Curtis of 1857—and Robert G. Shaw, Jr. This group had prayed Congress "to render effectual . . . the privileges of citizenship secured by the Constitution of the United States" in the matter of these Negro seamen.[41] The majority of the committee agreed with the petitioners that, in addition to the charges that the laws by which these imprisonments were effected violated the commerce power of the federal government and the American Convention of 1815 with Great Britain, they also violated the privileges and immunities clause of the Constitution. Some States, the report pointed out, recognised no distinction of color in citizenship: "Their citizens are all free; their freemen all citizens." [42] In Massachusetts, it continued, Negroes had been recognised as full citizens since 1780 and so were such when the Constitution of the United States was adopted. This entitled them to the full protection of that document.[43] The committee argued as Curtis was to argue in the Scott case.

A minority report was submitted by Kenneth Rayner, of North Carolina. Rayner pointed out that the restrictive laws in question had been passed upon the discovery of a plan for a Negro insurrection which was being fomented by some Negro sailors. South Carolina had acted from stern necessity. Glossing the privileges and immunities clause, Rayner advanced the idea that these words "must refer to those of the States *in* which, and not to the State *from* which, the citizen happens to be." [44] He warned the memorialists that their request, if it were to be granted, should work reciprocally. If the relationship that existed between black and white in Massachusetts were to be forced on South Carolina by Congress, then that body should enforce the South Carolina code in New England.[45] Congress did nothing about the situation.

In 1844, John C. Spencer, then Secretary of the Treasury, wished to know whether or not free Negroes could benefit by the Preemption Act of 1841. Attorney General Legaré was of the opinion they could. He felt no need to discuss citizenship "in the highest sense of the word," since only aliens were meant to be excluded by the act. Free Negroes were not aliens. Perhaps, he hazarded, they should be called denizens, a term Judge Mills had applied to free Negroes in Kentucky.[46] The anomalous position of the free Negro was emphasized by Attorney General Caleb Cushing in 1856. Robert McClelland, the Secretary of the Interior, wanted information on the citizenship of Indians. Cushing, in discussing citizenship in general, said that only citizens "in the highest political sense" constituted civil and political society. The right to vote, he pointed out, was no test of citizenship, for a person could be an elector without being a citizen. Mere birth in a State was not the basis of citizenship, he continued, and Story and Rawle were wrong when they said that citizenship in a State made a man a Federal citizen.[47] Legaré was following the dictates of his heart and not his head in the opinion he had given to Secretary Spencer, Cushing continued. On the general question, the Attorney General concluded there was no answer in United States law.[48]

It was from this mass of conflicting argument, assumption and logic that the judges who treated the question of Scott's right to sue in the Federal courts on the basis of diversity of citizenship were, theoretically, to draw their answer. The two protagonists on the bench, Taney and Curtis, had expressed themselves on the question previously; the former in his opinion of 1832, the latter in the endorsement of the petition to Congress that resulted in Winthrop's report of 1843.[49] Neither had changed his mind. Taney's opinion flowed from his theory of the Federal Union. As he saw it, the Constitution had brought into being a new political community, the United States, without obliterating the sovereignty of the commonwealths who formed it. Sovereignty, consequently, was not only divisible but actually divided, and on this point, which was and is basic to any thinking on the relationship which exists between the States and the national government, Taney parted company with the States Rights school. Their basic dogmas were that the Union possessed "no innate sovereignty, like the States; it was not self-constituted; it is conventional, and of course subordinate to the sovereignties by which it was formed." [50] For them sovereignty was "an entire thing;—to divide, is,—to destroy it." [51] Sovereignty, for Taney, resided in the people of the United States who had expressed their will that it be divided between a national and various local governments. Dual sovereignty was the intention of the people, and it was the function of the representatives of the people, in all the branches of the government, to fulfill their intention. Neither the State governments nor the national government were to be allowed to aggrandize themselves at the expense of the other. Dual sovereignty implied dual citizenship. The States were to decide the question of State citizenship for themselves; but they were not to decide who were to be citizens of the Union and it was not, since the adoption of the Constitution, in their power to admit new members into the national body politic. State citizenship did not imply Federal citizenship. The bestowal of the latter, since the adoption of the Constitution, was in the hands of Congress.[52] Curtis's opinion, that a citizen of a State was, by that very fact, a citizen of the Union, had the support of Justice Story and had been the guiding norm in the decision of certain early cases in Louisiana.[53] Implicit in Curtis's argument was the equation of the terms "subject" and "citizen" which had been the norm in Judge Gaston's opinion in The State vs. Manuel and in the Virginia decision in Barzizas v. Hopkins and Hodgson.[54] It was also the reasoning followed by a majority of the justices of the Supreme Judicial Court of Maine who, a short time after the Dred Scott decision, were requested for their opinion on the subject by the State Senate. Five of the six judges, while admitting that "the political status of that portion of the African race in this country, which is not in a state of slavery, has long been a matter of contestation," agreed that, since before the Revolution all native-born free men, irrespective of color or descent, were subjects of Great Britain by the common law, by that upheaval these same subjects of the King became citizens of the United States.[55]

The crux of the matter, for Taney, was the position of free Negroes at the time of the adoption of the Constitution. The Federal government had not bestowed citizenship on them. The only way that Dred Scott could be a citizen of the United States, as the Chief Justice saw it, was by descent from a free Negro who had been a citizen of a State in 1787 and had become a citizen of the United States at the formation of the Union. He inferred—an inference based on the discriminatory legislation on the statute books of the various States in existence in 1787—that no State regarded them as constituent members of the body politic at that time. So, no free Negroes were citizens of the United States. Implicit in this argument is Wirt's idea that only those who possessed all the privileges and immunities of citizens in the various States were citizens of the United States. Curtis rebutted this by asserting that certain States in 1787 regarded their free colored members

106

as citizens, no matter how they discriminated against them legally or in practice. From this fact, Curtis could conclude, legitimately, that some free Negroes, those descended from this particular group, were citizens of the United States. He would then have to prove that Scott was of this class or to argue that all free Negroes were citizens of the United States or that free Negroes in Missouri were, at least to such an extent that they could sue in the Federal courts.

This confusion in the judicial mind, caused in the last analysis by what Acton has termed "the process of development by which the America of Tocqueville became the America of Lincoln," [56] was shared by the whole country. Edward Bates, Lincoln's Attorney General, writing near the end of this process, expressed his chagrin at the vagueness of the term, "citizen of the United States": "I have often been pained by the fruitless search in our law books and the records of our courts, for a clear and satisfactory definition of the phrase *citizen of the United States*." Even holding office and voting were not sure criteria.[57] When the conflict, of which this question of the condition of the African race in American life was no small part, was over, the winning side felt the need of affirming the citizenship of free Negroes in a constitutional amendment and of settling the broader questions of the source of national citizenship and the nature of the Union by the same method.[58] The realities of the situation are still working themselves out.

NOTES

1. Cf., above, Chapter 5, p. 55, and note 18; Chapter 6, pp. 71-72, and note 20. To the layman, Judge Thompson's statement, cited by Judge Curtis on the technical point, would seem categorical: "But the present case being brought here on a writ of error, the whole record is under the consideration of the court," United States Bank vs. Smith, 11 Wheaton 171. The question is discussed in Connor, *John Archibald Campbell*, pp. 59-60; in Martin Van Buren, *Inquiry into the Origin and Course of Political Parties in the United States* (New York: Hurd and Houghton, 1867), pp. 860-861; in Elbert W. R. Ewing, *Legal and Historical Status of the Dred Scott Decision* (Washington: Cobden Publishing Co., 1909), pp. 40-44; and in Horace Hagen, "The Dred Scott Decision," *Georgetown Law Journal*, XV (1926), pp. 95-114.

2. Article 4, Section 2, Paragraph 1.

3. Article 2, Section 1, Paragraph 5.

4. Cf., above, Chapter 6, pp. 62-65 for Taney; Chapter 7, pp. 83-84 for Curtis. According to Taney, free Negroes were not recognised as citizens by the various States at the time of the adoption of the Constitution because of their degraded condition as exemplified by State laws discriminating against them. An answer to this rather embarrassing inference was given in *The New Englander*, where the reviewer of Appleton's edition of the decision wrote: "We admit the fact [of dis-

criminatory legislation]. We reject the inference. We oppose to *the inference* drawn from the degradation of the free negro, *the fact* that in spite of that degradation they were *citizens* of a majority of the states at the adoption of the Constitution, and *the concession* of Judge Taney, if they were so, they were citizens of the United States." The writer admitted that all parties involved in the question, from the founders to himself and Taney, were inconsistent but asked, "in order to be consistent shall we renounce the very fundamental principles of our government?" (*The New Englander*, XV [1857], pp. 478-526). The fact that free Negroes were regarded as citizens in several states, on the theory that the term inhabitant and citizen were synonymous, has been established by Gordon E. Sherman, who also points out that the trend to regard them as a third class, midway between citizens and aliens, did not become strong till after 1800. The fact that they were so regarded, however, depended on a theory that was not part of the Constitutional law of the country but was based on the common law of England, not necessarily binding on the judges of the Supreme Court in interpreting the Constitution of the United States. Cf. Gordon E. Sherman, "Emancipation and Citizenship," *Yale Law Journal*, XV (April, 1906), pp. 263-282.

5. For a summary of this legislation, cf. John C. Hurd, *The Law of Freedom and Bondage in the United States* (Boston: Little, Brown and Company, 1858), I, p. 436.

6. James Madison to James Monroe, November 19, 1820, *Letters and Other Writings of James Madison* (New York: R. Worthington, 1884), III, p. 187.

7. 1 Opinions of the Attorneys-General 506-509. Wirt confirmed his position by arguing that, if free Negroes were not excluded from Federal citizenship, a person, born and raised, for example, in Virginia and having none of the characteristic privileges of a citizen of that commonwealth, going into another State, and being a citizen of the United States, would be entitled, by the privileges and immunities clause of the Constitution, to rights he did not have in his own. He even, Wirt said, could become President. So, a free Negro was not a citizen in any sense in which that word was used in the Constitution.

8. Amy, a woman of color, v. Smith. 1 Littell 333.

9. *Ibid.* 334.

10. *Ibid.* 335-336.

11. Rankin v. Lydia, 2 A. K. Marshall 476; Holly v. Matthew Thompson et al., 3 A. K. Marshall 981-985.

12. 1 Littell 342, Amy a woman of color, v. Smith. This argument was used by Montgomery Blair in his plea for Scott. Cf., above, Chapter 4, pp. 33-34.

13. Barzizas v. Hopkins and Hodgson, 2 Randolph 276-294; the point is discussed on page 278.

14. 2 Peters 664-670. For Blair, cf., above, Chapter 4, p. 35.

15. 2 Peters 664.

16. *Ibid.*

17. 19 Howard 424-425.

18. 2 Opinions of the Attorneys General 427-442.

19. *Ibid.* 474-477.

20. Mss., State Department, National Archives.

21. *Ibid.* It is to be noted that the Attorney General was and is the government's lawyer whose principal duties were and are the argument of government cases in the Supreme Court of the United States and the giving of legal advice to the President and the heads of departments in connection with official business. For this reason, their opinions may not necessarily reflect their own private convictions any more than a lawyer's necessarily reflect those of his client. The same caution must be exercised, for example, in considering Taney's plea for Jacob Gruber, a Methodist minister, who was indicted for inciting slaves to rebellion in Western Maryland (cf. Swisher, *Roger B. Taney*, pp. 95-98).

22. Fisher's Negroes v. Dobbs and others, 14 Tennessee 126.

23. *Ibid.* 126-127.

24. *Ibid.* 131.

25. Crandall against the State of Connecticut, 10 Connecticut 344.

26. *Ibid.* 347.

27. *Ibid.* 366-372. In June, 1865, the judges of the Superior Court of Connecticut gave their opinion, in reply to a resolution of the General Assembly, that a free colored person, born in Connecticut, was a citizen of the State and of the United States. In March, 1857, Judge Bissell wrote to Judge Williams, complaining that the Crandall case was being abused. According to Bissell, only Daggett had held the doctrine that free Negroes were not citizens (32 Connecticut 565).

28. Hobbs and others *against* Fogg, 6 Watts 553-560.

29. *Ibid.* 556.

30. *Ibid.*

31. *Ibid.* 560.

32. *Ibid.* 558.

33. The State vs. Claiborne, 1 Meigs 331-341. Thomas's argument is on page 336.

34. *Ibid.* 339.

35. 4 Devereux and Battle 20-39.

36. *Ibid.* 23.

37. *Ibid.* 26.

38. Cf., above, pp. 98-99.

39. The State vs. Elijah Newsom, 5 Iredell 250.

40. *Ibid.* 252. For Gibson, cf., above, pp. 101-102.

41. 27 Congress, 3 Session, Reports of the Committees of the House of Representatives, I, Report 80, p. 7.

42. *Ibid.,* p. 2.

43. *Ibid.,* pp. 2-3.

44. *Ibid.,* p. 39.

45. *Ibid.*

46. 4 Opinions of the Attorneys General 147. Spencer later defended the Secretary of State Clayton for refusing passports to free Negroes, saying that the question was "in its nature a judicial question and that it would have been the height of presumption in the Secretary of State to depart from the cautious course of all his predecessors, including John Quincy Adams, and undertake its decision in anticipation of the Supreme Court" (*New Hampshire Patriot and Gazette,* June 24, 1857).

47. Rawle stated, without reference, that "The citizens of each state constituted the citizens of the United States when the constitution was adopted . . . and he who was subsequently born the citizen of a state became at the moment of his birth a citizen of the United States" (William Rawle, *A View of the Constitution of the United States of America,* Philadelphia: H. C. Carey and I. Lea, 1825, p. 80). Story declared, "Every citizen of a state is *ipso facto* a citizen of the United States," citing only the above sentence from Rawle as his authority (Joseph Story, *Commentaries on the Constitution of the United States,* Boston: Charles C. Little and James Brown, 1851, section 1693).

48. 8 Opinions of the Attorneys General 748-752.

49. For Taney, cf., above, pp. 99-100; for Curtis, pp. 102-103.

50. John Taylor, *New Views of the Constitution of the United States* (Washington City: Way and Gideon, 1823), p. 37.

51. Richard Crallé, *The Works of John C. Calhoun* (New York: D. Appleton and Co., 1854-57), I, p. 146.

52. This brief summary of Taney's views is based on Charles W. Smith, Jr., *Roger B. Taney: Jacksonian Jurist* (Chapel Hill: University of North Carolina Press, 1936), pp. 82-105.

53. Joseph Story, *Commentaries on the Constitution of the United States,* Section

1693. Desbois' Case, 2 Martin 185-202; United States v. Laverty et al., 3 Martin 733-740.

54. Cf., above, pp. 99, 102-103.

55. Judge Hathaway held that free Negroes were not citizens and that the Dred Scott case was binding on this point. Judge Appleton spoke for four of the judges. Judge Davis gave a brief opinion which agreed with Appleton's. Cf. 44 Maine Reports 505-595. Judge Appleton's discussion runs from page 521 to page 576.

56. John Dalberg-Acton, *The History of Freedom and Other Essays* (London: Macmillan and Co., 1922), p. 582.

57. 10 Opinions of the Attorneys General 383.

58. Article 14, section 1; article 15, section 1. Cf. 59 Congress, 2 Session, Document 326, *Citizenship of the United States, Expatriation, and Protection Abroad"* (Washington, D. C.: Government Printing Office, 1907). The authors remark: "The status of free, native born negroes before the adoption of the fourteenth amendment is no longer of practical importance so far as the Negro is concerned . . ." (p. 62). They treat it briefly for the light it may throw on the status of the inhabitants of our island possessions.

9

THE TERRITORIAL ISSUE

WHEN THE CHIEF JUSTICE AND JUSTICES WAYNE, GRIER, DANIEL, Campbell, and Catron asserted, for various reasons, that congressional power to govern the territories of the United States did not extend to the exclusion of slaves from them, the arguments and theories they advanced to sustain this conclusion had been in existence almost as long as there was territory at the disposal of Congress and for which that body had to make rules and regulations. When Justices McLean and Curtis countered with the opinion that Congress could prohibit slavery in those regions, they, too, said nothing new.

In 1803, the year the Louisiana Territory had been acquired, and for several years thereafter, the Federalist minority had strenuously opposed the constitutionality of extending the United States beyond the original limits of the country. They were not reluctant to acquire territory, but they had no desire to see such acquisitions incorporated into the United States on an equal footing with the older commonwealths. In such a procedure they saw a violation of the original compact of 1787 and a loss of sectional power and prestige.[1]

The Supreme Court, through Chief Justice Marshall, disposed of this difficulty, the right of the United States to acquire territory, by assuming that the nation possessed it. In 1810, the court stated, in a case coming from the Orleans Territory, "The power of governing and of legislating for a territory is the inevitable consequence of the right to acquire and hold territory."[2] This statement, which, on its face, removed the whole problem of acquisition and government from the order of conjecture, was immediately qualified by Marshall, who continued, "Could this position be contested, the Constitution of the United States declares that, 'Congress shall have power to dispose of and make all needful rules and regulations respecting the territory or other property belonging to the United States.'[3] Accordingly we find Congress possessing and exercising the absolute and undisputed power of governing and legislating for the territory of Orleans." [4] Marshall, having left in doubt whether he held that the position that the right to govern flowed from the right to acquire was questionable, or, whether he based the power of Congress to govern on the constitutional provision, did not settle the matter. Perhaps, like John Adams writing to Josiah Quincy on the same subject, he wished "the Constitution had been more explicit." Perhaps, again like the ex-President, he felt that "Congress have not entertained any doubts of their authority, and I cannot say they are destitute of plausible arguments to support their opinion." [5]

The disturbing question, the right of Congress to govern acquired territory, particularly how far that right extended, first agitated the country in 1819 when the admission of Missouri, a State formed out of the Louisiana Purchase, was before Congress. It had caused a slight flurry in the previous year. On November 23, 1818, Representative James Tallmadge, of New York, objected to the incorporation of Illinois into the Union on the ground that its constitution, while not adopting slavery, did not sufficiently prohibit it.[6] Poindexter, of Mississippi, rose to give the answer that was soon to become standard in the Missouri debate. That slavery was an evil, the southerner said, was a question upon which all were agreed. But, he continued, his colleague's proposal was an attempt to fetter a sovereign State, which, in the American system of government, was impracticable.[7] After some more debate, during which Anderson, of Kentucky, having cast doubt on the power of Congress to pass the Ordinance of 1787, made the ominous remark, "Serious doubts had arisen . . . whether Congress had a right to prescribe any condition respecting slavery," [8] Illinois was admitted.

On February 13, 1819, Tallmadge moved an amendment to the Missouri admission bill, by which all slaves, born in the State after its reception into the Union, were to be free and all those already there were to be gradually emancipated. The House adjourned before the question on this proposal was taken.[9] When the House met again on the fifteenth, the debate commenced. It centered about two questions, one of right and one of expediency. Did Congress have the power to prescribe any of the details of a State government, other than that it should be republican in form? If Congress had such power, should it use it in the admission of Missouri?

Taylor, of New York, coming to the support of his colleague,

Tallmadge, adverted to the fact, which he did not intend to discuss, that the country was expanding too rapidly. This situation, he felt, was closely connected with the disputed question. Breaking abruptly from this typically eastern train of thought, he informed his hearers that the territorial provisions of the Constitution [10] provided adequate sanction for Tallmadge's amendment. It would be difficult, he thought, to devise a more comprehensive grant of power. Since it was a matter of congressional discretion whether a State should be admitted or not, surely the national legislature, by fair inference, could lay down conditions of admission. It had already done so in the act of 1802 by which Ohio was received into the Union. Turning his attention to the argument that the proposed amendment violated the third article of the treaty of 1803 by which the region had been acquired from France,[11] Taylor remarked that a treaty could not change the Constitution and that the President and the Senate could not, by using the treaty-making power, bind Congress to admit new States. He then asked the important question. Did the Tallmadge amendment violate the treaty because it impaired the property right of a master in his slave? He answered with the assertion, later to be enlarged upon by Webster and Benton, that the sovereignty of Congress, while limited in regard to the States, was unlimited over the territories. "Missouri was purchased with our money, and, until incorporated into the family of States, it may be sold for money" was his unvarnished description of the absolute power of the Federal government. Such being the case, he concluded, Congress could certainly limit the further increase of slavery in those possessions.[12]

Barbour, of Virginia, conceded the force of the constitutional provision, but reminded Congress that the question before the House was not the government of a territory but the hobbling of a sovereign State, in clear opposition to the second section of the Fourth Article of the Constitution which guaranteed the equality of the States and their title to like privileges and immunities.[13]

Scott, the territorial delegate from Missouri, rose to defend the rights of the future State. Dismissing the States which had been formed out of territory whose organic law had been the Northwest Ordinance as not constituting precedent in this matter of slavery restriction, Scott turned to the treaty. It had been made by the competent arm of the government, it had been ratified by the Senate, it had been sanctioned by the House by the acts which made appropriations for carrying it into effect. It was a part of the supreme law of the land. If it were in the power of Congress to restrict slavery in Missouri, it was equally in its power to say "what color the inhabitants of the proposed State should be, what description of property, other than slaves, those people should or should not possess, and the quantity of property each man should retain, going upon the Agrarian principle. He would go even further, and say, that Congress had an equal power to enact to what religion the people should subscribe; that none other should be professed, and to provide for the excommunication of all those who did not submit." [14] This appeal to the bill of rights, outlining an argument which was, eventually, to culminate in Taney's use of the Fifth Amendment, fell upon hostile ears and the House passed the amendment.

The next day, February 14, Taylor raised the question of congressional power over the territories directly by proposing to amend the Arkansas Territory Bill in the same way that Tallmadge had amended the Missouri Enabling Act. He wished, Taylor said, one little portion of the country left open to the enterprise of the free men of the north and the east.[15] To this, Walker, of North Carolina, rejoined with the argument Scott had used the day before. He contended that Congress had "no legitimate power to legislate on the property of the citizens, only to levy taxes. We might, with the same right, prohibit other species of property from crossing the Mississippi." He was for letting the people of the territory decide whether it would be slave or free, a solution that was to appeal strongly to the country in the eighteen-fifties.[16] McLane, of Delaware, after expressing his sympathy for the aims of the northern gentlemen, said that, in his opinion, Congress did not have the power to pass the proposed restriction, which amounted to the emancipation, without compensation, of the slaves then resident in Arkansas and their issue. Congress had no right "to invade any other species of property whatsoever." A slave was property. Whoever stole one committed a felony. McLane then invoked the third article of the treaty, which protected all property rights, concluding that not only was the proposal beyond the power of Congress but that it was also in violation of the treaty with France,[17] arguments that were to appeal strongly to Judge Catron. Whitman, of Massachusetts, was sure that Congress had the power to pass the restriction. The territories were "under the absolute control of the United States." This fullness of power was clearly implied in the constitutional provision which placed the

114

admission of new States in the hands of Congress, and by reason of it that body could "require any stipulation relative to their internal police or municipal regulations" it pleased. However, Whitman admitted, a concession that was to embarrass the property-conscious representatives from the north and east all through the slavery controversy and to which the south was to return again and again, Congress could not require anything repugnant to the fundamental articles of the Federal government.[18]

On February 15, the Arkansas bill passed without the restriction, but the Fifteenth Congress closed without admitting Missouri into the Union. The debate continued when Congress reconvened in December, though Elliott, of Georgia, asked that the question of the extent of congressional power over the territories should not be allowed to cloud the point under discussion, the admission of a State. The former question could be settled when it arose.[19] But the vexing matter, in reality, closely connected with the subject of incorporation into the Federal body, would not rest. The constitutional provision was exegeted and re-exegeted. Morril, of New Hampshire, could feel sure that it gave Congress all the power it needed. As for the treaty with France, all its conditions were fulfilled.[20] Walker, of Georgia, "would hardly have supposed" that the phrases, which contemplated "only a temporary arrangement in relation to the territory and property of the United States," would be taken as conferring such absolute authority.[21] Mellen, of Massachusetts, supporting congressional power, was followed by Leake, of Mississippi, who advanced the interpretation of the word, "territory," which was to become increasingly popular in the south. "Sir," he said, "the word 'territory,' being immediately followed by the words, 'or other property,' proves, satisfactorily, to my mind, that the word 'territory' was there intended to mean, the domain, which Congress may dispose of by sale or otherwise, and may make such needful regulations respecting its protection from waste or other injury, and to preserve their rights to it unimpaired." [22]

Lowrie, of Pennsylvania, raised the question which was at the heart of the legal controversy over slavery when he asserted that "slaves" and "property" were not convertible terms.[23] This was a point which troubled Gross, of New York, who found the proposal to free the slaves in Missouri a violation of the Fifth Amendment to the Constitution, which prohibited the taking of private property without due process of law. He thought that the House could not entertain a proposition which was in direct hostility to this provision, one that was contained in every State constitution as well as in the Federal. It would be demanding of Missouri to do what all her sister States declared could not be done.[24] It was a point which Scott, of Missouri, assumed as the basis for his argument on February 25. Commencing from the premise that governments were instituted for the protection of the property as well as the persons of the governed, he contended that the restriction in question was *ex post facto* as regarded the Missourians because it deprived them of a vested right in freeing their slaves. If the prohibition became law, "that amendment to the 5th article of the Constitution which declared that no person should be deprived of life, liberty, or property, without due course of law, became inoperative, and the citizen was divested of his property without Constitution, or law, or judge, or jury." [25] The same point was to prove convincing to Chief Justice Taney.

In the confusion attending the solution of the Missouri question, Madison was turned to in an effort to find out what the document, so largely the work of his hands, really meant. In a long letter to the Philadelphian, Robert Walsh, the ex-President gave his opinion. The terms of the constitutional provision, he said, "though of a ductile character, cannot well be extended beyond a power over the territory, as property, and a power to make the provisions really needful or necessary for the government of settlers until ripe for admission as States into the Union." Whatever its import, he assured Walsh, it had nothing to do with a State.[26] Monroe, the harassed President, wrote to Judge Spencer Roane in a vein that Taney was later to find rich in argument. He felt that the phrases of the Constitution, "the only check on the power of Congress," referred solely to "the old controversy between the United States and individual states, respecting vacant lands, within their chartered limits, whose relative claims it was intended to preserve." As far as he could see, they had no operation on the present case and the power granted applied only to territory ceded by the individual States to the United States. Any restraint on the power of Congress, Monroe continued, must be sought in other parts of the Constitution. As slavery was recognized by that instrument, Monroe was of the opinion that it was "very unjust to restrain the owner from carrying his slave into a Territory, and retaining his right to him there; but whether the power to do this has not been granted" was a point on which he doubted.[27]

116

He took his doubts to Madison. They proved to be both practical and speculative. Madison replied that he agreed with Monroe in a suspicion they shared with the young Senator from New York, Martin Van Buren.[28] As Monroe had intimated, the real object of those who so zealously opposed "the extension, so called, of slavery" was "to form a new state of parties founded on local instead of political distinctions, thereby dividing the Republicans of the North from those of the South, and making the former instrumental in giving to the opponents of both an ascendancy over the whole," a strategy that it took forty years to implement.[29] To prevent its fulfillment in 1820, Madison recommended a conciliatory attitude in relation to the admission of Maine. Several days later, he gave his view on the theoretical problem. In applyplying a restriction on the introduction of slaves into a territory, Congress could find sanction for its action only in the third section of the Fourth Article. As to the right there conferred, two considerations arose. The power to regulate the territories, being given from the necessity of the case, was a suspension of the great right of self-government. As a consequence, it ought not to be extended further nor continued longer than the occasion might require. On the other hand, Madison wrote, again using his highly descriptive adjective, the constitutional provision, as actually interpreted in practice, was "ductile" and left much to legislative discretion. The questions for Monroe and his cabinet to decide were two. Was a territorial limitation on the extension of slavery an assumption of illegitimate power? If it were not, was it prudent to do so? On the first point, the legitimacy of the act, Madison admitted there was certainly room for difference in opinion, though, for himself "I must own that I have always leaned to the belief that the restriction was not within the true scope of the Constitution." If Congress had the power, his second alternative came up for consideration, the expediency of the act. In the circumstances, Madison felt "the cool and the candid" could not blame compromise.[30]

In 1828, Marshall was again confronted with the problem of the power of Congress over the territories. The circumstances in which the issue arose were rather unusual. A man named David Canter had bought three hundred and fifty-six bales of cotton at a public auction at Key West, Florida Territory. The sale had been made at the order of a territorial court which consisted of a notary and five jurors. This court had been set up by act of the governor and legislative council of the Territory and it had given its decision by virtue of another act of the same body, which awarded to salvors seventy-six percent of the net proceeds of the sale. A district court had declared these proceedings a nullity. The Federal court had reversed the decision of the district court. In giving his opinion, Judge Johnson, the presiding judge of the last-named court, pointed out that the solution of the case depended on a just idea of the relation in which Florida stood to the United States. "At the time the constitution was formed," he elaborated, "the limits of the territory over which it was to operate were generally defined and recognized." [31] It consisted, in part, of organized States and, in part, of territories, "the absolute property and dependencies of the United States." These States, this territory, and future States to be admitted into the Union were the sole objects the Constitution had in view. There was no provision in the Constitution by which territory might be acquired and there was none for the government of such acquisitions outside the original limits of the Union. Johnson concluded that the right to acquire territory was incidental to the treaty-making power and "perhaps to the power of admitting new states into the Union; and the government of such acquisitions is, of course, left to the legislative power of the Union, so far as that power is uncontrolled by treaty." [32]

The insurance companies, who were interested in the case, appealed it to the Supreme Court. They argued, through counsel, that the court at Key West was not legally organized nor of competent jurisdiction. To prove these contentions they held that the Constitution and laws of the United States were of full force in the territory of Florida, the position Calhoun was later to adopt. Consequently, the subject of salvage was beyond the authority of the territorial legislature, superior courts alone having jurisdiction in admiralty cases.

The case was not without its difficulties. On the territorial issue, Whipple, of counsel for Canter, countered Ogden's theory of the extension of the Constitution to the territories by asserting the full power of Congress over those regions. He described this authority as equal to that which "Congress and the legislature of a state have over a state." [33] Webster, appearing on the same side, was more graphic. "What is Florida?" he asked. It was not a part of the United States, he answered. The territory, and all within it, were to be governed by the acquiring power, unchecked

118

save by treaty reservations. "What has Congress done?" he queried. His reply was that "she might have done anything—she might have refused the trial by jury, and refused a legislature." [34] The law establishing the court at Key West, Webster insisted, did not come within the restrictions of the Constitution, because that instrument did not extend over territories.

Marshall, to decide whether or not Canter was entitled to seventy-six percent of the proceeds from the sale of three hundred and fifty-six bales of cotton, was forced, like Judge Johnson, to consider the relationship that existed between Florida Territory and the United States. He agreed with his brother justice that the treaty and war powers implied the power to acquire territory. He agreed with Webster and Whipple that the inhabitants of Florida did not share in the government until the territory became a State. He was sure that Florida was a territory and that Congress had the right to govern it. He was not sure of the source of this right. He said, "In the meantime, Florida continues to be a territory of the United States; governed by virtue of that clause in the Constitution, which empowers Congress 'to make all needful rules and regulations, respecting the territory, or other property of the United States.' " But of this he was not certain, though he seemed to have been in the Orleans case of 1810.[35] "Perhaps," he doubted, "the power of governing a territory belonging to the United States, which has not, by becoming a state, acquired the means of self government, may result necessarily from the fact, that it is not within the jurisdiction of any particular state, and is within the power and jurisdiction of the United States. The right to govern may be the inevitable consequence of the right to acquire territory. Whichever may be the source whence the power is derived, the possession of it is unquestioned." [36] Having the power, Congress could act. Territorial courts were not constitutional courts but legislative courts, erected "in virtue of the general right of sovereignty which exists in the government, or in virtue of that clause which enables Congress to make all needful rules and regulations, respecting the territory belonging to the United States." Consequently, the constitutional limitations on admiralty jurisdiction did not extend to the territories over which Marshall said, repeating Whipple's words, "congress exercises the combined power of the general, and of a state government." [37] So, a notary and five jurors were competent to dispose of salvage cases in a territory.

119

While Marshall may have doubted the source of the power by which the legislature was to govern territories acquired since the adoption of the Constitution, he was sure that the constitutional provision for territories covered those in American possession at the time of its ratification. The power bestowed was of a most plenary kind and the words, "rules and regulations," included complete jurisdiction, he stated in another case, since "it was necessary . . . to enable the new government to redeem the pledge given by the old, in relation to the formation and powers of the new states." [38]

The case of the United States vs. Gratiot was notable for the strict interpretation of the territorial provision of the Constitution used by Senator Benton. Attorney General Gilpin had held that, whatever the passage meant in its fullness, it certainly gave the government enough authority to lease land in the territories. The Missouri Senator, on the other hand, argued that the only power given was the power to dispose of the public lands and to make rules and regulations "respecting the preparation of them for sale." [39] Judge Thompson, in giving the opinion of the Court, over which Taney was now presiding, held that the word territory, as used in the provision, was "merely descriptive of one kind of property; and is equivalent to the word lands." [40] Congress had the same power over these lands as it had over any other property belonging to the United States and it had it without limitation. So, he concluded, the government could lease such property. As a matter of fact, he added, this provision had been considered the foundation upon which territorial governments rested.[41]

The following year, 1841, a case came before the Supreme Court which involved a conflict between a provision of the constitution of the State of Mississippi and the commerce power of the Federal government. Mississippi had intended to prevent the purchase of Negroes from other States. It was argued that this was a violation of the interstate commerce clause of the Constitution. The case was settled on a technicality, the Court holding that the State provision needed legislation to implement it, which legislation had not been passed. Webster, who was of counsel, gave a strong argument in proof of the fact that slaves were property. "What is the foundation of the right to slaves?" he asked. Expounding the custom theory of slavery, he continued, "There is no law declaring slaves property any more than land. Slaves are property by the term 'slaves.' The master has a right to their

120

services and labor. This is property." Instancing the fugitive slave provision of the Constitution, Webster urged "The right to take them up, is an acknowledgment of the right to property in them." [42]

Judge Baldwin, in his opinion, agreed with Webster. Though, perhaps, he stood alone among the members of the Court, he said, he would not be deterred from affirming that slaves were property. They were such by the laws of the States before the adoption of the Constitution and this property right existed independently of that document, which did not create it but recognized and protected it from violation. Baldwin, after summarizing what he considered practical constructions of the Declaration of Independence by Congress, various discriminatory acts, some of which equated slaves and property, proceeded to invoke the Fifth Amendment. "Being property by the law of any state, the owners are protected from any violation of the rights of property by Congress under the fifth amendment of the constitution; these rights do not merely consist in ownership; the right of disposing of property of all kinds is incident to it, which Congress cannot touch." [43] The arguments to be used in the Scott Case were taking more definite shape.

The acquisition of another great land mass after the Mexican War—in fact, the very prospect of such an acquisition—again raised the question of the extent of congressional power over slavery in the territories. On August 8, 1846, President Polk asked Congress for two million dollars to be placed "under the control of the executive." Admitting that the request was unusual, Polk stated that it was not unprecedented, citing the appropriation made at Jefferson's request at the time of the last great westward expansion, the purchase of Louisiana. [44] A bill to secure the money was proposed in the House, which David Wilmot, a Pennsylvania Democrat, proposed to amend. This famous provision which, in the "ism-filled" forties gave rise to another "ism," Wilmotism, read: "Provided, that, as an express and fundamental condition to the acquisition of any territory from the Republic of Mexico by the United States, by virtue of any treaty which may be negotiated between them, and to the use by the Executive of the moneys herein appropriated, neither slavery nor involuntary servitude shall ever exist in any part of the said territory." [45] Polk's bill, so amended, passed in the House, but the Senate adjourned before a vote was taken there. At the next session, a bill to appropriate three million dollars for the same purpose was introduced and again Wilmot moved what has become known as his Proviso. The amended bill passed, again to be refused consideration in the Senate which passed an appropriation bill of its own. After bitter debate, in which the question of congressional power over the territories was thoroughly aired, the House concurred in the Senate bill and Polk got the desired sum.

It was with truth that Wilmot, defending his amendment, could retort to Rhett, who had attacked it, that "every argument of the gentleman against the amendment was [urged] with equal force against the ordinance of 1787 and the Missouri Compromise." The Pennsylvanian drew the line of argument sharply. "If this proposition," he said, "invades the rights of the South, then the Missouri Compromise line invades the rights of the South. If we have no right to say to them that slavery shall not exist in California and New Mexico, we have no right to say to them that it shall not go north of the Missouri Compromise Line," [46] a logic that was to appeal strongly to his southern hearers, who were to conclude that that was just what was the matter with the Missouri Compromise line.

Apart from arguments already familiar, this debate over California and New Mexico, in which the government of the Oregon Territory was also involved, brought to completion the southern theory on their position as a minority group in the Union.[47] It was first proposed in the Senate on February 19, 1847, by Calhoun, who rose to offer the quasi-official answer to the south to this new challenge from the north. He prefaced his remarks by calling attention to the fact that, in every branch of the government, except the Senate, the south was in a hopeless numerical position. Iowa and Wisconsin would soon send four senators to Washington and the last defense of the south would be gone unless the Constitution offered a remedy. Fortunately, he found that it did. "Ours is a Federal Constitution," he said; "the States are its constituents, and not the people. . . . It did not look to the prosperity of individuals as such." Rather, every State, as a constituent member, was, in equal measure, to enjoy all rights. There was to be no monopoly of the public domain which was the common property of the States of the Union. He then pointed out the new line of defense for the south: "Let us be done with compromises. Let us go back and stand upon the Constitution." This new creed Calhoun reduced to the form of resolutions. Starting with the basic principle that the territories of the United States belonged to the several States as joint and common property, Calhoun passed to his second premiss, that Congress, as the joint agent and representative of the States, had no right to pass any legislation that would, in effect, discriminate against the full and equal rights of the States in any territory already acquired or to be acquired. A law, he continued, that would "deprive the citizens of any of the States of the Union from emigrating with their property into any of the territories of the United States" would be discriminatory and a violation of the Constitution because it derogated from the perfect equality of the States, a step that, if taken, would "tend directly to subvert the Union itself." He closed with a final article, asserting that the people, in forming a constitution, were to be subject to one condition only, that it be republican. Any further action by Congress would violate this sacred right.[48]

These resolutions, which Benton called "a string of abstractions" less pressing than ordinary business,[49] were but a refinement of the "common sword and common purse" argument of the smaller states of the Confederation, a very conscious minority, who feared, before the adoption of the Constitution, that they would be swallowed up by their larger neighbors. The south, which had played a very active part in the war with Mexico, was determined to share, in the way she pleased, in the fruits of victory. In particular, she had no intention of seeing herself swallowed up by a continually expanding north.

The new creed was expressed, in catechetical form, by Senator Yulee, of Florida, in response to the questions of Dickinson, of New York, who had expressed a desire to ascertain his views more fully. Dickinson proposed an hypothesis. "Suppose," he asked, "Canada should be annexed to the United States without any change in her laws: Would the institution of slavery exist there without any legislation?" To this Yulee replied, "If Canada was acquired as territory, any citizen of a State of this Union could go upon it with his family and property, slaves as well as others, and would be entitled to reside there, securely, under the guarantee of the Constitution, while it continued to be a part of the territory belonging to the United States." Dickinson proposed a second question. Could Congress, he asked, "or any other legislative body," having in mind a territorial legislature, exercise any authority over slavery in the territory so long as it remained in that status? Yulee answered that no legislative body could pass a law "by which the property of a citizen, going rightfully upon such territory, could be divested—no matter whether such property consisted in slaves or anything else." On the contrary, Congress, "as the common agent of the people of the Union," would be bound to pass all the laws necessary to protect such a citizen "in the undisturbed tenure of such property." [50] Calhoun's abstractions were becoming more concrete.

Henry C. Murphy, of New York, outlined, in the House, the argument Taney was to use. Congress, he said, had the power to legislate for the territories and, consequently, can legislate on the question of slavery there. He was, he made haste to assure his hearers, no Wilmotist, inflating an amendment to an appropriation bill into a philosophy of life. Neither, on the other hand, was he a southern fire-eater. The power that Congress had over the territories, at least those acquired since the adoption of the Constitution, was incident to the right to acquire such regions. It was not, however, an absolute power, but was restrained, on the one hand, by the conditions on which the territory was ceded and, on the other, by the limitations of the Constitution. To maintain this view of Federal power over the territories, which, substantially, was to be that of the Chief Justice, Murphy, like Taney, had to dispose of certain arguments, drawn from precedent. The Northwest Ordinance, he declared, referred only to the territory for which it had been devised, the constitutional provision considered territory only as property, and the decision of the Supreme Court in the Insurance Companies case left the source of congressional power ambiguous. The power of Congress was real but, like all power in the United States, limited. Murphy did not consider the specific limitation on the authority of Congress over slavery. [51]

Venable, of North Carolina, was more precise. The power to govern, he said, stemmed from the right to acquire territory. But such government must be in accordance with the Constitution. "Congress," he informed his hearers, "could have no power to establish religion or to create titles of nobility in the territories, because expressly denied by the Constitution; and when the laws of the United States are extended over a territory, it must be understood that the Constitution and laws are so extended that nothing repugnant to the Constitution can be in force as law." From this general principle, he deduced the fact that Congress could not touch slavery in the territories. Slaves, he stated, were property at the time the Federal government came into existence.

Whatever was property, at that time, so far as the Federal government was concerned, remained so and the government was bound to enforce the constitutional guarantees which secured all the holders of such property in peaceful tenure.[52]

On June 1, Houston, of Texas, proposed to his fellow Senators a solution that was beginning to have considerable appeal to the more conservative and peace-loving elements of the country. The right to bring slaves into a territory, he thought, was "a question to be determined by the Judiciary of the United States, and any law enacted by Congress that would be incompatible with the Constitution would be utterly void." [53]

Senator Pettit, of Indiana, summed up the nationalistic position in incisive words. He informed the Senate that the true doctrine was "that this power to legislate for the Territories was in the United States, and any other doctrine could not stand the test of reason, of the judicial decisions, elementary reading, or the uniform practice of the United States ever since their existence as a power of the earth," [54] citing, as had often been cited before and would be cited again till their use by Justices McLean and Curtis, Story, Kent, Rawle, Sergeant and the Insurance Companies and Cherokee Nation opinions.

Horace Mann spoke on the subject at some length in the House. He regarded the southern interpretation of the word "territory" in the constitutional provision as "a new and most extraordinary doctrine," apparently unaware that it was neither. He himself regarded the express words of the Constitution as "ample and effective in conferring all the power claimed." "The right to dispose of," he reasoned, "means to sell. A seller may lay down conditions. I want, therefore, no better foundation for legislating over the Territories than the fact of ownership in the United States," Mann said, echoing Taylor's argument during the struggle over the admission of Missouri. The educator amplified this logic with an example. In Massachusetts, he said, temperance was regarded as a great blessing and virtue; its opposite, a great curse and sin. Manufacturers there, who had purchased great tracts of land on which to carry on their enterprises, knowing full well the dangers of a lack of sobriety to themselves and their workmen, would not dispose of such land unless there were incorporated in the deed the fundamental condition that ardent spirits would never be sold there. No court could challenge this right, for the owners were but passing needful rules and regulations. "If tipplers," he continued, "do not like them, let them stagger away and seek their residence elsewhere." Pointing his moral, Mann said that the fact of ownership, added to the sovereignty of the United States, made the right to govern the territories clear.[55]

The two greatest arguments on the question, considered as a point in constitutional law, were those of Dix, of New York, and Berrien, of Georgia. When the New Yorker arose to speak on the question of a territorial government for Oregon, he was prepared to be very thorough, and opened by asking a very comprehensive question: "Has Congress the right, under the Constitution, to legislate for the territory of the United States, organize governments for the inhabitants residing in such territory, and regulate within it all matters of local and domestic concern?" He believed that the answer was affirmative. His reasons fell under three headings, the intention of the framers of the Constitution, judicial interpretation of that document, and the whole practice of the government from its foundation.

Dix was sure that the founding fathers regarded the territorial provision of the Constitution as a plenary grant of power to Congress. His certitude rested on circumstantial evidence. On August 18, 1787, he recounted, Madison had introduced two resolutions by which Congress was to be authorized "to dispose of the unappropriated lands of the United States" and "to institute temporary governments for new States arising therein." These resolutions, Dix admitted, had not been adopted by the Convention. On the other hand, he urged the fact that they had not been formally rejected by that body, never having been voted upon. The most that could be said about them, in strict accuracy, Dix urged, was that the Committee on Style of the Convention was not in favor of their original form. The present constitutional provision, Dix said, making somewhat of a leap, was, "from its terms, subject matter and attendant circumstances, intended as a substitute for Madison's proposals," and so, in the minds of the framers, intended to give as complete power. The attention of the Convention had been explicitly called to the problem by Madison, Dix pointed out, and the bestowal of the power to regulate which, according to Dix, meant, at that time, to legislate, supported his construction of the clause.

The fact that the Ordinance of 1787 was beyond the power of the body that passed it, Dix continued, had no bearing on the power of Congress, under the Constitution, to prohibit slavery in the territories. When Madison, in *The Federalist,* asserted the nullity of the Ordinance,[56] he did not do so for its own sake. He was urging that a defect in the Articles of Confederation be remedied as it would be by the new constitution. The passage under consideration should be taken in conjunction with Madison's remarks in a later number of *The Federalist.*[57] There, discussing both sections of the Fourth Article of the Constitution, Madison showed that, under the Articles, the admission of new States into the Federal compact had been overlooked, a lack the new form of government supplied. In the same context, Madison referred to the power to regulate the territories as "a power of very great importance." This did not sound to Dix as though the Virginian were referring to a mere power of sale. Taking these two articles of *The Federalist* and joining to them Madison's subsequent action in legislation based upon territorial passage of the Constitution, his interpretation of the phrase was clear. It gave Congress the power it needed.[58]

Dix then turned to the decisions of the Supreme Court, and, after a consideration of the opinions in the Insurance Companies, Cherokee Nation and Gratiot cases, came to the conclusion that the Court also held that Congress had the necessary power to deal with slavery in the territories.[59] Having demonstrated, at least to his own satisfaction, that the authority was vested in the national legislature, Dix turned to the expediency of passing such laws as would restrict the institution in the territories. He came to the conclusion that they were highly desirable, because by such restrictions alone could this country be kept under white influence.[60]

After Calhoun had reiterated his general theory of the trusteeship of Congress over the territories,[61] Berrien rose to answer Dix more in detail. His general statement was that the constitutional provision did not grant to Congress authority to legislate on the internal policy of the territories. The purpose of those phrases was readily understood when it was remembered that the unsettled land to the west, which had been ceded to the general government by the various States, was looked to as a source of revenue and that Congress was to establish a system for their disposal. Territory, in the context, meant land. The following clauses in the passage under discussion furnished additional reason for the interpretation. By them, Congress was to be restrained from disposing of any land the title to which was contested by any State.[62]

Berrien then challenged the inference Dix had drawn from the fact that Madison's resolutions had not been formally rejected. The second of these, by which Congress was to have jurisdiction over persons in the territories, was not adopted and a provision, applicable to property alone, was inserted. The fairer deduction from these circumstances, Berrien argued, was that the Convention was unwilling to give this jurisdiction over persons to Congress. As for the citations from *The Federalist* which Dix had advanced, Berrien said that all Madison had said was that the new form of government would take care of the admission of new States, legalizing what had been done out of necessity. Of the territorial provision, Madison said that it was important and left it at that.

The former Attorney General then took up the matter of legislative precedents. The Ordinance of 1787, its re-enactment by Congress in 1789, and its application by that body to the several States created under it had nothing to do with the power of Congress, under the Constitution, to inhibit slavery in the territories. When Virginia had made her act of cession, she was a completely sovereign State, possessed of full jurisdiction over persons in the territory as well as being proprietor of the soil. By reason of this fullness of power, she was competent to abolish slavery there, or to declare in advance that it should not exist there. The rights she possessed she could transfer to others, and she did so to the United States. Congress received the cession and was bound to fulfill the obligations she had undertaken. It was "an engagement entered into before the adoption of the Constitution," [63] and so was as valid against the United States, under the Constitution, as it had been under the Articles of Confederation. All the acts, then, Berrien concluded, by which Congress applied the provisions of the Ordinance to the States formed out of the Northwest Territory were passed to fulfill the compact that had been made with Virginia. The acts which prohibited the importation of foreign slaves into Mississippi and Louisiana were exercises of the commerce power.

Berrien next turned to the decisions of the Supreme Court on the matter. In general, he asserted, they decided nothing on the point at issue. Everyone, he said, admitted the constitutionality of a territorial government. What the source of the power was by which such a government was erected was the precise point under discussion, and about this the Supreme Court had said nothing of any exactitude. The case of the Cherokee Nation turned on whether or not an Indian tribe was a foreign nation, and to prove that it was not one of the judges instanced the founding of territorial governments in regions still occupied by Indians. The Gratiot Case had as its issue whether or not the United States could lease as well as sell land. The Insurance Companies Case left the matter unsettled.

Berrien urged that the source of congressional power was, not the constitutional provision, but "our nationality—from the power to make war, and to conclude treaties, and the consequent right to acquire territory. The right to acquire includes the right to use—to enjoy; and government is indispensable to use and enjoyment." This principle which was to become the guiding norm of the nation's judiciary in regard to the territory acquired after the Spanish-American War, did not, according to Berrien, confer unlimited power. It was an authority limited to the single purpose of governing the territory till it was fit to govern itself. As a result of this restriction, the Senator concluded, "it cannot violate the right of a citizen, which is derived from or recognized by the Constitution. It cannot indefinitely prolong the tutelage of the territory. In relation to a common property, it cannot violate the equality of right which belongs to every citizen." To inhibit slavery would be such a violation for slaves were but property, recognized as such by the constitution and laws of the United States.[64]

This speech, which contained many of the arguments as well as having the same general framework of Taney's opinion, along with that of Dix, contains practically all that could be said on the power of Congress in the territories. Dix said the framers of the Constitution must have meant to give Congress the power. This was, substantially, what Curtis said. Berrien said that, if they meant to give the power, they should have said so. This was echoed by Taney. During the debate, Phelps, of Vermont, challenged the south to produce more than theories and generalizations. "Let gentlemen refer us to the article, the section, the clause in the Constitution of the United States which interferes in this particular with the general legislative power of Congress." No one had so far, Phelps said mistakenly, and he was confident no one would.[65]

In the light of all this reasoning and counter-reasoning, it is not surprising that the thoughts of certain men, feeling that Congress itself was incapable of solving the problem, should turn to a co-ordinate branch of the government, the judiciary. On July 18, 1848, Senator Clayton, of Delaware, reported a bill to establish territorial governments for Oregon, California, and New Mexico, a bill that became known as the Clayton Compromise. It was the fruit of the deliberations of a select committee which had been appointed on July 12 to consider the Oregon Territorial Bill and those passages in Polk's message to Congress which concerned the new western acquisitions. In presenting the bill, Clayton gave some of the details of the committee's conferences. Atchison, of Missouri, Benton's arch foe and, subsequently, one of the leaders of the violently pro-slavery group in his native State, had proposed, rather surprisingly, that "the spirit of the Missouri Compromise be adopted to govern the settlement of all the Territories of the United States." The committee, by a vote of five to three, decided to proceed in this spirit. Bright, of Indiana, went a step further. He moved the adoption of the Missouri Compromise Line as the norm of freedom and slavery in the new territory. Underwood, of Kentucky, moved to amend this proposition to the effect that all the territory in New Mexico and California, south of thirty-six degrees, thirty minutes, be placed in the same position as to slavery as Louisiana was when it was a territory. On this the committee split, four to four. Clayton commented that "At this stage of the proceedings all compromise appeared hopeless." However, the committee continued its efforts and evolved a bill. Oregon was to be organized as a territory as the people there desired, the laws prohibiting slavery being temporarily adopted until the territorial legislature could act upon the subject. California and New Mexico were to be organized, also, along traditional lines, but without the power to legislate on slavery. The right to introduce or prohibit slavery was to depend "on the Constitution, as the same should be expounded by the judges, with a right of appeal to the Supreme Court of the United States." The whole question was to be left to "the silent operation of the Constitution itself." [66]

This solution met with a mixed reception in the Senate. Despite the fact that Clayton said that any man who opposed the bill showed his preference for discord and civil war, there were many who did. Niles, of Connecticut, wished to know how this proposal settled either of the two issues, the right of Congress to legislate on slavery in the territories and, if the right existed, the expediency of using it. Clayton replied that Niles was missing the whole point of the bill. It was not intended to settle those questions. It did not affirm or deny the power, but left the question for the decision of the proper constitutional tribunal. Niles retorted that this solution was that of Calhoun and the south, and he saw no compromise in it. Calhoun begged Niles not to regard him as an advocate of slavery. He, and those who agreed with him, only claimed the rights which belonged to them as members of the Union and they were willing to rest their rights "upon the high ground on which the Senator from Delaware had placed them, where our forefathers placed them, and where we place them." [67] Dickinson, of New York, rose to defend the bill and the committee of which he had been a member. The peculiar merit of the bill, in his eyes, was that it encroached neither upon the north or the south. The subject of slavery was left where the committee found it, while, at the same time, the territories were organized and on their way into the Union. Niles prefaced his reply with a warning to Dickinson to mend his ways or he would be in trouble with his constituents. Passing from this personal aside to the principle of the bill, he attacked it on the grounds that a question of political regulation was not one to be settled by the courts. It was an unmanly shrinking from its own task on the part of the legislature. Dickinson countered by telling Niles that his constituents were his own business, that, if he were interested, Calhoun's approval of the measure had not been complete, and closed by recalling to Niles that the Constitution itself was made up of compromises on the subject of slavery and that all action in regard to it must be in the same spirit.[68] Phelps, of Vermont, another committee member, rose to explain the bill. Great insistence, he said, had been placed on the fact that the Constitution precluded legislation on the subject of slavery in the territories. The question would keep recurring no matter how much legislation Congress passed. "If this bill leaves the question to the constitutional expounders," he asked, "can gentlemen complain that we have not attempted to do that which the Constitution has put out of our power, but have left the subject where the Constitution placed it?" a thought that would play a large part in his fellow Vermonter's, Roswell Field's, interest in the case several years later.[69] Miller, of New Jersey, found the bill entirely southern in its bias. Furthermore, he asked, striking a warning note, were the Senators sure the country would acquiesce in a decision of the Supreme Court? [70] Corwin, of Ohio, called the bill an effort in evasion on the part of Congress. He expressed distrust of the

131

Court; were not five of its members from the south? [71] Underwood, of Kentucky, described, rather accurately, the public reaction to a decision in favor of the south. "The gentleman from Ohio [Corwin] will be ready to exclaim, 'I told you so; I knew they could not be trusted; I foresaw the wonderful influence which geographical lines possess and exercise over the human intellect. . . ' And what will the great northern public say and do? Sir, they will denounce the Supreme Court, and clamor for congressional interference to avert the consequences of a corrupt decision." [72] Reverdy Johnson, of Maryland, rose to defend the Court. He warned his hearers that "it is this bill, or it is nothing." He could not see how the issue, since it was a case arising under the Constitution, could be taken away from the Court.[73] Dayton, of New Jersey, on the other hand, felt "an utter aversion, an invincible repugnance" to throwing the question on the Court. "Let us blow off our own political steam," he urged, "and that of our constituents, if we can. That court is the sheet anchor of the hopes of conservatism in this country; if public feeling be excited—as it is said to be—I do not wish unnecessarily to see the court stagger under the weight of this question. . . . Drag that court and your judges into this scene of political strife, and the consequences may yet be deplored by us all." [74]

Despite these sombre warnings, the bill passed in the Senate, by a vote of thirty-three to twenty-two, on July 27th. While a respectable majority of the elder statesmen of the country was willing to pass the question on to the Supreme Court, the proposal received short shrift in the House. When it appeared there the day after the Senate had passed it, Stephens, of Georgia, moved that it be laid on the table, which it was by a vote of one hundred and twelve to ninety-seven. Bowdon, of Alabama, who supported the measure, described the scene quite vividly. "Gray-headed Senators sat in the other end of the Capitol, day after day, and night after night, near the close of their labors, after a session of near twenty-four hours, embracing the entire night, when, worn with fatigue," they passed the Clayton bill. "What did we do with it?" he asked. "In a few hours after that time, when many rejoiced that the rainbow of peace was again to span the horizon, this House assembled, every bosom heaving with interest, every eye beaming forth the intense interest of the heart, almost every cheek blanched with paleness. The Speaker took his seat. The fell purpose of predetermination was about to be realized. The fatal edict

132

had gone forth and no time was to be lost. A gentleman . . . the gentleman from Georgia [Stephens] rose in his place, and in that shrill voice that made me for a time almost imagine John Randolph had risen from the dead and reappeared in the theatre of his old renown, uttered the significant words. . . ." [75]

Stephens' own explanation of his motion was less dramatic. He opposed the bill because it referred the matter of slavery in New Mexico and California to the judiciary alone. While the Constitution recognized slavery where it existed by the law of the State or the place, it did not establish it where it was prohibited. The Mexican laws, prohibiting slavery in those regions, were still in force. The courts, consequently, would be constrained to decide that slavery did not exist in the recent acquisitions. The bill, in other words, was a total surrender of southern rights to the fruits of the Mexican War. [76]

While the legislature was struggling to find a solution of the vexing question of slavery in the territories, the general question of the power of the Federal government in those dependencies was engaging the attention of the Supreme Court, to whose care the conservative elements of the country would have liked to confide the whole matter. Early in 1847, Polk had empowered the military commander in California to set up both military and civil governments there in virtue of the right of conquest. An official, Edward Harrison by name, was authorized to impose duties. Certain California traders contested the right of the military commander so to act and sued the government for the duties they had paid from February 3, 1848, the date of the treaty of Guadalupe-Hidalgo, to November 13, 1849, the date when the collector appointed by the President arrived. Justice Wayne delivered the opinion of the Court which sustained the collector, Harrison, basing his argument on the power conferred by the constitutional provision respecting the territories and buttressing it with references to the Insurance Companies and Gratiot cases. The fact that military government continued was due to the inactivity of Congress, which failed to provide a more regular form of organization. [77]

The arguments that were heard in 1820 and in 1848 were heard again in 1854 when the question arose over the organization of the Nebraska Territory. Senator Jones, of Tennessee, introduced what he considered a new slant on the whole problem of the power of Congress over the territories carved out of the

133

Louisiana Purchase. The Constitution, he urged, made all treaties the supreme law of the land. By article three of that treaty, he continued, by which the domain was acquired from France, all property rights in the territory were to be respected.[78] Among such rights were those in slaves which were owned at the time of purchase by the inhabitants of the territory. A law of Congress which abrogated these rights was null and void. He professed himself at a loss to perceive how gentlemen could get around this argument.[79] His fellow Tennessean, Judge Catron, would be equally at a loss in 1857.

In a speech in the House, picturesquely entitled, "No Slavery in Nebraska; No Slavery in the Nation; Slavery an Outlaw," Gerrit Smith, the New York abolitionist, expounded those portions of the Constitution which, to him, clearly proved its anti-slavery character. Ironically, he saw the end of American slavery in that provision which read, "No person shall be deprived of life, liberty, or property, without due process of law." [80] He was aware, he went on, of the claim that "inasmuch as the slave is held by law . . . and, therefore, by due process of law, nothing can be gained for him from this provision." This, he declared, resulted from a confusion of the laws by which persons were held in slavery with due process of law, a point he did not clarify. He closed by recommending Lysander Spooner's *Unconstitutionality of Slavery* to the House, if any member felt he needed further argument.[81]

The roving eye of reform, in the north, had not confined itself to the subject of slavery, an evil that existed at a distance. Besides slaves, there was another form of property which, in the opinion of many, was of dubious morality. This majority made it the law in several States that alcohol, in any form that might be called potable, was beyond the pale of protection, and was to be confiscated if found in private possession. Judges, in deciding the cases which came before them as a result of these liquor laws, availed themselves of a line of reasoning which had been used to decide a case which had nothing to do with slavery or alcohol. This was the case of Taylor v. Porter and Ford which had been decided by the Supreme Court of New York in 1843. The point at issue was a statute which allowed a private road to be laid out over another's land without his consent. The court declared it void, Justices Bronson and Cowen concurring, Chief Justice Nelson, the later Justice Nelson, dissenting. Judge Bronson, who wrote the opinion, commenced by challenging the supremacy of the Legislature. It was not the sole but only one of the organs "of that absolute sovereignty which resides in the whole body of the people." It could only exercise such powers as had been delegated to it, and when it went beyond this grant of authority its acts were void. This question was not to be considered solely in the light of that section of the State Constitution which dealt with legislative power. "The people have added negative words," he said, "which should put the matter at rest." He then cited from the New York Constitution the provision that "No member of this state shall be disfranchised, or deprived of any of the rights or privileges secured to any citizen thereof, unless by the law of the land, or the judgment of his peers." [82] The words, "law of the land," as used in this provision, the judge explained, did not mean "a statute passed for the purpose of working the wrong." This would be to make the provision a useless trifle whose interpretation would be "You shall not do the wrong, unless you choose to do it." More than legislation was required by this provision; the matter must be adjudged against a man on trial. But a following section of the same article put the matter beyond doubt. "No person shall be deprived of life, liberty, or property without due process of law, nor shall private property be taken for public use, without just compensation." Even as regarded the point at issue, the laying of a road on private property, Bronson felt that the prior section, on due process, was more applicable than the latter, providing for just compensation. Due process could not mean anything less "than a prosecution or suit instituted and conducted according to the prescribed forms and solemnities for ascertaining guilt, or determining the title to property." The same protection against legislative encroachment was extended to property as to life and liberty. If property could be taken without trial, all life was insecure.[83]

Chief Justice Nelson dissented on the grounds that the road was public. He found the reasoning of Bronson novel. The privileges of the Constitution and the statute under discussion had stood together for fifty-six years, he pointed out, and no one had noticed the contradiction.[84]

These arguments of Justices Bronson and Cowen were found quite convincing some nine years later by Judge Curtis. In May, 1852, Rhode Island, following the lead of Maine, passed a statute entitled An Act for the Suppression of Drinking Houses and Tippling Shops. By November, the validity of the law was the point at issue in a case that came before the judge while on circuit. Curtis, with District Judge Pitman concurring, found the act unconstitutional because it violated the due process clause of the State Constitution. In interpreting the phrase, "law of the land," the Justice held that it certainly did not mean "any act which the Assembly may choose to pass," echoing Judge Bronson's earlier statement. After citing the New York judge, Curtis concluded that, if the provision of the Constitution did not act as a check on the Legislature, "the legislative will could inflict a forfeiture of life, liberty, or property without a trial." Liquor was still property, despite the Rhode Island Legislature. What most aroused the ire of the judges in this case, however, was the summary procedure prescribed by these acts in confiscating this form of property.[85] At the November term, 1854, Curtis, again on circuit, found another act of the Rhode Island Assembly, drawn along similar lines, void for the same reasons. In this case, the Supreme Court of the State had anticipated the Justice and he declared his full concurrence in their opinion.[86]

In view of these two decisions, Curtis should not have found Taney's reasoning on the Fifth Amendment in the Scott case very novel, especially since he had called the Chief Justice's attention to it. After he had given his opinion in the first of the Rhode Island liquor cases, Curtis was attacked by Horace Greeley in the *Tribune*. His uncle, George Ticknor, was disturbed over the assault and Curtis wrote him to describe his own reactions. He told Ticknor that he had had no doubt, when he gave the decision, that it would be attacked, "not by reasoning, for that I did not fear, but by abuse, which I feared as little." [87] He regarded it as a fact of some significance, an illustration of the position of the judiciary in the country in 1853, that he had been criticised, in the same year, once for trenching on the right of trial by jury, and again for extending that right unduly. He pointed out to his uncle that, in the one instance, he was repelling the presumption of those who would make the jury judges of the law as well as the facts, a position destructive of liberty; in the other, he was restraining those "who, in the pursuit of an object deemed by them of great importance, have disregarded principles contained in Magna Charta, and affirmed in every American Constitution which has been formed since 1776." It was the Justice's conviction that neither Greeley nor any one else could overthrow the opinion. He admitted that he might have made mistakes and would probably make more, but he did think he did know when he had arrived at "the primitive foundations, whose *situs* will never be disturbed until our political fabric breaks up; and be sure this opinion rests upon them." Judges Nelson and Grier, he continued, had both read the opinion before it was delivered. He had discussed the reasoning of the case and its underlying principles with the Chief Justice. All had approved. It was Curtis's opinion that "the members of the judiciary department of the government must make up their minds to being treated hereafter by the press with very little deference, and no more fairness than other people." He was determined, he told his uncle, to do his duty to the best of his ability and "let the country take care of the consequences." [88] Taney had but to change the word, "liquor," in Curtis's opinion, to the word, "slave," and he had the substance of the argument by which he invalidated the eighth section of the Missouri Compromise Act. Although the argument from the Fifth Amendment, in reference to the exclusion of slavery from the territories, already had a long, if not too prominent, legislative and legal history, it is possible that Curtis's use of it in the defense of alcohol may have prompted Taney's defense of slavery by the same means, with the same intentions as Curtis and with the same resignation to the expected onslaughts of the fourth estate.

When the New York law on ardent spirits came before the courts, it, too, was found wanting. The Court of Appeals, citing Taylor v. Porter, found it void. "Such an act as the legislature may, in the uncontrolled exercise of its power, think fit to pass," said Judge Henry Edwards, with the hearty concurrence of Judge Denio, "is, in no sense, the process of law designated by the Constitution." The construction of Judge Bronson was so sound, Edwards felt, that the mere statement of it was sufficient.[89] Another act, with the same purpose, passed in place of the former, met a like fate at the hands of Judges Brown, Strong and Rockwell of the Supreme Court. Brown held that the due process provision of the State Constitution, to be of any value, "must have a fixed permanent signification, one that shall remain unchanged by circumstance, or time, or the caprice of those to whom the restraining words may become offensive or troublesome." Strong, concurring, found the act in question to be, "with a single exception," the only instance of an attempt to legislate any species of property substantially out of existence. The exception was the abolition of slavery, by statute, in the State. However, he continued, slaves were not considered property at common law. If they had been, "it might have been a grave question, whether their owners could have been deprived even of such property without compensation." [90] In 1856, another case involving the constitutionality of the New York law was decided along the same lines for the same reasons.[91]

NOTES

1. Everett S. Brown, *The Constitutional History of the Louisiana Purchase* (Berkeley: University of California Press, 1920), pp. 14-74. Gouverneur Morris expressed Federalist opinion on this subject rather forcibly. Writing to Henry Livingston on November 25, 1803, he assured him that, in drafting the territorial provisions of the Constitution, he "had it not in contemplation to insert a decree *de coercendo imperio* in the Constitution of America." Among other reasons which would have prevented him from incorporating such a limitation, he told Livingston, was the fact that he "knew as well then, as I do now, that all North America must at length be annexed to us. Happy, indeed, if the lust of dominion stop there. It would, therefore, have been perfectly Utopian to oppose a paper restriction to the violence of popular sentiment in a popular government." In another letter to Livingston of December 4, 1803, he stated that it was his opinion that Congress could not admit, as a new State, "territory which did not belong to the United States when the Constitution was made." He had always thought that, "when we should acquire Canada and Louisiana, it would be proper to govern them as provinces, and allow them no voice in our councils" (Max Farrand, [ed.], *The Records of the Federal Convention of 1787*, New Haven: Yale University Press, 1923, III, p. 401).
2. Seré vs. Pitot, 6 Cranch 336.
3. Article 4, Section 2, Paragraph 3.
4. 6 Cranch 336. This position was, substantially, that of Albert Gallatin. Cf. Gallatin to Thomas Jefferson (n.d.), cited by Brown, *The Constitutional History of the Louisiana Purchase*, pp. 20-22.
5. John Adams to Josiah Quincy, Feb. 9, 1811, Charles F. Adams (ed.), *The Works of John Adams* (Boston: Little, Brown and Co., 1854), IX, p. 631.
6. *Congressional Globe*, 15 Congress, Session 2, p. 306.
7. *Ibid.*, p. 307.
8. *Ibid.*, p. 309.
9. *Ibid.*, p. 1166.
10. Article 4, Section 3.
11. "The inhabitants of the ceded territory shall be incorporated in the Union of the United States . . . as soon as possible . . . and in the meantime they shall be maintained and protected in the free enjoyment of their liberty, property, and the religion which they profess. . . ." William Malloy (ed.), *Treaties, Conventions, International Acts, Protocols and Agreements between the United States of America and Other Powers* (Washington: Government Printing Office, 1910), I, p. 509.
12. *Congressional Globe*, 15 Congress, Session 2, pp. 1173-1174.
13. *Ibid.*, pp. 1181-1183.
14. *Ibid.*, pp. 1198-1200.
15. *Ibid.*, pp. 1222-1223.
16. *Ibid.*, pp. 1226-1227.
17. *Ibid.*, pp. 1230-1232.
18. *Ibid.*, pp. 1276-1277.
19. *Congressional Globe*, 16 Congress, Session I, p. 131.
20. *Ibid.*, pp. 135-155.

21. *Ibid.*, p. 169.

22. *Ibid.*, pp. 198-199.

23. *Ibid.*, pp. 205-206.

24. *Ibid.*, p. 1262.

25. *Ibid.*, p. 1521.

26. James Madison to Robert Walsh, Nov. 27, 1818, *Letters and Other Writings*, III, pp. 152-153.

27. James Monroe to Spencer Roane, Feb. 16, 1820, Stanislaus M. Hamilton (ed.), *The Writings of James Monroe* (New York: G. P. Putnam's Sons, 1898), VI, pp. 160-161.

28. John C. Fitzpatrick (ed.), *The Autobiography of Martin Van Buren* (Washington: Government Printing Office, 1920), p. 139.

29. James Madison to James Monroe, Feb. 10, 1820, *Letters and Other Writings*, III, p. 165.

30. James Madison to James Monroe, Feb. 23, 1820, *ibid.*, pp. 167-169.

31. *American Insurance Company and Ocean Insurance Company*, Appellants, vs. 356 Bales of Cotton: David Canter, Claimant and Appellee, 1 Peters 518. Hereafter referred to as Insurance Companies vs. Canter.

32. *Ibid.* 518.

33. *Ibid.* 534.

34. *Ibid.* 538.

35. Cf., above, pp. 111-112.

36. I Peters 542.

37. *Ibid.* 545.

38. Cherokee Nation vs. Georgia, 5 Peters 43.

39. 14 Peters 531-532.

40. *Ibid.* 536.

41. *Ibid.* 537.

42. Groves vs. Slaughter, 15 Peters 495.

43. *Ibid.* 513-515.

44. *Congressional Globe*, 29 Congress, Session 1, p. 1211.

45. *Ibid.*, p. 1217.

46. *Ibid.*, Session 2, p. 355.

47. Jesse T. Carpenter, *The South As a Conscious Minority, 1789-1861* (New York, New York University Press, 1930), pp. 3-5.

48. *Congressional Globe*, 29 Congress, Session 2, pp. 453-455.

49. *Ibid.*, p. 455.

50. *Congressional Globe*, 30 Congress, Session 1, Appendix, p. 305.

51. *Ibid.*, Appendix, pp. 579-582.

52. *Ibid.*, Appendix, p. 653.

53. *Ibid.*, Appendix, p. 699. Cf., above, Chapter 2, pp. 14-15.

54. *Ibid.*, Appendix, p. 717.

55. *Ibid.*, Appendix, p. 833.

56. William J. Ashley (ed.), *The Federalist* (New York: E. P. Dutton and Company, 1911), No. 38, p. 189.

57. *Ibid.*, No. 43, pp. 220-221.

58. Dix cited the re-enactment of the Ordinance of 1787 by the first Congress of the United States, an act of Congress of April 7, 1798, organizing the Mississippi Territory, in which the importation of foreign slaves was prohibited, another, of 1800, which re-enacted the Ordinance of 1787 for the Indiana Territory, and several other territorial acts (*Congressional Globe*, 30 Congress, Session 1, Appendix, pp. 863-864).

59. Cf., above, pp. 117-120.

60. *Congressional Globe*, 30 Congress, Session 1, Appendix, pp. 865-868.

61. *Ibid.*, Appendix, p. 870.

62. Article 4, Section 3, Paragraph 2.
63. Article 6, Section 1, Paragraph 1.
64. *Congressional Globe,* 30 Congress, Session 1, Appendix, pp. 874-875.
65. *Ibid.,* Appendix, p. 880. Cf., above, pp. 199-200, 203-204, 212-213.
66. *Ibid.,* Appendix, pp. 1139-1140. On the Clayton Compromise, cf., above, Chapter 2, pp. 14-15.
67. *Ibid.,* Appendix, pp. 1140-1141.
68. *Ibid.,* Appendix, p. 1143.
69. *Ibid.,* Appendix, p. 1155.
70. *Ibid.,* Appendix, p. 1157.
71. *Ibid.,* Appendix, pp. 1157-1164.
72. *Ibid.,* Appendix, p. 1169.
73. *Ibid.,* Appendix, pp. 1171-1172.
74. *Ibid.,* Appendix, p. 1185.
75. *Ibid.,* Appendix, p. 1058.
76. *Ibid.,* Appendix, p. 1107.
77. Cross vs. Harrison, 16 Howard 193. Wayne, in giving the Court's opinion, stated that the sovereignty receiving the cession of California was "the United States, under the Constitution, by which power had been given to Congress to dispose of and make all needful rules and regulations respecting the territory or other property belonging to the United States, with power also to admit new states into this Union, with only such limitations as are expressed in the section in which this power is given." It was this statement that prompted Catron to write to Treat, after the Dred Scott decision, "Wayne came in, in the face of his opinion in Cross v. Harrison" (John Catron to Samuel Treat, May 31, 1857, Treat Papers, Missouri Historical Society, St. Louis, Mo.).
78. Cf., above, p. 113, note 11.
79. *Congressional Globe,* 33 Congress, Session 1, p. 342.
80. Fifth Amendment.
81. *Congressional Globe,* 33 Congress, Session 1, Appendix, p. 524.
82. Article 7, Part 1, New York Constitution.
83. 4 Hill 145-147.
84. *Ibid.* 152-153.
85. "Greene v. Briggs *et al.,*" 1 Curtis 311-339, at 325 and 328.
86. "Greene v. James," 2 Curtis 187-189. Note Curtis's words in Murray vs. Hoboken Land and Improvement Company: "The article is a restraint on the legislative as well as on the executive and judicial powers of the government, and can not be so construed as to leave Congress free to make any process 'due process of law' by its mere free will." 18 Howard 276. In this connection note also the use of the Fifth Amendment to the Constitution in the argument of George T. Curtis and Senator Geyer. Cf., above, pp. 87, 90.
87. Benjamin R. Curtis (ed.), *A Memoir of Benjamin Robbins Curtis,* I, p. 172.
88. *Ibid.,* I, p. 173.
89. Westervelt vs. Gregg, 12 New York Reports 209, 212.
90. People vs. Philip Berberrich, 11 Howard Practice Reports 322, 339-340.
91. People vs. Wynehamer, 3 Kernan 378-395.

10

CONFLICT OF LAWS

THE THIRD MAJOR ISSUE INVOLVED IN THE SCOTT CASE WAS WHETHER Dred's residence in the free State of Illinois so affected his relationship to Dr. Emerson that, in the words of Chief Justice Taney, "he was not again reduced to a state of slavery by being brought back to Missouri." [1] Here, to an even greater degree than in granting or refusing to grant free Negroes citizenship, we can see the disruptive forces engendered by slavery at work and the Federal Union, as a result, tottering and about to fall. For the cement which held that edifice together, before the Civil War, was largely compounded of comity which, on an international level, meant a disposition to accommodate, by reason of which the courts of justice of one sovereignty would grant recognition to the laws of another within its own boundaries. From this conciliatory attitude arose a body of private international law, a system of rules to prevent the conflict of laws. Such a conflict arose when a person's rights were affected by the laws of two or more jurisdictions, laws which, ordinarily, had a contrary effect on the rights of the person involved. This branch of law, which was of relatively recent origin, was, as Story pointed out, of the greatest interest and importance to the United States, "since the union of a national government with already that of twenty-six distinct states [1834], and in some respects independent states, necessarily creates complicated private relations and rights between the citizens of those states which call for the constant administration of extra-municipal principles." [2] It was in the nature of things that the laws of the free and slave States should conflict on the matter of the peculiar institution and it was equally natural that, as slavery became a continually growing source of irritation between the States, there should be manifested by the courts of these commonwealths a decreasing tendency to accommodate their laws on the subject to one another.

The acknowledgment of the rights of a master in a slave by a State which did not recognise that relationship in its own law and the effects of such non-recognition were questions that began to trouble lawyers at the time of the reintroduction of slavery into Europe in the late fifteenth century and the Justices of the Supreme Court of the United States in 1857 had considerable law at their disposal from which they could draw precedents and guiding norms. Jean Bodin, who was of the opinion that slavery had ceased in France in the twelfth century, had recounted several cases to prove that the slaves of foreigners, who had been brought by their masters into France, became free. These decisions, however, appear to have been based on statutes peculiar to certain localities rather than on any general law of the kingdom.[3]

That, however, there arose in France in later years considerable uncertainty on the subject, as well as repugnance to the institution, is demonstrated by the felt necessity of some declaration on the part of the government with regard to the slaves of the French colonists in the West Indies. Colonials who desired to visit the mother country wished assurance that their servants, who were slaves, would not be taken from them on their arrival in France. This was given to them by a royal edict of October, 1716, in which the king, having been informed that the colonists wished to send Negroes to France, "to confirm them in the teachings and exercise of our religion, and to have them learn, at the same time, some art and profession, from which the colonists would receive great use," [4] decreed that slaves could come, provided that their masters had the permission of the governor of the colony and that they were registered at their place of residence and on their arrival in France. If these conditions were fulfilled, they could not be freed and they could be sent back to the colony. However, if consent to their marrying were given, while they were in France, they were free.[5] This edict, which settled three problems which were to vex English and American judges for many years to come, was still in force in 1788.[6]

The force of this decree was tested in a case in which Jean Boucaux, "négre creole," sued for his freedom. Jean had been born in Santo Domingo, the slave of the governor of Cap François, and he had passed, on the death of the governor, to his widow, who was known as La Dame de Beaumanoir. She, in 1734, had married one Verdelin and they had brought Jean to France as their cook. He was freed because his owners had not complied with the terms of the edict. The Verdelins were given three days to fulfill the requirements of the law with regard to two other slaves, Colin and Bibiana. The lawyers in the case had indulged in considerable rhetoric on the liberating qualities of French soil, but the case really turned on the failure of Verdelin to meet the technical requirements of the Code Noir.[7]

What the English law on the subject was became a matter of concern about the same time as it did in France, and for the same reason, the possession of slaves by English colonists who wished to return home to visit. As there had been in France, so there was also, in England, a tendency to regard all slavery as outlawed. In the "Eleventh of Elizabeth," as the lawyers in the celebrated case of Somerset were to discover, one Cartwright brought a slave from Russia to England and "would scourge him." It was resolved "That England was too pure an air for slaves to breath in."[8] But, when England became a country that encouraged slavery in her colonies, and, even more so, when she became deeply involved in the slave trade, the question was not so simple. While Chief Justice Holt might still hold that, "as soon as a Negro comes into England, he becomes free," he also told the defendants that they should have said in their declaration that the sale, of which there was question, had taken place in Virginia, in which region Negroes were saleable. The laws of England, he said, did not extend to Virginia, since it was a conquered country whose law was what the king pleased.[9]

In 1729, a plain question received a plain answer. In that year, Sir Philip Yorke, then Attorney General and, later, Lord Chancellor Hardwicke, and Mr. Talbot, then Solicitor General and, later, Chief Justice, were asked by interested merchants whether a slave, coming to Great Britain or Ireland, with or without his master, became free. They replied that he did not and that "his master's property or right in him is not thereby determined or varied; and baptism doth not bestow freedom on him, nor make any alteration in his temporal condition in these kingdoms." Further, a master could legally compel his slave to return to the plantations.[10]

Twenty years later, Yorke, as Chancellor, found, in the case of Pearne v. Lisle, that a Negro slave was "as much property as any other thing." Referring to Holt's opinion,[11] Hardwicke said that the case really had been decided "on the want of proper description." The papers had said nothing about the man being a slave, but, merely, that he was a Negro. "The reason said at bar," the Chancellor continued, "to have been given by Lord Chief Justice

143

Holt, in that case, as the cause of his doubt, *viz*. That the moment a slave sets foot in England he becomes free, has no weight with it, nor can any reason be found, why they should not be equally so when they set foot in Jamaica, or any other English plantation." [12]

Such were the contrary opinions on the subject of slaves in England when the celebrated case of Somerset v. Steuart came before the Court of the King's Bench in 1771. On December 3rd of that year, Thomas Walklin, Elisabeth Cade, and John Marlow filed affidavits that James Somerset, a Negro, was confined in irons on board the brig, *Ann and Mary*. The brig, John Knowles commanding, lay in the Thames, bound for Jamaica. On these informations, Lord Mansfield issued a writ of *habeas corpus*, requiring Knowles to bring Somerset before him and to show cause why he detained him. Six days later, Knowles came before Mansfield with Somerset and gave as his reason for confining him that Somerset was the slave of Charles Steuart who had placed Somerset in Knowles' custody so that he might take him to Jamaica and sell him. Somerset, who had been bought by Steuart in Virginia, had run away from his master on his arrival in England and the latter had had him taken on board the brig. Steuart himself was but sojourning in London. It was his intention to return to America. [13]

The case was not immediately argued, Somerset's counsel requiring time for preparation. In fact, it was not thoroughly discussed till Easter Term, 1772. Hargrave, appearing for Somerset, went into the question of slavery most comprehensively. After a long historical discourse on the nature and origins of slavery, ancient and modern, [14] he advanced, as his basic argument for the Negro, the plea that the law of England would not admit a new slavery, different from ancient villenage. The law of the realm, he said, excluded every form of slavery not commencing in England. Any slavery, even though it commenced in England, which was not "ancient and immemorial" was likewise illegal. Villenage was the only form of slavery which could answer to such a description and that had long since expired. So, there was no slavery in England and there could be none "until the legislature shall interpose its authority." [15]

After noticing several arguments against his position, Hargrave took up that based on comity. It had been urged that, since slavery was lawful in America, the laws of that region should prevail in England and the master's right should not be impaired.

144

This argument, based on the third axiom of the Dutch lawyer, Huber,[16] according to Hargrave, labored under a limitation. No state was under any obligation to receive the law of another if grave inconvenience ensued,[17] as Huber had clearly said. Nothing, he declared could be more inconvenient than the admission of slavery into England. "To prevent the revival of domestic slavery effectually . . . its introduction must be resisted universally . . . the *lex loci* must yield to the municipal law," Hargrave concluded. Alleyne, for Somerset, laid down another principle that was to enter largely into the American law on slavery. Slavery, he said, was not a natural relationship but a municipal one, by its nature confined to certain places, and one that necessarily ceased when the slave passed into a State where laws maintaining the connection did not exist.[18]

During the course of the argument, Lord Mansfield had made several observations. He remarked of the opinion of Hardwicke and Talbot,[19] that it was given in answer to a petition presented to them after dinner at Lincoln's Inn and "probably, therefore, might not, as he believes the contrary, is not unusual at that hour, be taken with much accuracy." The principal question to which these gentlemen had replied, Mansfield asserted, was whether a slave became free by being baptized.[20] At another point, he advised the interested merchants to apply to Parliament for protection. Later, he urged the parties involved to come to a private agreement, "as he had done previously in five or six cases." But, if the parties would have it decided, he would have to give an opinion.[21] The question to be settled, in Mansfield's mind, was "Whether any dominion, authority, or coercion can be exercised in this country on a slave, according to the American laws?" In other words, should comity be extended by England to her colonies in this matter? But, said Mansfield, agreeing with Somerset's counsel, Hargrave, the difficulty of adopting the relationship, without adopting it in all its consequences, was extreme and many of these consequences were opposed to the law of England. Finally, the Chief Justice exclaimed, "If the parties will have judgment, *fiat justitia, ruat caelum;* let justice be done whatever be the consequence." A loss to the owners of slaves to the extent of seven hundred thousand pounds sterling might follow his decision. But he still hesitated, and allowed the matter to stand over, saying, "if we are called on for a decision, proper notice shall be given." [22]

The parties persisted and, on June 22, 1772, Mansfield gave

his decision. He said that the only question before the court was: "Whether the return on the cause was sufficient?" This was that the slave refused to serve, "whereupon he was kept to be sold abroad." Such an high act of dominion, the Justice said, must be recognized by the law of the country where it was attempted. He went further. The state of slavery, he declared, was of such a nature that it could not be introduced, "on any reasons, moral and political, but only by positive law. . . . It was so odious, that nothing could be suffered to support it but positive law. Whatever inconvenience, therefore, may follow from the decision, I cannot say this case is allowed or approved by the law of England; and therefore the black must be discharged." [23]

Some thirteen years later, Mansfield commented on this decision in the case of Somerset. "The determinations," he said, "go no further than that the master cannot by force compel him [a slave] to go out of the kingdom. The case of Somerset is the only one on this subject." As for England, he continued, villens in gross, the form of villenage most akin to Negro slavery, "may in point of law subsist to this day." [24]

It was a very narrow point, then, that the Chief Justice decided, a slave could not be forcibly deported from England. But the opinion that slavery needed positive law to exist, which Mansfield himself regarded as *obiter dictum*, became part of American law on the subject on the authority of the Chief Justice.

In America, a case in point appeared before Judge Mills, of Kentucky, in 1820. A slave named Lydia had been born in that State and had been taken by her then master, one Warwick, to Indiana Territory in 1807. Warwick sold Lydia to a man named Miller in 1814. Miller, in turn, sold her to a third master, Robert Todd, who brought her back to Kentucky and sold her to John Rankin, whom she sued for her freedom. Mills decided in favor of Lydia's freedom. He based his opinion on the principle that residence in the Indiana Territory extinguished any right to Lydia's services. "This right, then," he argued, "during the seven years residence of Lydia, in Indiana, was not only suspended, but ceased to exist; and we are not aware of any law of this state which can or does bring into operation the right of slavery when once destroyed." In according this full recognition to the laws of Indiana, Mills made a strong plea for comity on this subject, urging that it should prevail more among sister states than foreign nations.[25]

Mills' contention that residence on free soil destroyed the right of the master in his slave received a blow in the High Court of Admiralty at the hands of Lord Stowell. In 1822, a Mrs. Allan, of Antigua, had come to England on a visit, bringing with her a slave named Grace. The following year, Mrs. Allan and Grace returned home, the latter quite willingly. Things went quietly for some time, until, on August 8, 1825, a man named Wyke, who had come to Antigua on the same boat as Mrs. Allan and Grace and who was now the collector of customs there, seized Grace on the grounds that she had been imported into the island illegally. The case finally came before Stowell. The question posed by the case, his lordship commented, was whether slavery was so divested by landing in England that it would not revive on a return to the place of servitude. After adverting to the negligence of Wyke, in allowing a matter he was so thoroughly aware of to run for two years, Stowell placed the burden of proving her freedom on Grace. The only basis for her plea was residence in England. To this Stowell answered, "If she depends on such a freedom, conveyed by mere residence in England, she complains of a violation of right which she possessed no longer than whilst she resided in England, but which had totally expired when that residence ceased and she was imported into Antigua." He then reviewed the course that English law had taken on the subject of slavery. He found that the judgment of Talbot and Yorke, "pronounced in full confidence, and without a doubt upon a practice which had endured universally in the colonies, and (as appears by these opinions) in Great Britain," had been, "in no more than twenty-five years afterward reversed by Lord Mansfield." Public and authorized traffic in slaves, Stowell continued, had existed in London as well as in the West Indies. What was more, Mansfield, as was evident from his many delays, tried to avoid a judgment. However, Stowell pointed out, as Mansfield himself had, "the real and sole question" in the case of Somerset was whether a slave could be forcefully taken from England and sold. In deciding this point, the Chief Justice, in his final judgment, had amplified the subject largely. His statement that slavery depended on positive law was, in particular, *obiter dictum*, Stowell asserted, since ancient custom is also a foundation of law. Slavery was reimposed on the slave who returned to the colonies, Stowell ruled, "by the same title by which it grew up originally. It was never in Antigua the creature of law, but of that custom which operates with the force of

147

law; and when it is cried out that *malus usus abolendus est,* it is first to be proved that, even in the consideration of England, the use of slavery is considered as a *malus usus* in the colonies." It was supported there by all the legal power in England. He closed by recommending those opposed to such laws to appeal to Parliament.[26]

While Stowell seemed certain enough of the correctness of his judgment in its final expression, the case really had weighed heavily on him. He wrote to Judge Story, with whom he had corresponded, that he had been very much engaged "in an undertaking perfectly novel to me, and which has occasioned me great trouble and anxiety, and that was the examination of a new question, namely—whether the emancipation of a slave, brought to England, insured a complete emancipation to him upon his return to his own country, or whether it only operated as a suspension of slavery in this country, and his original character devolved upon him again, upon his return to his native Island." [27] He told Story that the question had not been examined in fifty years, but that the usual practice was that, on his return to his place of servitude, the slave resumed his original character. Story, who was in Washington at this time, did not reply. Stowell wrote again. He did not wish to be understood, he told Story, as having decided the case as he did because he thought the slave trade legal. He was but endeavoring to answer "merely this narrow question, whether the Court of King's Bench, in the case of Somerset, meant to declare that our non-execution of the slave code in England was a new suspension of it as respected England, but left it in full operation with respect to the colonies." His clear opinion was "for its limited effect. The execution of the Code laws is suspended in England, as being thought inconsistent with the nature as well as the institutions of this country . . . it does not at all derogate from the law of the colonies upon the return there of the person so far liberated in England." [28]

Story, in his reply, fully concurred with Stowell's reasoning. If he had been called upon to pronounce a judgment in a like case, he assured his English friend, he would have arrived at the same result, though, he added modestly, he would not have been able to present his findings in so striking and convincing a manner. In Massachusetts, he informed Stowell, slavery was not legal, and yet, "if a slave should come hither, and afterwards return to his own home, we would certainly think that the local law would reattach upon him, and that his servile character would be reintegrated." The decision appeared to him to be impregnable. It had been widely read in America, "where questions of this nature are not of unfrequent discussion," and the approbation of it was universal.[29]

In 1833, a case came before Chief Justice Lemuel Shaw, of Massachusetts, which involved the narrow question decided by Lord Mansfield. It concerned the status of a slave girl, Med, who had been brought to Boston by a Mrs. Slater of New Orleans. While she was absent for a few days from Boston, the child was left in the care of her father, Thomas Aves, and it was he who was accused by Levin Harris of unlawfully restraining Med of her liberty. Benjamin Curtis, then practicing law in Massachusetts, appeared for Aves and argued that a slave-holder, making a temporary sojourn in Massachusetts, could restrain his slave to the extent of taking his property out of the State and back to his own place of residence. The law of Massachusetts should so far give effect to that of Louisiana and it was in the power of the court to extend such comity for which no legislation was necessary. Status, he urged, depended on domicile and here there was no change of residence intended. Mrs. Slater was to return to New Orleans in several months. The temporary residence of Med in Boston worked no injury to Massachusetts. Considering the case of Somerset, Curtis pointed out that British practice did not bear out Mansfield's contention that all the consequences of slavery necessarily followed upon its temporary admission in certain cases. What was more, Mansfield's assertion that slavery needed positive law to sustain it was wrong, if by positive law he meant legislation. Slavery was the creature of custom though, Curtis admitted, some law was necessary to allow the master to exercise his rights. Curtis closed, instancing Judge Mills' plea for comity between the States.[30]

Ellis Loring appeared for the State. He argued that comity was not to be extended in doubtful cases. In such situations, the State, which was to decide, was bound to resolve the doubt in its own favor. In this particular matter, that of slavery, comity was not to be extended because there existed no reciprocity, the southern States all holding that color created the presumption of slavery. What was more, no State had to recognize an institution which offended morals, contravened policy, violated public law, and offered a pernicious example.[31]

149

In his opinion, Judge Shaw distinguished the relationship of master and slave which was established, he said, by the local law of particular States from those natural relationships which were recognized everywhere such as that between husband and wife. The right of property was one of these latter relationships. This appeared to Shaw to answer the argument advanced by Curtis that the right of property adhered to a person and by the comity of nations must be recognised wherever he was. "It is obvious," Shaw concluded, "that, if this were true, in the extent in which the argument employs it, if slavery exists anywhere . . . the law of slavery must extend to every place where such slaves may be carried. The maxim, therefore, and the argument can apply only to those commodities which are everywhere, and by all nations, treated and deemed subjects of property." [32] So Shaw, who had found no case on the subject, was of the opinion that Massachusetts should not extend comity to Louisiana and, by implication, to any other southern State, in the matter of slavery, even for a temporary stay, because the institution was, "repugnant to our laws, entirely inconsistent with our policy and our fundamental principles." [33]

In 1834, Joseph Story published his *Commentaries on the Conflict of Laws, Foreign and Domestic,* a work which became of almost paramount authority in its field, rapidly superseding the three other English treatises on the subject, those of the Englishmen Jabez Henry and Fortunatus Dwarris, and that of the American civil lawyer, Samuel Livermore.[34] Story derived his system of private international law largely from the highly simplified maxims of the seventeenth-century Dutch publicist, Ulric Huber, the source upon which Hargraves had relied in the Somerset case in his argument for the Negro. He differed with Huber, however, on the extent to which personal qualities, acquired in one jurisdiction, should be recognised in another.[35] Story subjected these qualities, which Huber had exempted from the operation of his highly nationalistic principles, to the same limitation that bound any extra-territorial law, namely, the policy and interests of the particular State in which the person enjoying qualities conferred by another jurisdiction found himself, policy and interests which, especially in the United States, could be determined either by legislative act or judicial decision. This departure from Huber's departure from his own principles, a step already taken by Chief Justice Shaw when he refused the comity of Massachusetts to Louisiana in his opinion in Commonwealth vs. Aves, had considerable effect on Story's discussion of slavery in Prigg vs. Pennsylvania and upon the opinions of Justices Scott and Ryland, of the Missouri Supreme Court, and Chief Justice Taney and Justice Nelson, of the United States Supreme Court, when they were called upon to determine the effect on Dred Scott's status of his residence in the free State of Illinois.[36]

The general principles of Story on the matter of comity received the sanction of the Supreme Court of the United States in 1839, when, in a case concerning the status of foreign corporations, Taney held that "In the silence of any positive rule, affirming or denying, or restraining the operation of foreign laws, courts of justice presume the tacit adoption of them by their own government, unless they are repugnant to its policy, or prejudicial to its interests." [37] Another application of the same principle was made in 1851, when the Supreme Court decided that the law of a State alone decided the status of persons domiciled within its territory, an application having direct effect on the Scott case. The question arose due to the fact that a Kentuckian, Graham, had allowed his slaves to make occasional trips into Ohio, where they played at various balls and dances. It was claimed that they were free by virtue of the laws of Ohio or the Northwest Ordinance. The court decided that the whole matter rested with Kentucky, an opinion in line with Story's doctrine of comity.[38]

These were the principles and precedents on which the Supreme Court of Missouri decided the case of Dred Scott. In rendering the decision, Judge Scott remarked that cases in which persons sued for freedom because they had been held in slavery in territories or States in which the institution was prohibited were not strangers in Missouri courts. Earlier cases seemed to have been decided, he continued, on the presumed assent of the master, but more recent pleas have been based on the grounds that it was "the duty of the courts of this State to carry into effect the constitution and laws of other States and territories, regardless of the rights, the policy or the institutions of the people of this state." [39] This was in opposition to the accepted law of the country, since every State, Scott said, citing Story, had the right to determine how far, in a spirit of comity, it would respect the laws of other States. "The respect allowed them will depend," he concluded, "on their conformity to the policy of our institutions." [40] In support of his conclusion that the Scotts were not free, Scott instanced the reasoning of Stowell in the case of the Slave Grace and that of Taney in Strader v. Graham.

From this decision, Judge Gamble dissented. He held that the question was a settled one in Missouri. It would appear that it was. But there is point to Judge Nelson's conclusion that the only case really in opposition to the decision of Judge Scott and Ryland was that which involved the freedom of Rachel who had been bought, through an agent, from Major Brant, Benton's son-in-law, by an army officer named Stockton who was stationed at Fort Snelling and who had Rachel held at that fort and, subsequently, at Prairie du Chien, as a slave. Judge McGirk, in freeing Rachel, held that there must be something more than convenience to the owner to warrant his holding a slave in free territory. What was more, Stockton had been the resident of a free territory when he bought Rachel.[41] This decision was reversed in the opinion of the judges in the Scott case. But, as Nelson pointed out, the law expounded by Judge Scott was in conformity with numerous decisions in State courts, with the law of England, as stated by Stowell, with the opinions of Justice Story and Chancellor Kent, and with that of the Supreme Court of Massachusetts in Commonwealth vs. Aves.[42]

The refusal to extend comity in the matter of slavery, the refusal to enforce the Federal fugitive slave laws, went far to destroy what J. J. Crittenden had called, in his plea for Graham, the Kentucky slave-owner, before the Supreme Court, "that amenity of intercourse, that interchange of social courtesies that now exist, and which does so much to preserve those kindly and fraternal feelings upon which the success of our institutions so much depends." [43] It gave point to Lincoln's conclusion that the Union could not exist half slave and half free. Descending to the relatively trivial, it provided the background for the incident Senator Trumbull's wife described to her son. When the Georgian, Senator Toombs, was about to leave Washington for his native State in 1861, his coachman fled north. The dignified Mrs. Toombs was forced to use a public conveyance. In these reduced circumstances, she was met by Justice McLean's wife, who said, "Mrs. Toombs, are you going to leave us?" To which the lady replied, "I am glad enough to go; here I am riding in a hack!" Mrs. McLean then assured her, with satisfaction not untinged with malice, that this was just a beginning. Where one slave now escaped, hundreds would later and there would be no possibility of recapturing them.

All of which, Mrs. Trumbull, in common with many of her countrymen, found "very, very disgusting." [44]

NOTES

1. 19 Howard 452.

2. Joseph Story, *Commentaries on the Conflict of Laws*, 4th ed. (Boston: Little, Brown and Company, 1852), ix.

3. Jean Bodin, *Les Six Livres de la République* (n. p.: Gabriel Cartier, 1599), Book I, Chapter 5, p. 62.

4. *Le Code Noir* (Paris: Chez L. F. Prault, 1788), p. 172.

5. *Ibid.*, pp. 172-176. This condition, if the slaves married with consent, was due to the sacramental character of the marriage that would be contracted in France at this time.

6. *Ibid.*, pp. 507-509.

7. François Gayot de Pitaval, *Causes Célèbres* (Amsterdam: Z. Chatelain et Fils, 1776), 15, pp. 1-83.

8. 20 Howell 51.

9. 2 Salkeld 666.

10. 27 English Reports 47-48.

11. Cf., above.

12. 27 English Reports 47-48.

13. 20 Howell 1-22.

14. Hargrave rewrote his argument for publication, making many additions (*ibid.* 23).

15. *Ibid.* 23-48.

16. Ulricus Huberus, *"De Conflictu Legum in Diversis Imperiis"* (Friedrich Von Savigny, *A Treatise on the Conflict of Laws*, p. 509).

17. *Ibid.*, p. 514.

18. 20 Howell 68. This theory of the municipal character of slavery was to be the basis of Story's opinion in Prigg vs. Pennsylvania. Cf. 16 Peters 539.

19. 20 Howell 70.

20. *Ibid.* 79.

21. *Ibid.* 79.

22. *Ibid.* 79-80.

23. *Ibid.* 80-82.

24. King v. Inhabitants of Thames Ditton (99 English Reports 892).

25. Rankin v. Lydia (2 A. K. Marshall 813-819).

26. 2 Haggard 94-135.

27. William W. Story, *Life and Letters of Joseph Story* (London: John Chapman, 1851), I, pp. 552-553.

28. *Ibid.*, pp. 553-557. Justice McLean argued (19 Howard 559-560) that Lord Stowell's decision in the case of the Slave Grace did not apply to the Scotts because the record merely stated that the Scotts were "removed" to Missouri from Minnesota Territory (19 Howard 530) and it could not be inferred from this that they returned voluntarily. The fact that they did not resist their master forcibly was not sufficient to show that they returned of their own accord. Positive acts of the will were necessary to make the reasoning of the English judge hold and whether the Scotts elicited such acts, McLean said, was a fact for a jury to decide or, at least, the circumstance should be clearly admitted. It could not be presumed. Apart from the fact that Lord Stowell nowhere placed such stress on the voluntary character of Grace's return to Antigua, though the word "voluntary" did appear on the record in her case, the decision of Judges Scott and Ryland in the Missouri Supreme Court

did not depend on Stowell's opinion alone, or even primarily. It relied chiefly on Judge Story's principles on the conflicts of laws. Cf., above, Chapter 2, pp. 19-20.

29. Story, *op. cit.*, p. 558.

30. Commonwealth vs. Aves (18 Pickering 194-195).

31. *Ibid.* 201.

32. *Ibid.* 216.

33. *Ibid.* 218.

34. Henry's *The Judgment of the Court Demerara in the case of Odwin v. Forbes* and Dwarris's *A General Treatise on Statutes* had appeared in London in 1823 and 1830 respectively. Livermore's *Dissertations on the Questions which Arise from the Contrariety of the Positive Laws of Different States and Nations* was published at New Orleans in 1828. Livermore had been one of the lawyers in the case of Saul v. His Creditors (5 Martin La. 569) and had argued for the adoption of the principle of the civil law that a person clothed with certain rights by the operation upon him of the law of a particular place carried those rights with him, in justice and equity, wherever he went. Judge Porter, of the Louisiana Supreme Court, summarily rejected Livermore's argument and decided the case along lines Story was later to popularise. Livermore's book is an answer to the judge. Chancellor Kent, who was opposed to the introduction of the civil law into American jurisprudence, disapproved of Livermore. Kent himself had no doubts on the extra-territorial effect of laws. "There is no doubt of the truth of the general proposition," he wrote some four years before Story's work was to appear, "that the laws of a country have no binding force beyond its territorial limits, and their authority is admitted in other states, not *ex proprio vigore* but *ex comitate;* or, in the language of Huberus, *quatenus sine praejudicio indulgentius fieri potest.* Every independent community will judge for itself how far the *comitas inter communitates* is to be permitted to interfere with its domestic interests and policy" (James Kent, *Commentaries,* II, p. 570). Kent even went so far as to regard nuptial contracts, valid where they were made as subject to the perfect equality and entire independence of all states, for him the fundamental principle of public law (*ibid.,* II, p. 572, and I, p. 21). The origin and influence of Story's theory of the conflict of laws has been treated by William R. Leslie. See his "The Influence of Joseph Story's Theory of the Conflict of Laws on Constitutional Nationalism," *Mississippi Valley Historical Review,* 35 (1948), pp. 203-220, to which I am indebted for much of the material here.

35. Ulricus Huberus, *"De Conflictu Legum Diversarum in Diversis Imperiis."* Cf., above, Chapter 6, note 44. For Hargrave's use of Huber, cf., above, 144-145. Story's refusal to exempt personal qualities is discussed by Leslie, "The Influence of Joseph Story's Theory on the Conflict of Laws on Constitutional Nationalism," pp. 211-212.

36. For the opinion of Chief Justice Shaw, vid. sup. cf., above, p. 149. For Prigg vs. Pennsylvania, cf. 16 Peters 614-624. For the decision of the Missouri Supreme Court, cf., above, Chapter 2, pp. 19-20, and, above, pp. 151-152. For the opinions of Taney and Nelson, cf., above, Chapter 6, pp. 71, 73-74.

37. Bank of Augusta vs. Earle (13 Peters 599).

38. Strader vs. Graham (10 Howard 83-99).

39. 15 Missouri 582.

40. *Ibid.* Cf., above, Chapter 2, pp. 19-20.

41. 4 Missouri 350-354. Nelson (19 Howard 465) felt that to ascertain the law of Missouri on the subject of Dred's status it would be enough to refer to the judgment of the Supreme Court of that State on the case. But he also was of the opinion that it was due to that court to review the cases it had already decided in which the point at issue was like the Scott case. The crux of the matter in the cases of Winny vs. Whitesides (1 Missouri 472), La Grange vs. Chouteau (2 Missouri 20), Julia vs. McKinney (3 Missouri 270), and Wilson vs. Melvin (4 Missouri 592) was the intention of the master, implicit or explicit, of making a permanent residence in a free

state. The technical point, whether Dr. Emerson had a domicile at either Fort Armstrong or Fort Snelling, depended on two factors: his actual residence at both places, which no one could deny, and his intention of remaining at one or the other. Mere temporary absence, no matter how long continued, does not cause a person to lose his domicile, the classic example of such a case being that of a soldier in the army. Absence in the service of the government does not necessarily affect domicile. The intention of the person concerned must be considered. The peripatetic Dr. Emerson certainly had no intention of remaining anywhere but in the neighborhood of St. Louis. Cf., above, Chapter 1, pp. 5-6; Story, *Conflict of Laws 43*, and William E. Baldwin (ed.), *Bouvier's Law Dictionary* (Cleveland: Banks-Baldwin Law Publishing Co., 1934, pp. 316-318). Tramell vs. Adam (2 Missouri 155), Vincent vs. Duncan (2 Missouri 214) and Merry vs. Tiffin and Menard (1 Missouri 725) were decided in view of the Ordinance of 1787, the circumstances, on which the plea of freedom was based, having occurred before Illinois adopted her constitution.

42. 19 Howard 465-469. George T. Curtis, on the authority of Edwin Dickerson, a friend of Judge Grier, who said that he had the information from the judge in 1855, asserts that Grier's discussion of the binding effect of the decisions of state courts on the Supreme Court of the United States in the case of Pease vs. Peck (18 Howard 595-601) had a double purpose. The primary intention of the judges was to dispose of the case under consideration. The secondary one was to leave the judges free in regard to the last decision of the Missouri Supreme Court in the Scott case (Curtis, *Memoir*, I, pp. 209-210). Curtis regretted that Taney, in the Scott case, ignored this ruling of the court's and gave a "most stringent" effect to the decision of the Missouri Supreme Court (*ibid.*). The effect Taney attributed to the decision of the Missouri Supreme Court was that attributed to any state tribunal in the case of Strader vs. Graham, which had been decided in 1851 (19 Howard 452-453). Grier had declared that the Supreme Court was not bound to follow a State court's interpretation of its own laws when the court had first decided a question arising under State laws and there was a subsequent, contrary decision of a State court; when the decisions of a State court were not consistent, the Supreme Court did not feel itself bound to follow the last. While the Supreme Court was not bound to follow, it was also free to follow. While it was not bound to follow the last, it was also not bound to follow the earlier decisions.

43. 10 Howard 191.

44. White, *The Life of Lyman Trumbull*, p. 121.

11

WAR OF WORDS

OFFICIALLY, NOTHING REMAINED NOW BUT TO WIND UP THE CASE. An order to the Court of the United States for the District of Missouri was issued by the Supreme Court, informing the court that its decision in the case of Scott vs. Sanford was reversed and the cause was remanded to it to be dismissed for want of jurisdiction. Finally, the case of Scott vs. Emerson, which had been continued in the St. Louis Circuit Court, pending the decision of the Supreme Court of the United States, was decided in favor of the defendant and, on March 18, 1857, the Scotts, as well as being declared slaves, were ordered to pay costs.[1] The actual litigation was at an end. The press, the pulpits and politicians, however, took up the war of words where the judges had left it.

But, for a while, there was difficulty in gaining access to what the judges had said. On the last day of the term, March 7, 1857, Judge Curtis filed his opinion with the clerk of the Court, William Carroll. On the same day, the Washington agent of a Boston editor asked him for a copy of his opinion; the judge gave it to him and it was published in Boston a few days later.[2] By March 9, both the dissents were on file.[3] Four days later, the Chief Justice instructed the clerk to inform General Howard, the Supreme Court reporter, that the opinions were to be published in the order in which they now appear: his own first, then those of Wayne, Nelson, Grier, Daniel, Campbell and Catron. The two dissents were to be last; first McLean's, then Curtis's.[4] The opinions of all the judges, however, had not as yet been given to the clerk and soon the press of the country was clamoring for them. The Washington *Union* pointed out that McLean and Curtis had scattered their dissents widely; the Democratic press was being handicapped in its defense of the majority.[5] The St. Louis *Leader,* which had published a version of Taney's on March 13, promised its readers the other opinions as soon as it could get them.[6] The Washington correspondent of the New York *Journal of Commerce* wrote his paper on March 28 that there was no way of getting the official opinions

156

of the majority until Howard had printed them. It was expected that Taney would file his that day and that the others would be left with the clerk soon.[7]

The reasons for this delay were the subject of a heated correspondence between the Chief Justice and Judge Curtis, who, after a brief trip into Virginia, had arrived at Pittsfield, Massachusetts. Somewhere in his travels, he had been informed that Taney's opinion had been revised and "materially altered."[8] Wishing to know what changes had been made, Curtis wrote to Carroll, the clerk, requesting a copy of the Chief Justice's opinion when it had been printed for the Court records.[9] Carroll replied that neither Taney's, Wayne's, Nelson's, McLean's, nor Curtis's own opinion had yet been printed. He hoped to have them done in ten days. But, Carroll told the judge, the Chief Justice had instructed him not to release a copy of his opinion to any one, without his permission, before it was published by Howard, and he recommended that Curtis apply to Taney. To this the judge replied that "if by his opinion, you mean the opinion delivered by the Chief Justice as the opinion of the majority of the court," making a point of which the brothers Curtis were fond, the judge thought the restriction hardly applied to him, a member of the Court. If, however, Carroll had any doubt on this point, Curtis felt that it was certainly proper for the clerk to consult Taney.[10] This Carroll did. The Chief Justice told the clerk that he had understood him correctly and that Curtis, if he wished a copy of his opinion, would have to apply to Taney himself. To supplement his previous verbal instructions, he gave Carroll a written order placing an embargo on all the opinions, a move which was agreed to by Wayne and Daniel, the only two Justices still remaining in Washington. Taney gave as his reason for this restriction the fact that no one had a right to the opinion of the Court until it was published by the official reporter whose duty it was to bring the opinions of the Supreme Court "fully and fairly" before the public. He added the circumstance that the opinion of the Court had been "greatly misunderstood and grossly misrepresented in publications in the newspapers." Since it was impossible for any of the Justices to enter into discussions with "gentlemen who write for newspapers," it was due the Court and the public that the opinion should be allowed to speak for itself "and not be brought before the public garbled and mutilated, and with false glosses attached to it." Carroll replied to Curtis accordingly.[11]

In the meantime, speculation on the non-publication of the opinions was rife in Washington. James Harvey forwarded the current gossip to Judge McLean, telling him that there were "strong surmises about the manipulation to which the majority opinions have been submitted." Appleton and Company, the New York publishing house, had asked Harvey to get all the opinions for them and he had taken "some pains to inform myself about their *Status*—if you allow that word when not applied to slavery." As of a week ago, he went on, they had not been filed. Taney's, he stated, had been twice copied for revision. The *National Intelligencer* had been refused permission to reprint any of them. The "clause in Catron's, rebuking the discussion of the Merits of the Case, after the denial of the jurisdiction, has been expurgated," he continued, and only a single copy had been printed for Catron's own use. Campbell's was printed privately and the printer was forbidden to show it to anybody, "but especially to Grier, which was the unkindest cut of all." Appleton's had made a deal with General Howard, the reporter, and Harvey was no longer interested. In closing, he consoled the presidential aspirant with the news that "the sound judgment of the Country is up to the point of your position but not in favor of any fanatical crusade," an enterprise in which Harvey himself would not enlist.[12]

On receipt of Carroll's note, Curtis, rather nonplussed, wrote Taney that he could not suppose that "it was your intention to preclude me from having access to an opinion of the court in the only way possible for me to obtain it." If such were not the Chief Justice's intention, he asked Taney to direct Carroll to send him one. Ten days later, on April 28, the Chief Justice replied, enclosing a copy of the order he had given Carroll and explaining the reasons for the order. It was his conviction, one shared by Judges Wayne and Daniel, that the circumstances justified such procedure. They were also agreed that the opinions of the justices in the Scott case should be published in the usual manner and should not be separated from the other opinions given during the December term just ended. Above all, the opinions of the judges should not be hurried before the public in an unusual manner through the agency of the irresponsible reporters of a partisan press for party purposes. So the clerk had been instructed, verbally, not to give out any copies. Soon after this instruction, Mr. Charles P. Curtis (a distant relative of the judge's and his law partner), Taney continued, had applied to Carroll for a copy.

Carroll, thereupon, had inquired if Charles Curtis, because of his connection with the Justice, should be considered an exception to the order. Taney had asked why Charles Curtis wanted one. It appeared that he was going to publish his cousin's and wished a copy of Taney's to print with it. Taney denied the request as not being sufficiently considerate of the other justices, whose opinions would not be published, and as depriving General Howard of the just returns from his office. Carroll then, Taney went on, had shown him a copy of his, Judge Curtis's, letter and he had then issued the written order placing the restriction on the distribution of the opinions. From Curtis's letter, Taney continued, he presumed that the judge thought he had a right to the opinion because of his position, and this was true, if Curtis desired it for official use. But it was his understanding, Taney went on, that the judge did not wish the opinion for such a reason. "On the contrary," he remarked, "you announced from the bench that you regarded the opinion as extra-judicial, and not binding upon you or any one else." Curtis's position, then, did not differ from any other person's. What was more, Taney could not admit "that any one judge has the right to take away from the court the control of its own opinion before it is officially reported, or has the right to overrule its judgment, if he thinks proper, in a matter which nearly concerns its judicial character and standing, and more especially the judicial character and standing of the members of the court which gave the opinion." Taney closed, pointing out that the restriction applied to all the judges, "although it so happens that you are the only one who has applied for a copy." [13]

Curtis, deeply chagrined, replied that Taney had no right to presume that his intention was to make other than official use of the opinion. He knew nothing of Charles Curtis's purposes and the Chief Justice had no right to assume that there was any connection between his request and Taney's denial of his partner's. [14] He had thought, Curtis continued, that all the opinions of the judges were on file as the forty-second rule of the Supreme Court, on its face, would require. [15] He had but wanted to know what changes Taney had made in his opinion, particularly if they were material to his dissent, so that he could alter his own before it was printed. In his judgment, the sooner the opinions were published the better and, in a time of crisis, forms could be disregarded. It was on this assumption that he had given his to the Boston editor. [16]

Taney did not reply for almost a month, being at Richmond, holding the circuit court for the District of Virginia. By this time the opinions had been published.[17] The Chief Justice started by remarking that he would have been glad to find nothing in Curtis's letter that demanded an answer, but he felt called upon to tell the judge that there were no material alterations in his opinion. He did not intend, he continued, to ask Curtis where he had gotten the information that he had changed his opinion, but he felt constrained to remark that it would have been proper for Curtis to address himself on such a matter to the judge in whose opinion he was interested. "There is," he assured the Justice, "not one historical fact, nor one principle of constitutional law, or common law, or chancery law, or statute law, in the printed opinion, which was not distinctly announced and maintained from the bench; nor is there any one historical fact, or principle, or point of law, which was affirmed in the opinion from the bench, omitted or modified, or in any degree altered, in the printed opinion." Curtis would find in it, Taney went on, "proofs and authorities to maintain the truth of the historical facts and principles of law asserted by the court in the opinion delivered from the bench, but which were denied in the dissenting opinions. And until the court heard them denied, it had not thought it necessary to refer to proofs and authorities to support them. . . ."

If Curtis, Taney said, taking up another point, had thought that the usual mode of publication of the opinions of the Court should be altered, as he said he did, it would have been proper for Curtis to mention it to the Court. The Chief Justice remarked that he had had a letter from Curtis, the day after the decision had been given, in regard to the law library, but that Curtis had mentioned nothing about publishing his opinion nor had he intimated that another mode of publication of the opinions of the judges than the usual was desirable in the Scott case. In his opinion, Taney said, Curtis's behavior had made a fair judgment on the decision impossible. As far as he could see, Curtis had no reason to complain because he was not consulted when the restriction was placed on the publication of the opinions, in view of the fact that he had already published his own adverse opinion without consulting the other judges, "and I cannot see any just ground upon which you could claim the right to share in the control and disposition of the opinion of the court, when the avowed object of your dissenting opinion was to impair its authority and dis-

160

credit it as a judicial decision." [18] Curtis replied that he had never charged Taney with a breach of official duty, as the Chief Justice seemed to think and, what was more, Taney's assumptions, that he wished a copy of the opinion of the Court to pass it on to Charles P. Curtis or for partisan purposes, were unfair and groundless. He belonged to no party, Curtis said, and had no political end in view, "and no purpose whatever, save a determination to avoid misconstruction and misapprehension, from which I have suffered enough in times past." [19] Taney answered that he was glad to find there was nothing in Curtis's letter that required more than the acknowledgment of its receipt and the unpleasant correspondence ended.[20]

The party papers of the day did not feel the need for waiting for Howard's volume to appear, but, at once, attacked the decision and the Court, or defended both, as their policies required. The Republican and anti-slavery journals lost no time in searching the Old and the New Testaments, as well as less reputable sources, for appropriate epithets to hurl at the seven justices who had consigned the Scotts to slavery. The Democratic papers, feeling they had won a victory, were characterised, for a week or two, by a spirit of sweet reasonableness. They made painful efforts at logical demonstration. They reasoned with the opposition, but, eventually, they adopted the same tactics. The New York *Tribune* found the decision "to be entitled to just so much moral weight as would be the judgment of a majority of those congregated in any Washington bar-room." No matter how feeble Taney's voice had been, while reading his decision, the paper commented, "what he had to say was feebler." [21] The high point in its abuse was reached in a long despatch from Washington, dated March 13, 1857, which was the work of James S. Pike. He thought that it would not be amiss, at this juncture, to look at the personnel of the Court, "since the gentlemen composing it have chosen to thrust their political opinions upon the public under the garb and sanction of the judicial ermine." According to Pike, Taney, as Secretary of the Treasury, had been of considerable assistance to Reverdy Johnson when the latter had been involved in the failure of the Bank of Maryland. In gratitude, Johnson, and other Maryland Whigs, persuaded Clay to allow the nomination of Taney as Chief Justice to be confirmed, for which reason, Johnson had a "sinister" influence over Taney and because of this "he was procured to argue the Dred Scott case." Of Justice Wayne,

Pike remarked that he was "one of the Chivalry, and before he got too old the ladies used to be enamoured of his flowing locks and general beauty of appearance, to which he himself was not wholly insensible." Justice Daniel was described as "a tremulous, fidgety old man in glasses." Catron was a "robust, unintellectual man . . . whose erroneous opinions would, as a general rule, more often result from obtuseness than from original sin." Because of his stupidity, Pike thought, it was natural for Catron to "reject the Jesuitism, the sophistries, and the falsehoods by which Judge Taney would instinctively attempt to support the same conclusion." Judge Campbell, "more fanatical than the fanatics," was pictured as "a middle aged, middle sized man, bald, and possessed of middling talents." These five were "the High Priests of Slavery." The two northern concurring judges received similar handling. Nelson reminded Pike of "the wounded pigeon of the flock, essaying on broken wing to get a midway position of his own, from which he could either soar or descend, as circumstances might hereafter dictate." Grier, "a blond of rotund figure," was of "a soft and rosy nature." "Facile and easy of suggestion . . . ardent and impressible . . . fickle and uncertain," the judge's convictions were totally at the mercy of his brethren.[22]

The Washington *Daily Union*, the administration organ in that city, declared, on the other hand, that, "If the sectional question be not now settled, then we may despair of the republic." In electing Buchanan, "the people have decided that sectional agitation must cease, and the highest judicial authority has declared that the people have decided in accordance with the Constitution." The following day the paper entered a plea for sobriety. It warned the public, in Webster's words, that, "We have a race of agitators all over the country; their livelihood consists in agitating; their freehold, their copyhold, their capital, their all in all depend on the excitement of the public mind." For the next few days the paper continued to deprecate violence, but, on March 19, it undertook the offensive. The case, it pointed out, was not an administration move as had been charged but, on the contrary, "it has been done solely by those who now complain of the result. The suit was instituted and prosecuted" by anti-slavery men. On April 7, the editors, expressing their agreement with the Milwaukee *Daily News*, stated that the clamor raised by the opposition press arose from the fact that the ground has been taken out from under the Republican Party by the decision. It deprived that party "of the power to continue an excitement by which they hope to gain power and place. It is not the negro they care for." The paper's readers were urged to "look at the composition of their party" and they would realise the truth of the last statement —it was but an *omniumgatherum* for Whigs and Know-Nothings.[23] The *New Hampshire Patriot and Gazette,* a paper with a long tradition of virulent journalism, found that the decision made "Black Republicanism" unconstitutional. "It utterly demolishes the whole black republican platform and stamps it as directly antagonistical to the constitution. . . . This is the end of the matter. . . . That decision must be carried into effect—that interpretation must be acquiesced in and acted upon, *or* else it must be resisted by force." Its Washington correspondent commented on the fact that "Mr. Justice Curtis is no longer regarded by the freedom-shriekers as a *dough face per se,* but as a respectable gentleman, whose opinions are entitled to *considerable* weight upon grave constitutional questions." [24] It was soon addressing its opponents as "Ye generation of vipers" and urging them to clean their own houses of anti-Negro legislation before they turned to do good elsewhere.[25] The hypocrisy of abolitionist Congressmen Chaffee, Mrs. Emerson's second husband, was beyond its comprehension.[26]

A large section of the press took a moderate stand and deplored the "folly, treason and rebellion" counseled by some of the anti-slavery papers "stunned by these late tremendous blows from the Supreme Court." [27] But these were not the days for the *Times,* the *National Intelligencer* or *Harper's Weekly.* It was the heyday of the *Tribune,* the *Independent* and the *Charleston Mercury,* and the case, complex in itself, was shrouded in a fog of hysteria and calculated falsehood.

The ministry divided along the same lines as the press. Montgomery Blair told McLean that he had had the pleasure of rehearing the judge's opinion read "even in the house of God . . . and its exalted and Christian spirit made it worthy of meditation even there." [28] The St. Louis *Evening News* commented that "The recent Dred Scott decision of the Supreme Court has roused the lately torpid Northern pulpit into a factitious frenzy on the stale Negro question, and incited the preachers to a fresh crusade against the Judges." Outstanding for his attacks was the Reverend William B. Cheever, who urged rebellion against the decision as a Christian duty "like a regular Vesuvius, whose hebdomadal

163

eruptions the curiosity seekers of New York . . . flock to witness." [29] The Reverend Samuel Nott, after a reasonable discussion of the opinion of the Court, asked the still unsolved question, "Shall they [the slaves] be set free with full liberty to flood the North? Alas!" he pointed out, "it is one thing to denounce slavery, and another thing to receive the freed slaves with mutual advantages; one thing to keep up an outcry against the 'peculiar institution' of the South, and another to accept multitudes of African freemen as the new 'institution' of the North." [30] The Reverend James T. Brooke expressed concern over "the almost universal and contemptuous repudiation" of the decision by the Republican Party. He regarded it as "a sad indication of that disregard to constitutional obligations and judicial authority which, if not revolutionary in itself, is certainly so in its tendency." [31] After citing the laws of Ohio, Illinois, Indiana and Connecticut which had discriminated, or still did, against free Negroes and the opinions of Attorneys-General Wirt and Cushing on their status, Doctor Brooke wished to know "What ground is there, then, in view of such antecedents, to denounce the late decision of the Supreme Court as a kind of barbaric novelty, and the modern offspring of prejudiced and partisan judges?" [32]

The press and the clergy were not outdone by the politicians. The decision necessitated certain adjustments on the part of many, adjustments that were to prove quite painful to the persons involved and to the country at large. If, as Greeley had said, the Republican Party "must make a successful stand just here—in resistance to the assumed right of Congress to uphold, recognize, or in any manner legalize slavery in a Territory," then its central position had been seriously jeopardized by the decision, and the Republican cry of "So far, but no further," so far as slavery in the territories was concerned, lost legal meaning. Congress, according to the Supreme Court, had no power to prohibit at least one of the "two relics of barbarism—polygamy and slavery"—there.[33] The new-born party could either go out of existence, hope for a reversal of the decision, or reject the decision as no decision at all, insisting on regarding that part of it which concerned the power of Congress in the territories as *obiter dictum*. Most of its members chose the third alternative. In this they were supported by Benton, who considered it "a grave judicial solecism to try a man when the same court had decided he was not before it," the stand already taken by Judge Curtis.[34] The former Senator, after his unsuccessful campaign for the governorship of Missouri in 1856, was now engaged on his *Abridgement of the Debates of Congress*, having completed his autobiographical *Thirty Years' View*. The position taken by six members of the Court, that Congress had no power to prohibit slavery in the territories of the United States, contradicted the main thesis of his book, which was directed against the now dead Calhoun and all his works and pomps. In Benton's opinion, the Court "hunted for errors by virtue of a rule which did not apply, made a bridge to get from a case of personal rights to a question of political power; acted without necessity in a case of no consequence to the parties involved in a different case dreadfully momentous to the public." [35]

This became a staple argument for those who wished to talk the decision out of existence. One of the more celebrated attacks on the Court, that of Seward in the Senate on March 3, 1858, made good use of it, working up slowly to this point, prefacing it with the charge that the decision was the result of a pro-slavery conspiracy in which the prime movers were Buchanan and Taney. Lincoln was to add Pierce and Douglas.[36] "Before coming into office," Seward asserted, with more truth than he was aware of, "he [Buchanan] approached or was approached by the Supreme Court of the United States. On their docket was, through some chance or design, an action which an obscure Negro man in Missouri had brought for his freedom against his reputed master." [37] The Court, he went on, "had arrived at the conclusion, on solemn argument, that insomuch as this unfortunate Negro had, through some ignorance or chicane in special pleading, admitted what could not have been proved, that he had descended from some African who had once been held in bondage, and that therefore he was not, in view of the Constitution, a citizen of the United States, and therefore could not implead the reputed master in the Federal Courts; and in this ground the Supreme Court were prepared to dismiss the action, for want of jurisdiction over the suitor's person." [38] The case in the Supreme Court turned on the freedom of the Scotts primarily and only secondarily on their citizenship.

Seward, elaborating on his wrong opinion of what the Court had done and decided, remarked that a dismissal of the case for lack of jurisdiction on the grounds that Negroes were not citizens of the United States was repugnant to the Declaration of Independence and the spirit of the Constitution. Yet he would have preferred such a solution to what was done. To decide that the Scotts had no standing in the Federal courts would have exhausted the political possibilities of the case and this, according to Seward, was not regarded by the judges as desirable. Scott's counsel, he continued, who "had volunteered from motives of charity, and ignorant of course of the disposition that was to be made of the case," had argued that their client was free by reason of the Missouri Compromise Act. Opposing counsel, "paid by the defending slaveholder," claimed that this prohibition was unconstitutional. The Court seized upon "this extraneous and idle forensic discussion" and, in an effort to please the incoming President, pronounced an opinion that the act was void. That Montgomery Blair and George T. Curtis offered their services gratis, as Seward stated, is true. So did Reverdy Johnson.[39] But that they were naive enough to discuss the constitutionality of the Missouri Compromise Act, involving the most agitated question then before the country, the power of Congress over slavery in the territories, before the highest court in the land, under the impression they were indulging in idle declamation, is to make them ridiculous. Fortunately, the motives of these two well-known practitioners before the Supreme Court are known. Both Blair and Curtis were interested, and deeply so, in the question of the power of Congress over what Henry James termed "the cherished idiosyncrasy of one half of the country" and its extension into the territories. It was on this question that the Blair family had broken with the Democratic Party and it was to discuss this precise point that Curtis came into the case.[40] The Court did not seize upon the question at all, as Seward charged. It had decided to avoid it, leading McLean's friend, James Harvey, to call the judges "artful dodgers," [41] when it was brought to a decision by the action of the two dissenters in the case, McLean and Curtis, and by the pressure brought to bear on it by Buchanan and, through Wayne, it seems probable, of Alexander Stephens.[42]

Seward now became dramatic. "The day of inauguration came," he orated, "the first one among all the celebrations of that great national pageant to be desecrated by a coalition between the executive and judicial departments to undermine the National Legislature and the liberties of the people. The President, attended by the usual lengthened procession, arrived and took his seat on the portico. The Supreme Court attended him there, in robes which yet exacted public reverence. The people, unaware of the import of the whisperings carried on between the President and the Chief Justice, and imbued with veneration for both, filled the avenues and gardens as far away as the eye could reach. The President addressed them in words as bland as those which the worst of all the Roman Emperors pronounced when he assumed the purple. He announced (vaguely, indeed, but with self-satisfaction) the forthcoming extra-judicial exposition of the Constitution, and pledged his submission to it as authoritative and final. The Chief Justice and his associates remained silent. . . . The pageant ended. On the 5th of March the judges, without even exchanging their silken robes for courtiers' gowns, paid their salutations to the President in the Executive Palace. Doubtless the President received them as graciously as Charles I did the judges who had, at his instance, subverted the statutes of English liberty." Seward's picturesque description would be well received in New England and the Connecticut Reserve, but, since the people had just decided that their liberties were safer with the Democratic Party than with his own and since the President could safely presume that he had been elected by a majority that agreed with him, Seward's quasi-erudite references are beside the point. That the robes of the justices still exacted public reverence was through no fault of Seward and his colleagues in the Free-Soil movement who had been engaged for a number of years in a campaign to slander and slang the court at every opportunity.[43] It can seriously be doubted that Buchanan and Taney discussed the Dred Scott case on the portico for the very simple reason, if for no other, that they did not have to. The President was aware of what the disposition of the case would be from Catron's rather obviously obscure letter and Grier's quite open discussion of the case after his conference with Taney and Wayne.[44] Buchanan had only arrived in Washington the night before the inauguration and, since he and Taney had known one another for years, it is quite probable that they merely exchanged greetings.

Seward closed his attack on the decision by reiterating the Curtis-Benton charge that the decision, beyond the point of jurisdiction, was *obiter dictum* and by an inaccurate account of Dred's subsequent life. "Dred Scott," he said, "who had played the hand of *dummy* in this interesting political game, unwittingly, yet to the complete satisfaction of his adversary, was voluntarily emancipated; and thus received from his master, as a reward, the freedom which the court had denied him as a right."[45]

Some eight days later, Judah Benjamin, the Senator from Louisiana, replied to Seward and defended the Court and the decision. In the course of the same debate on the Lecompton Constitution during which Seward had attacked the court, Benjamin interrupted his speech on that issue. He had a duty to perform, he told the Senate, for, as a member of its Judiciary Committee, he felt it incumbent on himself to answer the charges brought against the Supreme Court, charges that disregarded "truth and decency." To Benjamin, the question appeared to be whether it lay in the competency of Congress to exclude slavery from the territories of the United States. The court affirmed that it did not and in this decision he agreed. "The radical, fundamental error which underlies the argument in affirmation of this power," he asserted, "is the assumption that slavery is the creature of the statute law of the several States where it is established; that it has no existence outside the limits of those States; that slaves are not property beyond those limits; and that property in slaves is neither recognized nor protected by the Constitution of the United States, nor by international law." [46] Benjamin proceeded to controvert these positions. He commenced with a long review of the history of modern slavery pointing out that, prior to 1606, the date of the first permanent English settlement in this country, the slave trade had been inaugurated in England, that Queen Elizabeth was a slave-holder, that the Stuarts had encouraged slavery and the trade, and that legislation on the part of the colonies to lessen this evil had been disallowed by the King in Council. The common law of the American colonies, he continued, at the time of the Revolution, regarded the Negro as "merchandise . . . property . . . a slave" and held that "he could only extricate himself from that status, stamped upon him by the common law of the country, by positive proof of manumission. No man was bound to show title to his Negro slave, but, the slave was bound to show manumission under which he had acquired his freedom, by the common law of every colony." Slavery, then, he said, was the creature of the common law, of custom, and it was universal in all the colonies. Slavery did not require statutory enactment to exist, but freedom did. "How came they free States? Did not they have this institution of slavery imprinted upon them by the power of the mother country? How did they get rid of it? All, all must admit that they had to pass positive acts of legislation to accomplish this purpose. Without that legislation they would

168

still be slave States. What, then, becomes of the pretext that slavery only exists in those States where it was established by positive legislation, that it has no inherent vitality out of those states, and that slaves are not considered as property by the Constitution of the United States." [47]

After a review of the English slave cases, Benjamin came to the decision of Lord Mansfield in the Somerset Case, remarking that it was not until 1771 that "the spirit of fanaticism . . . finally operated on Lord Mansfield, who . . . subverted the common law of England by judicial legislation . . . I say it not on my own authority . . . Lord Mansfield felt it. The case was argued before him over and over again, and he begged the parties to compromise . . . but the parties said no . . . and then . . . Lord Mansfield mustered up courage to say . . . that there was no law in England affording the master control over his slave." Benjamin found support for these charges against the opinion of Mansfield in the opinion of Lord Stowell in the case of the Slave Grace, unaware of the fact that he could have found it in Mansfield's own decision in the case of the King v. the Inhabitants of Thames Ditton. [48] Senator Collamer, of Vermont, Benjamin continued, had argued that a man cannot have title in property where the law does not give him a remedy by which he can assert that right, an argument Benjamin considered fallacious and resting on "the old confusion of ideas which considers a man's right and his remedy to be one and the same thing." Stowell and Story, Benjamin pointed out, both agreed that a slave did not cease to be his master's property on free soil, be it the soil of England or Massachusetts. His master only lost control of him in such places, "not by reason of the cessation of his property, but because those States grant no remedy to the master by which he can exercise control." [49]

The Senator then took up the question of jurisdiction, asking the Senate if that body wished to hear him read the charges of Seward, Fessenden, of Maine, and Collamer that the Court had decided that it had no jurisdiction and then went on to discuss the merits of the case as if it had. Fessenden interrupted. He explained that he was unable to recall the precise words he had used, but he was quite clear about the thought which he had wished to convey. He had intended to allude only to the opinion of the Court, not to those of the individual judges, in which the first point decided was that the circuit court had no jurisdiction because the plaintiff, having no standing in court, could not sue

169

and, as a result of this reasoning, they should, in Fessenden's opinion, have dismissed the question. He had not said that the judges themselves had admitted that they had no jurisdiction. Benjamin then described Fessenden as saying that, although the Supreme Court decided it had jurisdiction, it was wrong in his opinion. Fessenden retorted that that was not what he had said. Benjamin wished to know how it could be otherwise. Turning to the rest of the Senate, he said, "The Supreme Court of the United States was the only tribunal to determine in the last resort whether it had jurisdiction or not over the question. It determined that it had . . . the Senator [Fessenden] says that by the time they had got through stating the first half of their opinion, he has a right to shut their mouths." Benjamin closed his remarks on the decision with a reference to Seward's charge of conspiracy, pointing out that, if there was one, it was inspired by Free-Soilers since it had been brought to the Supreme Court by an anti-slavery lawyer, Roswell Field, and the subjects of the litigation were the property of an abolitionist congressman from Massachusetts, Calvin Chaffee. The Louisiana Senator apparently was unaware of the correspondence of Buchanan with Catron and Grier.[50]

The Senator most seriously hurt by the decision was Stephen A. Douglas, of Illinois. In addition to the hostility of the Buchanan administration, caused by his rejection of the Kansas Lecompton constitution, Douglas, soon to run for re-election to the Senate, was intellectually embarrassed by the opinions of the judges. According to the "Little Giant," the people's right to govern their own affairs was so basic to the American way of life that the inhabitants of a territory apparently possessed it the minute they had staked a claim. Let the people rule, he said over and over again, subject only to the Constitution of the United States. The Supreme Court had decided that, in the light of the Constitution, slavery in the territories was not under the control of Congress, that that body could not prohibit a slave-owner from taking his slave into the territories and, if it attempted to do so, its action was void. If Congress could not so act, how could a territorial legislature act? If a territorial legislature could not act, what became of popular sovereignty, what became of Douglas?

The Senator spoke publicly on this question for the first time on June 12, 1857, when he addressed the Grand Jury at Springfield, Illinois, at their request, on the state of the Union. He commenced by defending the Court. The judges, he declared, had not gone out of their way to decide all the questions they had touched upon and it was his opinion that, if the Court had availed itself of a technicality to avoid the main issues presented by the case and counsel, chiefly the power of Congress over slavery in the territories, the outcry against it would have been much worse. He then outlined his own solution by which the decision and popular sovereignty were to be reconciled. The Court, he said, had decided that a master could bring his slave into a territory and Congress could not prohibit the master from so doing, a right Douglas conceded. But, he continued, "While the right continues in full force under the guarantee of the Constitution, and cannot be divested or alienated by an act of Congress, it necessarily remains a barren and worthless right, unless sustained, protected and enforced by appropriate police regulations and local legislation, prescribing adequate remedies for its violation. These regulations and remedies must necessarily depend entirely on the will and wishes of the people of the territory, as they can only be prescribed by the local legislatures. Hence the great principle of popular sovereignty . . . is sustained and firmly established by the authority of the decision." [51] He then devoted the rest of his remarks to the questions of Negro citizenship and equality, stressing this portion of Taney's opinion. He was against both. Early in his campaign for re-election to the Senate, Douglas introduced the issue he was to stress all through it and on which he was to win over Lincoln, the question of Negro equality.[52]

Four days later, Lincoln addressed the State Republican Convention at Springfield which had just nominated him to run against Douglas. It was his opinion that agitation of the slavery question would never cease till some crisis had been reached and passed. Seeing that "A house divided against itself cannot stand," slavery would either be abolished or it would spread all over the Union. Lincoln saw a tendency to the latter alternative in "that now almost complete legal combination—a piece of machinery, so to speak—compounded of the Nebraska Doctrine and the Dred Scott decision. Let him [the listener] consider not only what work the machinery is adapted to do, and how well adapted; but also let him consider the history of the construction, and trace, if he can, or rather fail, if he can, to trace the evidence of design and concert of action among its chief architects, from the beginning." Lincoln then pointed out the connection, in his mind, between the Kansas-Nebraska Act, with its doctrine of popular sovereignty, the election of Buchanan and the delivery of the Dred Scott decision. The first move, the introduction of the idea of non-intervention on the part of Congress in the matter of slavery in the territories, was made by Douglas with his Kansas Bill. This doctrine was used to carry an election, Buchanan's, and to secure the appearance of a popular mandate. Then came the decision by which, according to Lincoln, "squatter sovereignty squatted out of existence, tumbled down like temporary scaffolding—like the mold at a foundry, served through one blast and fell back into loose sand." The several points of the decision, in conjunction with Douglas's assertion that he cared not whether slavery was voted up or down, constituted, Lincoln claimed, "the piece of machinery in its present state of advancement." By the decision, Negroes were excluded from citizenship and reduced to a permanently inferior class with no standing in the Federal courts, neither Congress nor a territorial legislature could exclude slavery from a territory, and, thirdly, questions of freedom were relegated to State courts. The next step, according to Lincoln, would be a decision by the Court that no State could exclude slavery from its borders, a step not to be taken immediately but to be made later. He admitted that it was not possible to know absolutely that these steps, the Kansas Bill, the election of Buchanan, the decision, the endorsement of the decision by Douglas, Pierce and Buchanan, were the result of design but, he went on, "When we see a lot of framed timbers, different portions of which have been gotten out at different times and places and by different workmen —Stephen, Franklin, Roger and James, for instance—and we see these timbers joined together . . . or, if a single piece be lacking, we see the place in the frame exactly fitted and prepared yet to bring such a piece in—in such a case we find it impossible not to believe that Stephen and Franklin and Roger and James all understood one another from the beginning, and all worked upon a common plan or draft before the first blow was struck." [53] The "place in the frame exactly fitted and prepared," by which slavery was to be made nationally legal, Lincoln found in the words of Justice Nelson, who had said that the law of a State is supreme over slavery within its jurisdiction "except in cases where the power is restrained by the Constitution of the United States." [54]

For the rest of the campaign, at Chicago, at Bloomington, at Springfield again, at Clinton, at Ottawa, Douglas and Lincoln continued to refine on the two speeches they had made at the beginning of their famous struggle at Springfield. At Ottawa, Lincoln modified his conspiracy charge. His main object in making it at Springfield, he said, "was to show . . . what I believed was the truth—that there was a tendency, if not a conspiracy, among those who have engineered this slavery question for the last four or five years, to make slavery perpetual and universal in this nation." [55] At Freeport, Lincoln asked Douglas to answer several questions, the second of which was: "Can the people of a United States Territory, in any lawful way, against the wish of any citizen of the United States, exclude slavery from its limits prior to the formation of a State Constitution?" The reply to this question, which Dogulas pointed out Lincoln had heard him make a hundred times from every stump in Illinois, was to become known as Douglas's Freeport Doctrine. It was but a rephrasing of the words he had spoken when he addressed the Grand Jury at Springfield. "It matters not," he said, "what way the Supreme Court may hereafter decide as to the abstract question whether slavery may or may not go into a Territory under the Constitution, the people have the lawful means to introduce it or exclude it as they please, for the reason that slavery cannot exist a day or an hour anywhere unless it is supported by the local police regulations. Those police regulations can only be established by the local legislature, and if the people are opposed to slavery they will elect representatives to that body who will by unfriendly legislation effectually prevent the introduction of it in their midst. If, on the contrary, they are for it, their legislation will favor its extension. Hence, no matter what the decision of the Supreme Court may be on the abstract question, still the right of the people to make a slave Territory or a free Territory is perfect and complete under the Nebraska Bill." [56]

Lincoln discussed this Freeport Doctrine at Jonesboro in "darkest Egypt," as Southern Illinois was known. In the first place, he said, "the Supreme Court of the United States has decided that any congressional prohibition of slavery in the Territories is unconstitutional—they have reached this proposition as a conclusion from their former proposition, that the Constitution of the United States expressly recognizes property in slaves; and from that other constitutional provision, that no person shall be deprived of property without due process of law. Hence they reach the conclusion that as the Constitution of the United States expressly recognizes property in slaves, and prohibits any person

173

from being deprived of property without due process of law, to pass an act of Congress by which a man who owned a slave on one side of a line would be deprived of him if he took him on the other side is depriving him of property without due process of law." How, then, Lincoln asked, could slavery be excluded from a territory without violating that decision? Before the decision, he continued, Douglas said it was for the Supreme Court to decide the question of slavery in the territories, while, after the decision, he said it was for the people of the territory. Lincoln could not see how this position could be sustained, since the Constitution guaranteed the right of property in slaves in the territories, according to the judges, and the members of the territorial legislature were under oath to support the Constitution. Could they refuse to protect slave property without violating their oaths? In the event they did, would not Congress be bound to respect the right of the slave owner and disallow the territorial legislation? Lincoln closed by asking Douglas if he would vote for a congressional slave code for the territories, a new southern demand.[57]

Douglas's doctrine of unfriendly local legislation, Lincoln surmised, would be as unpalatable south of the Ohio as his own Republican position. This thought may have occurred to Douglas also and he decided to make a trip through the South, which, in addition to being a pleasant way to return to Washington, would also give him a chance to test the southern reaction to his theory. Before leaving Illinois, he made his position on the question at issue clear in the Chicago *Times*. The Senator, the Douglas organ announced, supported the Dred Scott decision in the sense that it sought to assure the owners of slaves of equality with the owners of other property. If, after being placed on equality with other property, slaves required "higher and further affirmative legislation for its protection and security than is afforded to other property" and the territorial legislature should not accord it, that would be a "misfortune attending that description of property for which the Democratic party have no remedy and are not responsible." This was as far as the Democracy of Illinois would go and it would strenuously oppose a congressional slave code for a territory.[58]

Southern reaction was not long delayed in coming. Jefferson Davis, whom Douglas had quoted as an authority for his opinion that slavery, to exist, needed friendly legislation, promptly branded this position as heresy in a speech before the Mississippi

Legislature on Nov. 16, 1858.[59] On his arrival back in Washington, Douglas discovered that he had lost the chairmanship of the Committee on Territories, a post he had held for eleven years, and that his removal was not unconnected with his interpretation of the decision.[60] The opening oratorical shot against him was fired by Senator Albert G. Brown, of Mississippi, who expressed a common southern resentment against Douglas—having won in the Supreme Court, they would not be deprived of their victory by his logic chopping. The Constitution, as expounded by the Supreme Court, the Senator declared, awarded the right of protection to the slave-owner for his property in the territories and this the South demanded, this it meant to have. Some, he continued, contended that the right depended on action by the territorial legislature, a contention that confused power and right. "What I want to know," he asked, "is whether you will interpose against power and in favor of right? If the Territorial Legislature refuses to act, will you act? If it passes laws hostile to slavery, will you annul them and substitute laws favoring slavery in their stead?" If Congress did not so act, he concluded, the Union had become a despotism and he was for leaving it.[61] Mason, of Virginia, wished to know how a territorial legislature, a creature of Congress, could possess more power than its creator. If Congress could not prohibit slavery in the territories, how could a body created by Congress? [62] The demands of the south, the platform they wished adopted at the Charleston Convention to be held in April, 1860, were phrased as resolutions and introduced into the Senate by Davis. Of these, the one on which Douglas and the Democratic party split, declared that "neither Congress nor a Territorial Legislature, whether by indirect legislation or legislation of an indirect and unfriendly character, possesses power to annul or to impair the Constitutional right of any citizen to take his slave property into the common Territory and there hold and enjoy the same while the Territorial condition remains." Davis followed this with a demand that the Federal government act to protect such property, in substance a request for a congressional slave code, basing his position on that portion of the Dred Scott decision which invoked the Fifth Amendment to the Constitution to protect slave owners in the territories.[63] The south regarded such a device as unfriendly local legislation an effort to cheat it of its rights. With the split in the Democratic ranks, the election of Lincoln followed and with it the split of the Union. As Aristotle had remarked, "If a constitution is to survive, all the elements of the state must join in willing its existence and its continuance." The south no longer so willed.

While the halls of Congress rang with denunciations and defenses of the judges and with interpretations and counter-interpretations of their decision, the occasion of all this oratory, Dred Scott, was again in court. Alexander Sanford and his son, John, were dead; their logical successor in seeing to the interests of Emerson's widow and daughter, Henrietta, and in acting for them was Calvin Chaffee, the husband of Irene Emerson and the step-father of her daughter. He was considerably embarrassed by the role he was called upon to fill. The abolitionist Congressman did the best he could by writing a letter to the Springfield *Republican,* a letter which was later republished in various Republican papers. He felt that he had "lived to little purpose, if, after more than twenty years' service in the Anti-Slavery cause, it is now necessary that I should put in a formal disclaimer of my own participation in the sin and crime of slave-holding." But, for the benefit of those who were not too well aware of his beliefs and actions, he would declare, seemingly unaware of the death of his brother-in-law, that the only person in the Scott case "who had or has any power in the matter was and is" the defendant, Sanford. Neither he nor any member of his family, he continued, were consulted about the case or even knew of its existence till after it was noticed for trial. He promised his readers, apparently now aware of John Sanford's death, that, "if in the distribution of the estate, of which the decision affirms these human beings to be a part, it appears that I or mine consent to receive any part of the *thirty pieces of silver,* then, and not till then, let the popular judgment, as well as the public press" condemn him.[64] He then transferred the ownership of the Scotts, for a nominal sum, to Taylor Blow, the third son of Dred's original owner, Peter Blow, who on May 26, 1857, manumitted the Scott family, the papers being drawn by Abra Crane, before Judge Hamilton who had inherited the case from Judge Krum ten years before.[65]

Dred was now employed as a porter at Theron Barnum's Hotel at Second and Walnut Streets in St. Louis, enjoying, in his own way his national celebrity. At Mrs. Barnum's request, his portrait was painted by Louis Schultze, and, after some difficulty, the whole family were persuaded to have their pictures taken by Fitzgibbon, of St. Louis, for *Frank Leslie's Illustrated Newspaper.*[66] But, after a year of freedom, Dred, on September 17, 1858, succumbed to

176

rapid consumption and was buried in the Wesleyan Cemetery. Harriet followed soon after.[67] Eliza and Lizzie were the only ones of the little family who could have witnessed the scene at which the affairs of John Sanford in Missouri were finally settled. On March 30, 1859, the administrator's sale of his slaves, by public auction, took place on the east porch of the courthouse in St. Louis, looking over toward the Illinois shore. There, at twelve noon, "Fanny, with child," was sold to John R. Thompson for eight hundred and fifty dollars, Lucy was bid in for the same sum by James Ruppell, while William H. Smith bought Josephine and William for seven hundred dollars apiece.[68]

Several years later, only Lizzie, now Mrs. Henry Madison, was left to read or hear read "The Ordinance Abolishing Slavery in Missouri," a decree that was largely the work of one of her father's lawyers, Charles D. Drake, in which it was "ordained by the people of the State of Missouri in Convention assembled that hereafter in this State there shall be neither slavery nor unvoluntary servitude, except in punishment of crime . . . and all persons held to service or labor as slaves, are hereby DECLARED FREE." [69]

NOTES

1. Records, United States Supreme Court, "Dred Scott vs. Sandford" [sic]; Dred Scott Collection. According to Judge Treat, the original judgment was still, in 1894, in the United States Circuit Court and no mandate was ever issued, "supposedly because never called for." He also stated that the costs were never paid (Notes appended to a letter from Catron to Treat, May 31, 1857, Treat Papers, Missouri Historical Society, St. Louis, Mo.). The costs in the Supreme Court of the United States were paid by Gamaliel Bailey, who solicited seventy-five Republican members of Congress for two dollars each to meet the bill which came to one hundred and fifty-four dollars and sixty-eight cents. He himself contributed the four dollars and sixty-eight cents still needed (Gamaliel Bailey to Lyman Trumbull, May 12, 1857, Lyman Trumbull Papers, Library of Congress).

2. Curtis, *Memoir*, I, p. 211.

3. *National Intelligencer*, April 2, 1857.

4. Records, United States Supreme Court, "Dred Scott vs. Sandford" [sic].

5. Washington *Union*, March 18, 1857.

6. St. Louis *Leader*, March 23, 1857.

7. *National Intelligencer*, April 2, 1857, citing the New York *Journal of Commerce* for March 29, 1857.

8. Curtis, *Memoir*, I, p. 212.

9. *Ibid*. It was the practice of the clerk to prepare printed copies of all the opinions of the judges, filed in his office, before their publication by the official reporter of the Court.

10. Curtis, *Memoir*, I, p. 212.

11. *Ibid*., p. 216.

12. James Harvey to John McLean, April 3, 1857, McLean Papers, Library of Congress.

13. Curtis, *Memoir,* I, pp. 213-215.

14. *Ibid.,* p. 218. Justice Curtis added a note to this statement to the effect that Charles Curtis had applied to him for a copy of Taney's opinion and that he had replied that he did not know how his relative and associate could get one. The latter had then informed him that Carroll, the court clerk, had told him he could have one for sixty dollars.

15. "All the opinions delivered by the court since the commencement of the term [January 7, 1835] shall be forthwith delivered over to the court to be recorded. And all opinions here after delivered by the court shall immediately on the delivery thereof be in like manner delivered over to the clerk to be recorded."

16. Curtis, *Memoir,* I, pp. 217-221.

17. *National Intelligencer,* May 27, 1857.

18. Curtis, *Memoir,* I, pp. 221-225.

19. *Ibid.,* pp. 226-228. The late Professor Frank H. Hodder attributes to Curtis the major share of the responsibility for the decision as it was given. Summarily, Hodder says that Curtis, already having made his mind up to retire from the bench because of the inadequacy of the salary and to return to the practice of law in Massachusetts, felt the need of rehabilitating himself in the eyes of the citizens of that state who regarded him, because of his stand on the Fugitive Slave Law, as a "slave catcher." As a gesture to public opinion, then, Curtis gave his lengthy opinion in the Dred Scott case (Frank H. Hodder, "Some Phases of the Dred Scott Case," *Mississippi Valley Historical Review,* XVI [1929-1930], pp. 3-22). This idea, which had been developed at some length by Otto Gresham (*The Dred Scott Case,* Chicago: Barnard and Miller, 1908, pp. 16-20), fails to take into account the facts that Curtis was a follower of Webster and a strong Union man and that his views were characteristic of the conservative Whig opinion of Massachusetts. That the judge's views happened, at this juncture, to coincide with his interests is no reason to attribute to him a purely personal reason. Justice Curtis had already resisted public opinion when he thought it proper to do so.

20. Curtis, *Memoir,* I, pp. 228-229. Justice Curtis added several notes to this correspondence in one of which he says that Taney added, to his recollection, more than eighteen pages to his opinion (*ibid.,* pp. 229-230). According to his brother, George T. Curtis, the judge's resignation from the bench was, primarily, the inadequacy of the salary but, secondarily, "he no longer felt that confidence in the Supreme Court which was essential to its useful cooperation with its members, and with which he certainly began his connection with it." George Curtis stressed that the correspondence with Taney, given above, had nothing to do with his brother's determination, his mind having been made up before it started (*ibid.,* p. 243).

21. New York *Tribune,* March 7, 1857.

22. *Ibid.,* March 17, 1857. The press reaction to the decision has been ably treated by Warren, *The Supreme Court in United States History,* II, pp. 300-319. Taney's connection with Baltimore banks is treated in Swisher, *Roger B. Taney,* pp. 267-270.

23. Washington *Daily Union,* March 11, 12, 19, April 7, 1857. On the composition of the opposition to the decision, Taney wrote in a similar vein to Pierce: "You will see I am passing through another conflict much like the one which followed the removal of the deposits, and the war is being waged on me in the same spirit and by many of the same men who distinguished themselves on that occasion by the unscrupulous means to which they resorted" (Taney to Franklin Pierce, August 29, 1857, *American Historical Review,* X [1904-1905], p. 359).

24. *New Hampshire Patriot and Gazette,* March 18, 1857.

25. *Ibid.,* April 29, 1857.

26. *Ibid.,* June 3, 1857. Cf., p. 76, above, for Congressman Chaffee's connection with the Scotts.

27. New York *Herald,* March 7, 1857.

28. Montgomery Blair to John McLean, March 8, 1857, McLean Papers, Library of Congress.

29. St. Louis *Evening News,* March 20, April 15, 1857.

30. Samuel Nott, *Slavery and the Remedy; or, Principles and Suggestions for a Remedial Code* (Boston: Crocker and Brewster, 1857, 6th ed.), p. 135. Dr. Nott sent a copy of this edition of his pamphlet to Taney, which drew from Taney a letter of thanks and some interesting private opinions of his on slavery. "Every intelligent person," the Chief Justice said, "whose life has been passed in a slave-holding State, and who has carefully observed the character and capacity of the African race, will see that a general and sudden emancipation would be absolute ruin to the Negroes, as well as to the white population." As for himself, he went on, he was not a slave-holder and more than thirty years had passed since he had manumitted every slave he owned except two who were too old to provide for themselves when they became his property and whom he supported as long as they lived. He had never regretted emancipating the others who, by their actions, had proved worthy of their freedom (Roger B. Taney to Samuel Nott, August 19, 1857, *Proceedings of the Massachusetts Historical Society,* XII, 1871-1873, pp. 445-447).

31. James T. Brooke, *Short Notes on the Dred Scott Case* (Cincinnati: Moore, Wilstach, Keys and Co., 1861), p. 8.

32. *Ibid.,* pp. 8-9.

33. Republican Platform, 1856.

34. Thomas H. Benton, *Historical and Legal Examination of that part of . . . the Dred Scott Case Which Declares the Unconstitutionality of the Missouri Compromise Act, and the Self Extension of the Constitution to the Territories, Carrying Slavery Along with It* (New York: D. Appleton and Co., 1857), p. 8.

35. *Ibid.,* p. 12.

36. Seward's speech can be found in the *Congressional Globe,* 35 Congress, 1 Session, pp. 939-945. Lincoln's version on the conspiracy can be found in John G. Nicolay and John Hay (eds.), *Complete Works of Abraham Lincoln* (New York: Lamb Publishing Co., 1905), III, pp. 2-12.

37. Cf., above, Chapter 3, pp. 23-25, and Chapter 5, pp. 53-58, for a correct account of these phases of the case. Mention should also be made of the willingness of Sanford to go through with the suit. According to "Inspector" in the New York *Morning Courier and Enquirer* for March 16, 1857, who says he had the story from one of Sanford's relatives, the latter did not wish to contest the case in the Federal court in Missouri and never "willingly consented to appeal in the Supreme Court (a step he could not prevent). Sanford, according to the same source, intended to emancipate the whole family and "was badgered" into fighting the case by people with a political, not personal, interest in it and who were interested in the extension of slavery. Sanford's relative, according to "Inspector," said the trial was the cause of his breakdown.

38. Cf., above, Chapters 4 and 5 for the deliberations of the Court.

39. Cf., above, Chapter 3, p. 26, Chapter 5, p. 50. Whether Geyer was paid or not is not clear. There is no mention of any settlement among Sanford's papers in the probate court files in St. Louis.

40. Cf., above, Chapter 4, pp. 37-38, and Chapter 5, pp. 47-48.

41. New York *Tribune,* May 14, 1856.

42. Cf., above, Chapter 5, pp. 53-58.

43. Warren, *The Supreme Court in United States History,* II, pp. 270-278.

44. Cf., above, Chapter 5, pp. 53-58.

45. *Congressional Globe,* 35 Congress, 1 Session, p. 941. For the careers of the Scotts, subsequent to the decision, cf. pp. 175-177.

46. *Ibid.,* p. 1066.

47. *Ibid.,* p. 1068.

48. Cf., above, Chapter 10, p. 146.

49. *Congressional Globe,* 35 Congress, 1 Session, p. 1069.

50. Cf., above, Chapter 5, pp. 53-58.

51. Stephen A. Douglas, *Remarks . . . on Kansas, Utah, and the Dred Scott Decision* (Chicago: Daily Times Book and Job Office, 1857), p. 6.

52. *Ibid.,* pp. 7-15.

53. Nicolay and Hay (eds.), *Complete Works of Abraham Lincoln,* III, pp. 1-15.

54. 19 Howard 461. Nelson's exact words are "subject only to such limitations as may be found in the Federal Constitution."

55. Nicolay and Hay (eds.), *Complete Works of Abraham Lincoln,* III, pp. 236-237.

56. *Ibid.,* pp. 297-298.

57. *Ibid.,* IV, pp. 56-67.

58. George F. Milton, *The Eve of Conflict* (Boston: Houghton Mifflin Co., 1934), p. 358, citing the Chicago *Times* for November 11, 1858.

59. Dunbar Rowland, *Jefferson Davis, Constitutionalist* (Jackson, Miss.: Mississippi Department of Archives and History, 1923), III, pp. 339-360.

60. Milton, *The Eve of Conflict,* p. 363.

61. *Congressional Globe,* 35 Congress, 2 Session, pp. 1241-1244.

62. *Ibid.,* p. 1248.

63. *Congressional Globe,* 36 Congress, 1 Session, p. 658.

64. New York *Tribune,* March 17, 1857, citing the Springfield (Mass.) *Republican* of March 14, 1857.

65. Scharf, *History of St. Louis City and County,* I, p. 596; *Frank Leslie's Illustrated Newspaper,* June 27, 1858; Records, St. Louis Circuit Court. This transference to Blow was necessary in order to conform to the Missouri emancipation laws.

66. "Dred Scott Eulogy" by J. Milton Turner, Ms., Missouri Historical Society, St. Louis, Mo. Cf. Irving Dillard, "Dred Scott Eulogised by James Milton Turner," *Journal of Negro History,* XXVI, 1941, pp. 1-11; *Frank Leslie's Illustrated Newspaper,* June 27, 1858. Dred also helped his wife with a laundry business she ran.

67. Unsigned Ms., T. H. Chamberlin Collection, Missouri Historical Society, St. Louis, Mo., Bryan, "The Blow Family." The Wesleyan Cemetery being abandoned, Taylor Blow, who had become a Catholic, had Dred's body removed, on November 27, 1867, to Calvary Cemetery (J. Hugo Grimm to Charles Van Ravenswaay, October 29, 1946, citing the records of Calvary Cemetery). Of the four sons of Peter Blow, three, Peter, Taylor, and William, were southern sympathizers during the Civil War. According to Mrs. William Blow, the firm of Charless, Blow and Co., which by this time consisted of her husband and her brother-in-law, Taylor (Joseph Charless having been murdered in 1859), was ruined by the activities of the Provost Marshall during the war. Taylor Blow went into bankruptcy in 1867 and died in 1868 (Notes taken in a conversation with Mrs. William T. Blow by Mary Louise Dalton, February 18, 1907, Bryan, "The Blow Family"). Henry T. Blow became a Republican in 1860 and was a prominent radical in Missouri. Frank Blair, Jr., gave an outline of the political tergiversations of Blow in a letter to the St. Louis *Union,* October 10, 1863.

68. "John F. A. Sanford," Files, Probate Court, St. Louis.

69. Copy of the ordinance in the Slavery Folder, Missouri Historical Society, St. Louis, Mo. Of the convention that framed the ordinance, Judge Napton commented, "Mr. Drake and—have the chief management—the members are unknown hitherto in this State" (William B. Napton, Diary, p. 223, Missouri Historical Society, St. Louis, Mo.).

APPENDIX

Various reasons have been assigned as to why suit was originally brought by or for Dred Scott. According to one account,
which appeared in the Springfield (Mass.) *Republican* for Feb. 12,
1903, on the death of Mrs. Emerson, then Mrs. Chaffee, that lady
was about to leave St. Louis for Springfield when Dred returned
to the city. She left him "practically free." A young lawyer saw a
chance to make some money out of Dred by having him declared
free and then bringing suit for fourteen years' wages. Dred, at this
time, had three hundred dollars. The lawyer was assured of a fee
no matter what happened. The article contains a number of in-
accuracies. But the account has, in common with two other ver-
sions, the clear assertion that there was a financial angle to the case
in the beginning.

An unsigned manuscript in the Thomas H. Chamberlin Collection of the Missouri Historical Society states that, shortly after
his return to St. Louis, Dred was approached by two lawyers, Burd
and Risk, "who were called the nigger lawyers," and urged to sue
for his freedom on the grounds of residence in a free state and territory. These lawyers, the account continues, appeared for Dred
in the St. Louis Circuit Court and were unsuccessful. The lawyer
who first appeared for Dred in 1846 was Francis Murdoch, who
did have a reputation for taking cases that involved Negroes.
The reference in this manuscript might possibly be to the suit
mentioned by Emerson in 1838.[1] Here, again, we have Dred being
approached by a lawyer, though no motive, from the evidence, can
be ascribed to Murdoch.

A sketch of Dred and his family that appeared in the St. Louis
Evening News for April 3, 1857, states that Dred, on his return
from the southwest, applied to Mrs. Emerson in order that he
might purchase the freedom of himself and his family. He offered
to pay part of the money down, the rest of which was to be guaranteed by "an eminent citizen of St. Louis, an officer in the Army."
Mrs. Emerson refused, and Dred, "being informed that he was
entitled to his freedom by the operation of the laws regulating the
Northwest Territory, forthwith brought suit for it." This article

was written by someone who knew Dred and, from the context, was based on an interview with him. It agrees with another interview of Dred which appeared in *Frank Leslie's Illustrated Newspaper* for June 27, 1857, in the statements which are common to both.

There have been other conjectures. Some credit the start of the suit to Frank or Montgomery Blair, but merely assert this opinion.[2] Others have suspected Thomas H. Benton.[3] These efforts to find a political motive for the suit at its origin are interesting, particularly in view of the politics of the lawyers involved in the suit as friends of Mrs. Emerson or of Dred. Goode, Drake, and Bay are names with political connotations. Goode represents an extreme southern viewpoint on slavery; Drake was, later, a bitter Republican; Bay, who was to die soon, was a close follower of Benton. While their personal persuasions may account for their interest in the case, no evidence of a political cast to it can be found.

One fact that must be accounted for in any discussion of the case is the constant appearance of some member of the Blow family at every stage of its progress, except the actual inception of the suit. A possible version might be as follows. Dred, having saved some money and having secured the interest and patronage of an army officer whom he had met in his military sojournings, applied to Mrs. Emerson to purchase his own and his family's freedom. She refused. Dred's case became known to a lawyer interested in such suits for humanitarian or financial reasons or both. Realizing that Dred had a good case, he brought suit. The case moved slowly. Dred appealed to the sons of his old master, the Blows, for help. The original lawyer, Murdoch, dropped out, and, through the Blows, their brother-in-law, Charles Drake, took over the case and did the initial investigation. When the case was to be tried in court, he secured the aid of A. P. Field, a lawyer who was "great in all that class of cases which sounded in damages."[4] Drake left St. Louis in 1847, shortly after the death of his wife, Martha Blow Drake, and did not return until 1850, which explains why he did not continue with the case.[5]

NOTES

1. Cf., above, p. 6.
2. Otto Gresham, *The Dred Scott Case* (Chicago: Barnard and Miller, 1908), p. 3.
3. James M. Breckenridge, *William Clark Breckenridge, His Life, Lineage and Writings* (St. Louis: Published by the Author, 1932), pp. 200-201.

4. Frederick C. Pierce, *Field Genealogy* (Chicago: W. B. Conkey Co., 1901), II, pp. 1123-1126.

5. William Hyde and Howard L. Conard (eds.), *Encyclopedia of the History of St. Louis* (New York: Southern History Co., 1899), I, p. 588.

BIBLIOGRAPHY

PRIMARY SOURCES

Bates, Edward, *Diary*, Missouri Historical Society, St. Louis, Mo.
Jeremiah S. Black Papers, Library of Congress.
Blair Papers, Library of Congress.
James Buchanan Papers, Pennsylvania Historical Society, Philadelphia, Pa.
Thomas H. Chamberlin Collection, Missouri Historical Society, St. Louis, Mo.
The Congressional Globe.
The Congressional Record.
Benjamin R. Curtis Papers, Library of Congress.
The Debates and Proceedings in the Congress of the United States; with an Appendix, Containing Important State Papers and Public Documents, and All the Laws of a Public Nature; with a Copious Index. Washington: Printed and Published by Gales and Seaton, 1855.
Thomas Ewing Papers, Library of Congress.
Duff Green, *Letterbook*, Library of Congress.
John McLean Papers, Library of Congress.
Manuscripts, State Department, National Archives.
William B. Napton, *Diary*, Missouri Historical Society, St. Louis, Mo.
Official Opinions of the Attorneys General.
Records, City Clerk's Office, Springfield, Mass.
Records, Probate Court, St. Louis, Mo.
Records, Supreme Court of the United States, Washington, D. C.
Records, War Department, National Archives.
Dred Scott Collection, Missouri Historical Society, St. Louis, Mo.
Slavery Folder, Missouri Historical Society, St. Louis, Mo.
Samuel Treat Papers, Missouri Historical Society, St. Louis, Mo.
Lyman Trumbull Papers, Library of Congress.
United States Reports.
Martin Van Buren Papers, Library of Congress.

NEWSPAPERS

Daily Missouri Democrat
Frank Leslies' Illustrated Newspaper

185

National Intelligencer
New Hampshire Patriot and Gazette
New York Courier and Enquirer
New York Tribune
Springfield (Mass.) Republican
St. Louis Daily New Era
St. Louis Evening News
St. Louis Herald
Tri-Weekly Missouri Republican
Washington Daily Union

Secondary Sources

Auchampaugh, Philip, "James Buchanan, The Court and the Dred Scott Case," *Tennessee Historical Magazine,* 9, (January, 1926), 231-240.

Barns, Chancy R., editor, *The Commonwealth of Missouri; a Centennial Record.* St. Louis: Bryan, Brand and Co., 1877. Pp. xxiv, 936.

Barns, Chancy Rufus, editor, *Switzler's Illustrated History of Missouri from 1541 to 1877.* St. Louis: C. R. Barns, 1879. Pp. xviii, 601.

Bay, W. V. N., *Reminiscences of the Bench and Bar of Missouri.* St. Louis: F. H. Thomas and Company, 1878. Pp. x, 611.

Beckwith, Paul, *Creoles of St. Louis.* Nixon-Jones Printing Co., 1893. Pp. 169.

[Benton, Thomas H.,] *Historical and Legal Examination of That Part of the Decision of the Supreme Court of the United States in the Dred Scott Case Which Declares the Unconstitutionality of the Missouri Compromise Act and the Self-Extension of the Constitution to Territories, Carrying Slavery Along with It.* By the Author of the "Thirty Years' View." New York: D. Appleton and Company, 1857. Pp. 193.

Benton, Thomas H., *Thirty Years' View.* New York, D. Appleton and Company, 1858. 2 vols.

Beveridge, Albert J., *Abraham Lincoln, 1809-1858.* Boston: Houghton Mifflin Company, 1928. 2 vols.

Bikle, Henry W., *The Constitutional Power of Congress over the Territory of the United States.* (University of Pennsylvania, Publications of the Department of Law.) Philadelphia: 1901. Pp. x, 120.

69th Congress, Session 2, House Document 783. *Biographical Directory of the American Congress: 1774-1927.* Washington: United States Printing Office, 1928. Pp. 1740.

Black, Jeremiah S., *Observations on Senator Douglas's Views of Popular Sovereignty, as Expressed in Harper's Magazine, for September, 1859.* 2nd ed., Washington: Thomas McGill, 1859. Pp. 24.

Blackstone, William, *Commentaries on the Laws of England. With Notes and Additions by Edward Christian.* 17th ed. London: Thomas Tagg, 1830. 4 vols.

Blaine, James G., *Twenty Years of Congress, from Lincoln to Garfield with a Review of the Events Which Led to the Political Revolution of 1860.* Norwich, Conn.: Henry Bill Publishing Company, 1884. 2 vols.

Blair, Montgomery, *Address to the Democracy of Missouri.* [n.p., n.d.]. Pp. 12.

Bodin, Jean, *Les Six Livres de la Republique.* [n.p.:] Gabriel Cartier, 1599. Pp. 1059.

Breckenridge, James M., *William Clark Breckenridge, His Life, Lineage and Writings.* St. Louis: Published by the Author, 1932. Pp. 380.

Brooke, J. T., D.D., *Short Notes on the Dred Scott Case.* Cincinnati: Moore, Wilstach, Keys and Co., 1861. Pp. 29.

Bryan, James A., "The Blow Family of St. Louis," Mss., Jefferson National Expansion Memorial, National Park Service, Department of the Interior, St. Louis, Mo.

Burge, William, *Commentaries on Colonial and Foreign Laws Generally and in Their Conflict with Each Other and with the Law of England.* London: Saunders and Benning, 1838. 4 vols.

Burgess, John W., *The Middle Period: 1817-1858.* New York: Charles Scribner's Sons, 1901. Pp. xvi, 544.

Cairnes, John Elliott, *The Slave Power: Its Character, Career and Probable Designs.* London: Macmillan and Company, 1863. Pp. xliv, 410.

Carpenter, Jesse T., *The South As a Conscious Minority, 1789-1861.* New York: The New York University Press, 1930. Pp. x, 315.

Carr, Lucien, *Missouri: A Bone of Contention.* Boston: Houghton Mifflin and Company, 1894. Pp. x, 377.

Catterall, Helen T., *Judicial Cases Concerning American Slavery and the Negro.* Washington, D. C.: Carnegie Institution, 1937. 5 vols.

————, "Some Antecedents of the Dred Scott Case," *American Historical Review,* 30 (1924-25), 56-70.

Channing, Edward, *A History of the United States.* New York: The Macmillan Company, 1927. 6 vols.

Chase, Frederic H., *Lemuel Shaw, Chief Justice of the Supreme Judicial Court of Massachusetts, 1830 to 1860.* Boston: Houghton Mifflin Company, 1918. Pp. vi, 330.

59th Congress, Session 2, Document 326. *Citizenship of the United States, Expatriation, and Protection Abroad.* Washington: Government Printing Office, 1907. Pp. 538.

187

Clark, Victor S., "The Influence of Manufactures upon Political Sentiment in The United States from 1820 to 1860," *American Historical Review,* 22 (October, 1916), 58-64.

Cohn, Morris M., "The Dred Scott Case in the Light of Later Events," *American Law Review,* 46 (1912), 548-577.

Connor, Henry G., *John Archibald Campbell.* Boston: Houghton Mifflin Company, 1920. Pp. viii, 310.

Corwin, Edward S., *The Doctrine of Judicial Review, Its Legal and Historical Basis and Other Essays.* Princeton: Princeton University Press, 1914. Pp. vii, 177.

Cotterill, R. S., "The National Railroad Convention in St. Louis, 1849." *The Missouri Historical Review,* 12 (July, 1918), 203-215.

Coxe, Brinton, *An Essay on Judicial Power and Unconstitutional Legislation, Being a Commentary on Parts of the Constitution of the United States.* Philadelphia: Kay and Brother, 1893. Pp. xvi, 415.

Crallé, Richard K., *The Works of John C. Calhoun.* New York: D. Appleton and Company, 1859. 6 vols.

Cullum, George W., *Biographical Register of the Officers and Graduates of the United States Military Academy at West Point.* Boston: Houghton Mifflin Co., 1891. 2 vols. and 6 vols. of Supplement.

Culmer, Frederic A., *A New History of Missouri.* Mexico, Mo.: McIntyre Publishing Co., 1938. Pp. 592.

Current, Richard N., *Old Thad Stevens.* Madison: University of Wisconsin Press, 1942. Pp. v, 344.

Curtis, Benjamin R., Jr., *A Memoir of Benjamin Robbins Curtis, LL.D., with Some of His Professional and Miscellaneous Writings.* Boston: Little, Brown, and Company, 1879. 2 vols.

Darby, John F., *Personal Recollections.* St. Louis: G. I. Jones and Company, 1880. Pp. 480.

Delaplaine, Edward S., *The Dred Scott Case.* Frederick: Chief Justice Taney Home, 1934. Pp. 5.

Douglas, Stephen A., *Remarks of the Hon. Stephen A. Douglas on Kansas, Utah, and the Dred Scott Decision. Delivered at Springfield, Illinois, June 12th, 1857.* Chicago: Daily Times Book and Job Office, 1857. Pp. 15.

Drumm, Stella M., and Charles van Ravenswaay, "The Old Courthouse," *Glimpses of the Past,* 7 (Jan.-June, 1940), 3-41.

Edwards, Richard, and Menra Hopewell, *Edward's Great West and Her Commercial Metropolis . . . St. Louis.* St. Louis: Published at the Office of "Edward's Monthly," 1860. Pp. 604.

Elliot, Jonathan, editor, *The Debates in the Several State Conventions on the Adoption of the Federal Constitution as Recommended by the General Convention at Philadelphia in 1787.* Washington: Printed by and for the Editor, 1836. 4 vols.

Ewing, Elbert W. R., *Legal and Historical Status of the Dred Scott Decision*. Washington, D. C.: Cobden Publishing Company, 1909. Pp. 228.

Farrand, Max, *The Legislation of Congress for the Government of the Organized Territories of the United States, 1789-1895*. Newark: Wm. A. Baker, 1896. Pp. 101.

————, editor, *The Records of the Federal Convention of 1787*. New Haven: Yale University Press, 1923. 3 vols.

"Cecil" [Sidney George Fisher], *The Law of the Territories*. Philadelphia: C. Sherman and Son, 1859. Pp. xxiv, 127.

Fisher, Sidney G., *The Trial of the Constitution*. Philadelphia: J. B. Lippincott and Co., 1862. Pp. xv, 391.

Foot, Samuel A., *An Examination of the Case of Dred Scott Against Sanford, in the Supreme Court of the United States, and a Full and Fair Exposition of the Decision of the Court*. New York: William C. Bryant and Co., 1859. Pp. 19.

27th Congress, Session 3, Reports of the Committees of the House of Representatives of the United States. 4 vols. *Free Colored Seamen*, Report 80, Vol. 1. Pp. 58. Jan. 20, 1843. Majority Report, Robert Winthrop; Minority, Kenneth Rayner.

Gayot de Pitaval, François, *Causes célèbres*. Amsterdam: Z. Chatelais et Fils, 1776. 15 vols.

Goode, G. Brown, Virginia Cousins, *A Study of the Ancestry and Posterity of John Goode of Whitby*. Richmond: J. W. Randolph and English, 1897. Pp. xxxvi, 526.

[Gray, Horace,] *A Legal Review of the Case of Dred Scott as Decided by the Supreme Court of the United States*. Boston: Crosby, Nichols and Company, 1857. Pp. 62.

Greeley, Horace, *The American Conflict: A History of the Great Rebellion in the United States of America, 1860-1864*. Hartford: O. D. Case and Company, 1864. 2 vols.

Greeley, Horace and John F. Cleveland, compilers, *A Political Text-Book for 1860*. New York: Published by the Tribune Association, 1860. Pp. x, 254.

Gresham, Otto, *The Dred Scott Case*. Chicago: Barnard and Miller, 1908. Pp. 18.

Haggard, John, *Reports of Cases Argued and Determined in the High Court of Admiralty during the Time of the Right Hon. Lord Stowell and of the Right Hon. Sir Christopher Robinson*. Edited by George Minot. Boston: Little, Brown and Company, 1853. 3 vols.

Hamilton, Stanislaus M., editor, *The Writings of James Monroe*. New York: G. P. Putnam's Sons, 1898. 7 vols.

Heitman, Francis B., *Historical Register and Dictionary of the United States Army (1789-1903)*. Washington: Government Printing Office, 1903. 2 vols.

Hill, Frederick T., *Decisive Battles of the Law*. New York: Harper and Brothers, 1907. Pp. viii, 268.

Hoar, George F., *Autobiography of Seventy Years*. New York: Charles Scribner's Sons, 1903. 2 vols.

Hodder, Frank H., "Some Phases of the Dred Scott Case." *Mississippi Valley Historical Review*, 16 (June, 1929), 3-22.

————, "The Genesis of the Kansas-Nebraska Act," *Proceedings of the State Historical Society of Wisconsin, 1912* (Madison: Published by the Society, 1913), 69-86.

Howell, Thomas B., editor, *A Complete Collection of State Trials*. London: Printed by T. C. Hansard, 1814. 20 vols.

Hurd, John C., *The Law of Freedom and Bondage in the United States*. Boston: Little, Brown and Company, 1858-1862. 2 vols.

Hyde, William, and Howard L. Conard, editors, *Encyclopedia of the History of St. Louis*. New York: The Southern History Company, 1899. 4 vols.

Isely, Jeter Allen, *Horace Greeley and the Republican Party 1853-1861. A Study of the New York Tribune*. Princeton: Princeton University Press, 1947. Pp. xiii, 368.

Johnson, Allen, editor, *Dictionary of American Biography*. New York: Charles Scribner's Sons, 1928. Supplements.

————, *Stephen A. Douglas: A Study in American Politics*. New York: The Macmillan Co., 1908. Pp. lx, 503.

Kent, James, *Commentaries on American Law*. 8th edition, New York: Published by William Kent, 1854. 4 vols.

Lanman, Charles, *Biographical Annals of the Civil Government of the United States During Its First Century*. Washington: James Anglim, 1876. Pp. 676.

Lawrence, Alexander A., *James Moore Wayne, Southern Unionist*. Chapel Hill: University of North Carolina Press, 1943. Pp. xiv, 250.

Lawson, John D., *American State Trials*. St. Louis: Thomas Law Book Co., 1921. 17 vols.

Livermore, Samuel, *Dissertations on the Questions Which Arise from Contrariety of the Positive Laws of Different States and Nations*. New Orleans: Printed by Benjamin Levy, 1828. Pp. 172.

Livingston, John, *Portraits of Eminent Americans now Living*. New York: Cornish, Lamport and Co., 1853. 2 vols.

Luthin, Reinhard H., "Organizing the Republican Party in the 'Border-Slave' Regions: Edward Bates's Presidential Candidacy in 1860," *Missouri Historical Review*, 38 (October, 1933-July, 1934), 138-161.

McClure, Clarence H., *Opposition in Missouri to Thomas Hart Benton*. Nashville: George Peabody College for Teachers, 1927. Pp. 238.

McCormac, Eugene Irving, *James K. Polk: A Political Biography*. Berkeley: University of California Press, 1922. Pp. x, 746.

————, "Justice Campbell and the Dred Scott Decision," *Mississippi Valley Historical Review*, 19 (March, 1933), 565-571.

[Madison, James,] *Letters and Other Writings of James Madison, Fourth President of the United States*. New York: R. Worthington, 1884. 4 vols.

Malloy, William, editor, *Treaties, Conventions, International Acts, Protocols and Agreements between the United States of America and Other Powers*. 61st Cong., Sess. 2, Senate Document No. 357. Washington: Government Printing Office, 1910. 2 vols. [2 Supplements, to 1938].

Meigs, William M., *The Life of Thomas Hart Benton*. Philadelphia: J. B. Lippincott Company, 1904. Pp. 535.

Merkel, Benjamin, "The Slavery Issue and the Political Decline of Thomas Hart Benton," *Missouri Historical Review*, 38 (October, 1933-July, 1944), 388-407.

Milton, George Fort, *The Eve of Conflict*. Boston: Houghton Mifflin Company, 1934. Pp. xiii, 608.

Miller, Samuel F., *Lectures on the Constitution of the United States*. New York: Banks and Brothers, 1891. Pp. xxi, 765.

Moore, John B., editor, *The Works of James Buchanan, Comprising His Speeches, State Papers and Private Correspondence*. Philadelphia: J. B. Lippincott Co., 1908-11. 12 vols.

The National Cyclopaedia of American Biography. New York: James T. White and Co., 1892.

Nevins, Allan, *Frémont, Pathmarker of the West*. New York: A. Appleton-Century Co., 1939. Pp. xiii, 649.

Nicolay, John G., and John Hay, editors, *Complete Works of Abraham Lincoln*. New and Enlarged Edition. New York: The Lamb Publishing Co. [n.d.] 12 vols.

Parker, Joel, *Personal Liberty Laws, and Slavery in the Territories*. Boston: Wright and Potter, 1861. Pp. 97.

Phillips, Ulrich B., editor, *The Correspondence of Robert Toombs, Alexander H. Stephens, and Howell Cobb*. Washington: Annual Report of the American Historical Association for 1911, 1913. 2 vols.

Pierce, Frederick C., *Field Genealogy*. Chicago: W. B. Conkey Co., 1901. 2 vols.

Powell, Wm. H., *List of Officers of the Army of the United States from 1779 to 1900*. New York: L. R. Hamersby and Co., 1900.

Rawle, William, *A View of the Constitution of the United States of America*. Philadelphia: H. C. Carey and I. Lea, 1825. Pp. vii, 347.

Ray, P. Orman, *The Repeal of the Missouri Compromise*. Cleveland, Ohio: The Arthur H. Clark Company, 1909. Pp. 315.

————, "The Retirement of Thomas Hart Benton from the Senate and its Significance," *Missouri Historical Review*, 2 (January, 1908), 100-102.

Robertson, Max A., and Geoffrey Ellis, editors, *The English Reports*. London: Stevens and Sons, 1900-1930. 176 vols.

Roosevelt, Theodore, *Thomas Hart Benton*. Boston: Houghton, Mifflin and Company, 1899. Pp. 261-344.

Rhodes, James F., *History of the United States from the Compromise of 1850*. New York: Harper and Brothers, 1893. 7 vols.

Sergeant, Thomas, *Constitutional Law. Being a View of the Practice and Jurisdiction of the Courts of the United States, and of Constitutional Points Decided.* 2nd ed. Philadelphia: P. H. Nicklin and T. Johnson, 1830. Pp. xi, 440.

Scharf, J. Thomas, *History of St. Louis City and County*. Philadelphia: Louis H. Everts and Co., 1883. 2 vols.

Sedgwick, Theodore, *A Treatise on the Rules which Govern the Interpretation and Application of Statutory and Constitutional Law.* New York: John S. Voorhies, 1857. Pp. 712.

Sherman, Gordon E., "Emancipation and Citizenship," *Yale Law Journal*, 15 (April, 1906), 263-282.

Smith, Charles W., *Roger B. Taney: Jacksonian Jurist*. Chapel Hill: University of North Carolina Press, 1936. Pp. xi, 242.

Smith, Edward C., *The Borderland in the Civil War*. New York: Macmillan Co., 1927. Pp. 412.

Smith, Theodore C., *Parties and Slavery, 1850-1859*. New York: Harper and Brothers, 1907. Pp. xvi, 341.

Smith, William Ernest, *The Francis Preston Blair Family in Politics*. New York: The Macmillan Company, 1933. 2 vols.

Steiner, Bernard C., *The Life of Reverdy Johnson*. Baltimore: The Norman, Remington Co., 1914. Pp. v, 284.

————, *The Life of Roger Brooke Taney*. Baltimore: Williams and Wilkins Co., 1922. Pp. 553.

Stenberg, Richard R., "Some Political Aspects of the Dred Scott Case," *Mississippi Valley Historical Review*, 18 (March, 1933), 571-577.

Stewart, Alexander J. D., editor, *The History of the Bench and Bar of Missouri*. St. Louis: The Legal Publishing Co., 1898. Pp. 672.

Story, Joseph, *Commentaries on the Conflict of Laws, Foreign and Domestic, in regard to Contracts, Rights, and Remedies; and especially in regard to Marriages, Divorces, Wills, Successions, and Judgments.* 4th ed. Boston: Little, Brown and Company, 1852. Pp. xxxviii, 1072.

Story, Joseph, *Commentaries on the Constitution of the United States: with a Preliminary Review of the Constitutional History of the Colonies and States before the Adoption of the Constitution.* 2nd ed. Boston: Charles C. Little, and James Brown, 1851. 2 vols.

Story, William Wetmore, *Life and Letters of Joseph Story*. London: John Chapman, 1851. 2 vols.

Stroud, George M., *A Sketch of the Laws Relating to Slavery in the Several States of the United States of America*. Philadelphia: Kimber and Sharpless, 1827. Pp. vii, 180.

Swisher, Carl B., *American Constitutional Development*. Boston: Houghton Mifflin Company, 1943. Pp. xii, 1079.

————, *Roger B. Taney*. New York: The Macmillan Company, 1935. Pp. x, 608.

[Tanner, Henry,] *The Martyrdom of Lovejoy: An Account of the Life, Trials, and Perils of the Rev. Elijah P. Lovejoy Who was Killed by a Pro-Slavery Mob, at Alton, Ill., on the Night of November 7, 1857. By an Eye Witness*. Chicago: Fergus Printing Co., 1881. Pp. 233.

Taylor, John, *New Views of the Constitution*. Washington City: Way and Gideon, 1823. Pp. 316.

[Taney, R. B.,] *The Taney Fund. Proceedings of the Meeting of the Bar of the Supreme Court of the United States*. Washington City: M'Gill and Witherow, 1871. Pp. 8.

Thayer, James Bradley, *Cases on Constitutional Law*. Cambridge: George H. Kent, 1895. 2 vols.

Turner, Beatrice C., *The Chouteau Family*. [n.p., n.p.,] 1934.

Turner, Frederick J., *Rise of the New West, 1819-1829*. New York: Harper and Brothers, 1907. Pp. xviii, 366.

Tyler, Samuel, *Memoir of Roger Brooke Taney, LL.D.* Baltimore: John Murphy and Company, 1872. Pp. xv, 659.

Van Buren, Martin, *Autobiography*. Edited by John C. Fitzpatrick. Washington: Government Printing Office, 1920. Pp. 808. [Annual Report, A. H. A., 1918, Vol. II.]

————, *Inquiry into the Origin and Course of Political Parties in the United States*. Edited by His Sons. New York: Hurd and Houghton, 1867. Pp. ix, 436.

Vattel, Emmerich de, *The Law of Nations or the Principles of Natural Law Applied to the Conduct and the Affairs of Nations and of Sovereigns*. Translation of the edition of 1758 by Charles G. Fenwick. Washington: Carnegie Institution of Washington, 1916. Pp. 28(a), 398.

Von Holst, Hermann E., *The Constitutional and Political History of the United States*. Translated by John J. Lalor. Chicago: Callaghan and Company, 1889. 6 vols.

Von Savigny, Friedrich Carl, *A Treatise on the Conflict of Laws, and the Limits of Their Operation in Respect of Place and Time*. Translated by William Guthrie. With an Appendix Containing the Treatises of Bartolus, Molinaeus, Paul Voet, and Huber. 2nd edition. Edinburgh: T. and T. Clark, 1880. Pp. xii, 567.

Walsh, Edmund P., "The Story of an Old Clerk. Address before the Circuit Clerks and Recorders' Convention, St. Louis, July 14, 1908," *Glimpses of the Past,* 1 (July, 1934), 63-70.

Warren, Charles, *The Supreme Court in United States History.* Boston: Little, Brown and Company, 1932. 2 vols.

Weisenburger, Francis P., *The Life of John McLean.* Columbus: Ohio State University Press, 1937. Pp. lx, 244.

Wheeler, Jacob D., *A Practical Treatise on the Law of Slavery.* New York: Allan Pollock, Jr., 1837. Pp. xviii, 476.

White, Horace, *The Life of Lyman Trumbull.* Boston: Houghton Mifflin Co., 1913. Pp. xxxv, 458.

Williams, Walter, and Floyd C. Shoemaker, *Missouri, Mother of the West.* Chicago: The American Historical Society, Inc., 1930. 5 vols.

Willoughby, Westel W., *The Constitutional Law of the United States.* 2nd ed. New York: Baker, Voorhis and Company, 1929. Pp. lxxxviii, 2022.

Wilson, Henry, *History of the Rise and Fall of the Slave Power in America.* Boston: James R. Osgood and Co., 1872. 3 vols.

Wilson, James G., and John Fiske, editors, *Appleton's Cyclopaedia of American Biography.* New York: D. Appleton and Co., 1888.

Wise, John S., *A Treatise on American Citizenship.* Northport, N. Y.: Edward Thompson Company, 1906. Pp. vii, 340.

INDEX

Abolitionists, 20, 23, 26, 31 (n.23), 78, 134, 170

Abridgement of the Debates of Congress, 165

Acton, Lord, 107

Adams, John, 112

Adams, John Quincy, 13, 78, 109 (n.46)

Adams-Onís Treaty, 34

Address to the Democracy of Missouri, 37

Alabama, 1, 2, 9, 33, 75, 90, 92

Alienage, 34

Aliens, 65, 65, 88

Allison, John, 43

Alton, Illinois, 11

American and Ocean Insurance Companies vs. Canter, 68, 69, 80, 117-119, 124, 125, 127, 129, 133

American Party, 21 (n.29), 29 (n.5), 45, 78, 163

Amory, James S., 104

Amy vs. Smith, 33, 98, 108 (n.9)

Anderson, Catherine Thompson, 8 (nn. 19, 25), 12

Anderson, Richard C., Jr., 112

Anderson, William, 12

Anne Arundel County, Maryland, 99

Anti-Benton Democrats, 15, 17, 18

Antigua, 91, 147, 153 (n.18)

Anti-Masonic Party, 78

Appleton, John, 110 (n.55)

Appleton and Company, 158

Arkansas Territory, 114, 115

Articles of Confederation, 51, 66, 83, 127, 128

Articles of War, 52

Ashley, James M., 5

Atchison, David R., 130

Aves, Thomas, 149

Badger, George, 47

Bailey, Gamaliel, 26, 177 (n.1)

Bainbridge, Henry, 6, 7

Baldwin, Henry, 121

Bank of Augusta vs. Earle, 151

Bank of Maryland, 161

Bank of the United States, Second, 61

Bank of the United States vs. Smith, 83, 94 (n.21), 107 (n.1)

Barbour, Philip P., 113

Barnes, James, 15

Barnum, Theron, 176

Barzizas vs. Hopkins and Hodgson, 103, 106, 108 (n.13)

Bates, Edward, 16, 17, 39, 107

Bay, S. Mansfield, 13, 182

Bell, Henry, 11

Benjamin, Judah P., 168, 169, 170

Benton, Thomas H., 3-5, 9-11, 15-17, 20, 21 (n.27), 33, 38, 93, 113, 120, 123, 130, 152, 164, 165, 182

Berrien, John, 99, 126-129

Birch, James, 16-18

Bissell, Clark, 101, 109 (n.27)

Blair, Francis P., 10, 26, 93

Blair, Francis P., Jr., 10, 180 (n.67), 182

Blair, James, 26

Blair, Montgomery, 10, 25-28, 32, 33-40, 47, 48, 50, 52, 53, 59 (n.5), 66, 99, 108 (n.12), 163, 166, 182; argument of, at first hearing of Scott case by Supreme Court, 33-39; at second hearing, 47-48; briefs of, 32, 40, 45 (n.5), 59 (n.5)

Blair family, 37, 38, 166

Bloomington, Illinois, 172

Blow, Charlotte, *see* Charless, Charlotte B.

Blow, Elisabeth R., 1, 4, 7 (n.13)

Blow, Elisabeth Taylor, 1-3

Blow, Eugenie La Beaume (Mrs. Peter E.), 14

Blow, Henry T., 1, 2, 4, 7 (n.13), 9, 12, 14, 15, 180 (n.67)

Blow, James, 1

Blow, Julia W., 7 (nn.6, 13), 180 (n.67)

Blow, Martha Ella (Patsy), *see* Drake, Martha E. B.

Blow, Mary Anne (Key), 1

Blow, Minerva, 9

Blow, Peter, 1-4, 7 (nn.2, 3, 5, 6, 11, 13), 9, 176, 180 (n.67); will of, 3, 4, 7 (n.13)

Blow, Peter E., 1, 2, 4, 9, 23, 180 (n.67)
Blow, Taylor, 2, 4, 9, 25, 176, 180 (nn. 65, 67)
Blow, William Thomas, 2, 4, 9, 180 (n.67)
Blow Family, 1, 2, 7 (n.1), 14, 29 (n.5), 30 (n.23), 182
Bodin, Jean, 142
Bollinger, James, 8 (n.23)
Boston, Mass., 48, 149, 156
Boucaux, Jean, 142
Boutwell, George S., 82
Bowdon, Franklin W., 132, 133
Bowlin, James B., 21 (n.27)
Boyle, John, 33, 98, 100
Brant, Joshua, 4, 152
Breuil, Suzanne Chauvette du, 29 (n.5)
Bright, Jesse D., 130
Bronson, Greene C., 134-137
Brooke, James T., 164
Brown, Aaron, 54
Brown, Albert G., 175
Browning, Orville H., 44
Buchanan, James, 45, 47, 53-59, 74, 75, 89, 162, 165-167, 170, 172
Buckner, Alexander, 4

Calhoun, John C., 5, 9, 11, 12, 14, 15, 17, 21 (n.27), 38, 39, 50, 90, 95 (n.39), 118, 122-124, 127, 131, 165; Resolutions of 1847 of, 11, 122-124, 127
California, 14-16, 26, 34, 37, 122, 130, 133, 140 (n.77)
Calvert County, Maryland, 61
Campaign of 1848, 37
Campbell, John A., 33, 42, 54, 55, 57, 59 (n.20), 78, 90-93, 95 (n.39), 96, 111, 156, 158, 162; opinion of, in Scott case, 90-93, 156, 158
Campbell, Lewis D., 45
Canada, 123, 138 (n.1)
Canter, David, 117, 118
Cap François, 142
Carey, Mathew, 3
Carroll, William, 156-159, 178 (n.14)
Carter, John, 12
Carter, Stewart, 12
Cartwright's case, 143
Cass, Lewis, 4, 5
Catron, John, 32, 33, 40, 42, 52-58, 59 (n.20), 74-76, 77 (n.48), 95 (n.43), 96, 100, 101, 111, 114, 134, 140 (n.77), 156, 158, 162, 167, 170; opinion of, in Scott case, 74-76, 156, 158

Chaffee, Calvin C., 23, 29 (n.6), 163, 170, 176
Charles River Bridge Co., vs. Warren Bridge Co., 61
Charless, Charlotte Blow, 1-3, 7 (n.13), 14
Charless, Joseph, 3
Charless, Joseph, Jr., 3, 4, 7 (n.13), 9, 13, 180 (n.67)
Charless, Blow and Company, 9, 180 (n.67)
Charleston, So. Carolina, 103
Charleston *Mercury,* 163
Chase, Salmon P., 13
Chauncey, Charles, 93
Cheever, William B., 163
Cherokee Nation vs. Georgia, 120, 125, 127, 129
Chicago, 10, 172
Chicago *Times,* 174
Chouteau, Pierre, Jr., 4, 30 (n.9)
Church, Samuel, 101
Cincinnati, Ohio, 43, 78
Citizenship, 23, 24, 33-35, 37, 40-42, 48-50, 55, 57, 60 (n.21), 62-65, 72, 73, 78, 79, 83, 84, 87, 90, 96-110, 141, 165, 171, 172; acquired at birth, 34, 48, 49, 79, 84, 98, 105; by naturalisation, 33, 34, 49, 63, 64, 79, 84, 98, 106; and right to bring suit in Federal court, 24, 33-35, 40, 49, 62-65, 72, 79, 84, 96, 105, 107, 165; civil, and political rights of, 33, 34, 48, 63-65, 84, 96-98, 104; dual, 105, 106; Federal, 23, 33, 34, 48, 49, 62-65, 72, 79, 83, 84, 88, 96-100, 102, 104-106; Federal, conferred by treaties on Indians and free Negroes, 34; of free Negroes, 33-35, 37, 40-42, 48-50, 55, 60 (n.21), 62-65, 72, 73, 78, 79, 83, 84, 88, 90, 96-106, 107 (n.4), 108 (n.7), 141, 165, 171, 172; of free Negroes in Connecticut, 101, 109 (n.27); in Kentucky, 33, 34, 89; in Louisiana, 106; in Maine, 106, 110 (n.55); in Massachusetts, 104; in Missouri, 97, 107; in North Carolina, 34, 83, 103, 106; in Pennsylvania, 101, 102; in Tennessee, 100, 101; State, 23, 24, 34, 48, 49, 62-64, 72, 79, 83, 84, 96-98, 102, 104-106, 107 (n.4)
Civil rights, 33, 34, 63, 84, 96-98, 101, 102, 104
Clark, Miles, 12, 15
Clay, Henry, 3, 161
Clayton, John M., 14, 109 (n.46), 130, 131

196

197

199

in, 4-6; Calvary cemetery in, 180 (n.67); Circuit Court, 10-12, 156, 181; Courthouse in, 12, 23, 177; Wesleyan cemetery in, 177, 180 (n.67)

202

Thompson, Smith, 107 (n.1), 120
Ticknor, George, 41, 82, 136
Tocqueville, Alexis de, 107
Toombs, Robert, 152
Tramell vs. Adam, 155 (n.41)
Transylvania University, 3
Treat, Samuel, 9, 140 (n.77), 177 (n.1)
Trumbull, Lyman, 78, 152
Tyler, John, 32, 73

Underwood, Joseph R., 130, 132
United States, property of, 49, 67, 87, 91,
  115; right of, to acquire new territory,
  50, 69, 70, 80, 86, 87, 111, 118, 119,
  129, 138 (n.1)
United States Supreme Court, 15, 18,
  19, 25, 26, 28, 32, 37, 39-42, 45, 47, 48,
  52-58, 59 (n.20), 61, 63, 65, 66, 71-74,
  76 (n.19), 78, 79, 81-84, 86, 88, 93, 99,
  109 (n.46), 111, 118, 119, 128-132, 142,
  151, 155 (n.42), 163-168, 172; courtroom of (1856), 32, 61; jurisdiction of
  in Scott case, *see* Jurisdiction; personnel of (1856), 32, 161, 162; *see,* also,
  Scott case
United States vs. Gratiot, 120, 127, 129,
  133
United States vs. Laverty et al., 110
  (n.53)

Van Buren, Martin, 13, 32, 37, 53, 74,
  88, 93, 117
Vattel, Emmerich de, 89
Vaughan, Charles, 100
Venable, Abraham W., 124
Verdelin, Case of the slaves of, 142, 143
Vermont, 23, 30 (n.10), 131, 169
Villenage, 88, 144, 146
Vincent vs. Duncan, 155 (n.41)
Virginia, 1 (nn.2-3), 21 (n.27), 32, 36, 88,
  99, 108 (n.7), 113, 128, 143, 157, 175;
  Court of Appeals of, 36, 99

Walker, Felix, 114
Walker, Freeman, 114
Walsh, Robert, 116
War of 1812, 1, 5, 61, 74
Warren County, Ohio, 78
Washington, Bushrod, 34
Washington, D.C., 5, 26, 28, 39, 40, 53,
  58, 65, 90, 148, 157, 158, 161, 167, 174,
  175
Washington *Daily Union,* 7 (n.6), 8
  (n.19), 156, 162, 163
Wayne, James M., 32, 33, 42, 53, 55-57,
  60 (n.20), 78, 93, 95 (n.43), 96, 111, 133,
  140 (n.77), 156-158, 161, 162, 166, 167;
  opinion of, in Scott case, 93, 156, 157
Webster, Daniel, 48, 61, 82, 113, 118-121,
  162, 178 (n.19)
Wells, Robert, 23-25, 27, 28, 29 (n.1), 32,
  33, 37, 40, 42, 57
West Indies, 142, 147
West Virginia, 78
Western Star, 78
Westervelt vs. Gregg, 137
Wheatlands, 53, 58
Whig Party, 17, 18, 39, 61, 78, 161, 163,
  178 (n.19)
Whitman, Ezechiel, 114, 115
Whipple, John, 118, 119
Williams, Thomas S., 101, 109 (n.27)
*Willot, Sebastian, John McDonald and
  Joseph Hunn v. John F. A. Sandford,*
  24, 30 (n.9)
Willoughby, Westel W., 76 (n.19)
Wilmot, David, 11, 12, 39, 121, 122
Wilmot Proviso, 11, 121, 122
Wilson vs. Melvin, 154 (n.41)
Winny vs. Whitesides, 154 (n.41)
Winthrop, Robert, 103-105
Wirt, William, 65, 97, 98, 102, 103, 106,
  108 (n.7), 194
Wisconsin Territory, 74, 85

Yulee, David, 123, 124

Father Vincent C. Hopkins, S.J. was born in Brooklyn, New York, on September 30, 1912. He entered the Society of Jesus on September 23, 1929, received his B.A. and S.T.L. from Woodstock College and his Ph.D. from Columbia University. In 1951 he joined the faculty at Fordham University and taught in the Department of History and the Law School. He was Director of the Fordham University Press and President, in 1956, of the United States Catholic Historical Society. He wrote for *Thought,* the *Dictionary of American History* and contributed chapters to *Darwin's Vision and Christian Perspectives* (1960) and *In the Eyes of Others* (1962). He died at Georgetown University Hospital on April 3, 1964.

Atheneum Paperbacks

STUDIES IN AMERICAN NEGRO LIFE

Atheneum Paperbacks

HISTORY—AMERICAN—BEFORE 1900

Atheneum Paperbacks

HISTORY—AMERICAN—1900 TO THE PRESENT

Atheneum Paperbacks

Atheneum Paperbacks

THE NEW YORK TIMES BYLINE BOOKS

THE ADAMS PAPERS

ECONOMICS AND BUSINESS

PHYSICAL SCIENCES AND MATHEMATICS

Atheneum Paperbacks

LAW AND GOVERNMENT

DIPLOMACY AND INTERNATIONAL RELATIONS

Atheneum Paperbacks